CW00828469

Persecution and the Art of Writing

PERSECUTION AND THE ART OF WRITING

By Leo Strauss

THE UNIVERSITY OF CHICAGO PRESS

Chicago & London

The University of Chicago Press, Chicago 60637
The University of Chicago Press, Ltd., London

Printed in the United States of America

07 06 05 04   6 7 8

Library of Congress Cataloging in Publication Data

Strauss, Leo.
    Persecution and the art of writing / by Leo Strauss.
        p.   cm.
    Reprint. Originally published: New York : Free Press, c 1952.
    Includes bibliographical references and index.
    1. Judaism and philosophy.   2. Philosophy, Jewish.   3. Philosophy,
Medieval.   4. Philosophy and religion.   5. Maimonides, Moses,
1135–1204.   Dalālat al-ḥā'irīn.   6. Judah, ha-Levi, 12th cent.
Kitāb al-ḥujjah.   7. Spinoza, Benedictus de, 1632–1677.   Tractatus
theologico-politicus.   8. Persecution.   I. Title.
B755.S79   1988   88-17539
306'.42—dc19   CIP
ISBN 0-226-77711-1 (pbk.)

∞ The paper used in this publication meets the minimum
requirements of the American National Standard for
Information Sciences—Permanence of Paper for Printed
Library Materials, ANSI Z39.48-1992.

Contents

1
Introduction   7

2
Persecution and the Art of Writing   22

3
The Literary Character of the *Guide for the Perplexed*   38

4
The Law of Reason in the *Kuzari*   95

5
How to Study Spinoza's *Theologico-Political Treatise*   142

Index   203

PREFACE

These essays are here collected into one volume primarily with a view to the fact that they all deal with one problem: the problem of the relation between philosophy and politics. In the Introduction, I have tried to state this problem from the side of philosophy. In the article "Persecution and the Art of Writing," I have tried to elucidate the problem by starting from certain well-known political phenomena of our century. As I state in the Introduction, I became familiar with the problem mentioned while studying the Jewish and the Islamic philosophy of the Middle Ages. The three last essays deal with the problem as it appears from the writings of the two most famous Jewish medieval thinkers (Halevi and Maimonides) and of Spinoza who has been called, not altogether wrongly, "the last of the medievals."

For the Introduction I have made free use of my article "Fārābī's *Plato*" (*Louis Ginzberg Jubilee Volume*, American Academy for Jewish Research, New York, 1945, 357-393). "Persecution and the Art of Writing" was first published in *Social Research*, November, 1941, 488-504. "The Literary Character of *The Guide for the Perplexed*" was first published in *Essays on Maimonides*, edited by S. W. Baron, Columbia University Press, 1941, 37-91. "The Law of Reason in the *Kuzari*" was first published in the *Proceedings of the American Academy for Jewish Research*, XIII, 1943, 47-96. "How to Study Spinoza's *Theologico-Political Treatise*" was first published in the same *Proceedings*, XVII, 1948, 69-131.

I wish to thank the editors and proprietors of the above mentioned works or periodicals for their kind permission to reprint.

L. S.

INTRODUCTION

The subject matter of the following essays may be said to fall within the province of the sociology of knowledge. Sociology of knowledge does not limit itself to the study of knowledge proper. Being critical in regard to its own basis, it studies impartially everything that pretends to be knowledge as well as genuine knowledge. Accordingly, one should expect that it would devote some attention also to the pursuit of genuine knowledge of the whole, or to philosophy. Sociology of philosophy would thus appear to be a legitimate subdivision of sociology of knowledge. The following essays may be said to supply material useful for a future sociology of philosophy.

One cannot help wondering why there does not exist today a sociology of philosophy. It would be rude to suggest that the founders of the sociology of knowledge were unaware of philosophy or did not believe in its possibility. What one can safely say is that the philosopher appeared to them, eventually or from the beginning, as a member of a motley crowd which they called the intellectuals or the Sages. Sociology of knowledge emerged in a society which took for granted the essential harmony between thought and society or between intellectual progress and social progress. It was more concerned with the relation of the different types of thought to different types of society than with the fundamental relation of thought as such to society as such. It did not see a grave practical problem in that fundamental relation. It tended to see in the different philosophies, exponents of different societies or classes or ethnic spirits. It failed to consider the possibility that all philosophers

7

form a class by themselves, or that what unites all genuine philosophers is more important than what unites a given philosopher with a particular group of non-philosophers. This failure can be traced directly to the inadequacy of the historical information on which the edifice of sociology of knowledge was erected. The first-hand knowledge at the disposal of the early sociologists of knowledge was limited, for all practical purposes, to what they knew of nineteenth and early twentieth century Western thought.

To realize the necessity of a sociology of philosophy, one must turn to other ages, if not to other climates. The present writer happened to come across phenomena whose understanding calls for a sociology of philosophy, while he was studying the Jewish and Islamic philosophy of the Middle Ages.

There is a striking contrast between the level of present-day understanding of Christian scholasticism and that of present-day understanding of Islamic and Jewish medieval philosophy. This contrast is ultimately due to the fact that the foremost students of Christian scholasticism believe in the immediate philosophic relevance of their theme, whereas the foremost students of Islamic and Jewish medieval philosophy tend to regard their subject as only of historical interest. The rebirth of Christian scholasticism has given rise to a philosophic interest in Islamic and Jewish medieval philosophy: Averroes and Maimonides appeared to be the Islamic and Jewish counterparts of Thomas Aquinas. But from the point of view of Christian scholasticism, and indeed from the point of view of any position which accepts the very principle of faith, Islamic and Jewish medieval philosophy are likely to appear inferior to Christian scholasticism and at best only trail blazers for the approach characteristic of the latter.[1] If Islamic and Jewish medieval philosophy must be understood properly, they must be of philosophic and not merely of antiquarian interest, and this in turn requires that one ceases to regard them as counterparts of Christian scholasticism.

To recognize the fundamental difference between Christian scholasticism on the one hand, and Islamic and Jewish medieval philosophy on the other, one does well to start from the most

[1] Compare Isaac Abravanel's Commentary on Joshua X, 12 (ed. Frankfurt, 1736, fol. 21-22).

obvious difference, the difference in regard to the literary sources. This difference is particularly striking in the case of practical or political philosophy. The place that is occupied in Christian scholasticism by Aristotle's *Politics*, Cicero, and the Roman Law, is occupied in Islamic and Jewish philosophy by Plato's *Republic* and his *Laws*. Whereas Plato's *Republic* and *Laws* were recovered by the West only in the fifteenth century, they had been translated into Arabic in the ninth century. Two of the most famous Islamic philosophers wrote commentaries on them: Fārābī on the *Laws*, and Averroes on the *Republic*. The difference mentioned implied a difference, not only in regard to the content of political philosophy, but, above all, in regard to its importance for the whole of philosophy. Fārābī, whom Maimonides, the greatest Jewish thinker of the Middle Ages, regarded as the greatest among the Islamic philosophers, and indeed as the greatest philosophic authority after Aristotle, was so much inspired by Plato's *Republic* that he presented the whole of philosophy proper within a political framework. That of Fārābī's works which Maimonides recommended especially, consists of two parts, the first discussing God and the universe, and the second discussing the city; the author entitled it *The Political Governments*. A parallel work composed by him bears the title *The Principles of the Opinions of the People of the Virtuous City;* it is called in the manuscripts that I have seen "a political book." It is significant that Fārābī was definitely less known to Christian scholasticism than were Avicenna and Averroes.[2]

To understand these obvious differences, one must take into consideration the essential difference between Judaism and Islam on the one hand and Christianity on the other. Revelation as understood by Jews and Muslims has the character of Law (*torah, sharī'a*) rather than of Faith.[3] Accordingly, what first came to the sight of the Islamic and Jewish philosophers in their reflections on Revelation was not a creed or a set of dogmas, but a social order, if an all-comprehensive order, which regulates

---

[2] See *Church History*, XV, 1946, 62.—Louis Gardet and M.-M. Anawati, *Introduction à la théologie musulmane*, Paris, 1948, 245: ". . . les Fārābī, les Avicenne, les Averroès. Deux noms émergèrent (en chrétienté): Avicenne . . . et plus tard Averroès. . . ."

[3] Compare, e.g., Gardet-Anawati, *op. cit.*, 332, 335, and 407.

not merely actions but thoughts or opinions as well. Revelation thus understood lent itself to being interpreted by loyal philosophers as the perfect law, the perfect political order. Being philosophers, the *falāsifa*,[4] as they were called, attempted to arrive at a perfect understanding of the phenomenon of Revelation. Yet Revelation is intelligible to man only to the extent to which it takes place through the intermediacy of secondary causes, or to the extent to which it is a natural phenomenon. The medium through which God reveals Himself to man is a prophet, i.e., a human being. The *falāsifa* attempted therefore to understand the process of Revelation as essentially related to, or as identical with, a peculiar "connatural" perfection, and in fact, the supreme perfection, of man. Being loyal philosophers, the *falāsifa* were compelled to justify their pursuit of philosophy before the tribunal of the Divine Law. Considering the importance which they attached to philosophy, they were thus driven to interpret Revelation as the perfect political order which is perfect precisely because it lays upon all sufficiently equipped men the duty to devote their lives to philosophy. For this purpose they had to assume that the founder of the perfect order, the prophetic lawgiver, was not merely a statesman of the highest order but at the same time a philosopher of the highest order. They had to conceive of the prophetic lawgiver as a philosopher-king or as the supreme perfection of the philosopher-king. Philosopher-kings, and communities governed by philosopher-kings, were however the theme not of Aristotelian but of Platonic politics. And divine laws, which prescribe not merely actions but opinions about the divine things as well, were the theme of Plato's *Laws* in particular. It is therefore not surprising that, according to Avicenna, the philosophic discipline which deals with prophecy is political philosophy or political science, and the standard work on prophecy is Plato's *Laws*. For the specific function of the prophet, as Averroes says, or of the greatest of all prophets, as Maimonides suggests, is legislation of the highest type.

Plato's *Laws* were known in the period under consideration as "Plato's rational laws *(nomoi)*." The *falāsifa* accepted then the notion that there are "rational laws." Yet they rejected the

[4] The Arabic transcription of the Greek word for "philosophers."

notion of "rational commandments." The latter notion had been employed by a school of what one may call Islamic theology *(kalām)*, and had been adopted by certain Jewish thinkers. It corresponded to the Christian notion of "the natural law," which may be identified with "the law of reason" and "the moral law." By rejecting the notion of "rational commandments," the *falāsifa* implied that the principles of morality are not rational, but "probable" or "generally accepted." "The rational laws *(nomoi)*" which they admitted, are distinguished from "the rational commandments," or the natural law, by the fact that they do not have obligatory character. The Stoic natural law teaching, which was transmitted to the Western world chiefly through Cicero and some Roman lawyers, did not influence the practical or political philosophy of the *falāsifa*.

The philosophic intransigence of the *falāsifa* is not sufficiently appreciated in the accepted interpretations of their teachings.[5] This is partly due to the reticence of the *falāsifa* themselves. The best clues to their intentions are found in the writings of men like Yehuda Halevi and Maimonides. The value of the testimony of these great men may be thought to be impaired by the fact that they opposed the *falāsifa*. Yet at least some writings of Fārābī confirm the interpretation which Halevi and Maimonides suggest. In the present state of our knowledge it is impossible to say to what extent Fārābī's successors accepted his views in regard to the crucial point. But there can be no doubt that those views acted as a leaven as long as philosophy exercised an influence on Islamic and Jewish thought.

Fārābī expressed his thought most clearly in his short treatise on the philosophy of Plato.[6] The *Plato* forms the second and shortest part of a tripartite work which apparently was entitled *On the Purposes of Plato and of Aristotle* and which is quoted by Averroes as *The Two Philosophies*.[7] The third part, which

[5] See Gardet-Anawati, *op. cit.*, 268-272, and 320-324.

[6] The full title is "The philosophy of Plato, its parts, and the grades of dignity of its parts, from its beginning to its end." The original has been edited, annotated and translated into Latin by F. Rosenthal and R. Walzer (*Alfarabius De Platonis Philosophia*, London, 1943).

[7] The latter title is used also by a contemporary of Averroes, Joseph ibn Aknīn (see A. S. Halkin, "Ibn Aknīn's Commentary on the Song of Songs," *Alexander Marx Jubilee Volume*, New York, 1950, 423).

has not yet been edited, deals with the philosophy of Aristotle. In the first part *(On the Attainment of Happiness)*, Fārābī discusses the human things which are required for bringing about the complete happiness of nations and of cities. The chief requirement proves to be philosophy, or rather the rule of philosophers, for "the meaning of *Philosopher, First Leader, King, Legislator,* and *Imām* is one and the same." The Platonic origin of the guiding thesis is obvious and, in addition, pointed out by the author. He concludes the first part with the remark that philosophy as previously described stems from Plato and Aristotle, who both "have given us philosophy" together with "the ways toward it and the way toward its introduction after it has been blurred or destroyed," and that, as will become clear from the presentation of the philosophies of Plato and Aristotle in the two subsequent parts, the purpose of Plato and of Aristotle was one and the same. Two points in Fārābī's *On the Purposes of Plato and of Aristotle* strike one most. The work owes its origin to the concern with the restoration of philosophy "after it has been blurred or destroyed"; and it is more concerned with the purpose common to Plato and Aristotle than with the agreement or disagreement of the results of their investigations. What Fārābī regarded as the purpose of the two philosophers, and hence what he regarded as the sound purpose simply, appears with all the clarity which one can reasonably desire, from his summary of Plato's philosophy, and from no other source. This purpose is likely to prove the latent purpose of all *falāsifa* proper. Fārābī's *Plato* would thus prove to be the clue par excellence to the *falsafa*[8] as such.

According to Fārābī, Plato started his inquiry with the question regarding the essence of man's perfection or of his happiness, and he realized that man's happiness consists in a certain science and in a certain way of life. The science in question proves to be the science of the essence of every being, and the art which supplies that science proves to be philosophy. As for the way of life in question, the art which supplies it proves to be the royal or political art. Yet the philosopher and the king prove to be identical. Accordingly, philosophy by itself is not only necessary but sufficient for producing happiness: philoso-

[8] The Arabic transcription of the Greek word for "philosophy."

phy do̲es not need to be supplemented by something else, or by something that is thought to be higher in rank than philosophy, in order to produce happiness. The purpose of Plato, or of Aristotle, as Fārābī conceived of it, is sufficiently revealed in this seemingly conventional praise of philosophy.

The praise of philosophy is meant to rule out any claims of cognitive value which may be raised on behalf of religion in general and of revealed religion in particular. For the philosophy on which Fārābī bestows his unqualified praise, is the philosophy of the pagans Plato and Aristotle. In his *Enumeration of the Sciences,* he presents the "Islamic sciences" *(fiqh* and *kalām)* as corollaries to political science. By this very fact, the pursuits in question cease to be Islamic; they become the arts of interpreting and of defending any divine law or any positive religion. Whatever obscurity there might seem to be in the *Enumeration,* every ambiguity is avoided in the *Plato.* Through the mouth of Plato, Fārābī declares that religious speculation, and religious investigation of the beings, and the religious syllogistic art, do not supply the science of the beings, in which man's highest perfection consists, whereas philosophy does supply it. He goes so far as to present religious knowledge as the lowest step on the ladder of cognitive pursuits, as inferior even to grammar and to poetry. The purpose of the *Plato* as a whole makes it clear that this verdict is not affected if one substitutes the religious knowledge available in Fārābī's time for the religious knowledge available in Plato's time.

At the beginning of the treatise *On the Attainment of Happiness* with which he prefaces his summaries of the philosophies of Plato and of Aristotle, Fārābī employs the distinction between "the happiness of this world in this life" and "the ultimate happiness in the other life" as a matter of course. In the *Plato,* which is the second and therefore the least exposed part of a tripartite work, the distinction of the two kinds of happiness is completely dropped. What this silence means becomes clear from the fact that in the whole *Plato* (which contains summaries of the *Gorgias,* the *Phaedrus,* the *Phaedo,* and the *Republic),* there is no mention of the immortality of the soul: Fārābī's Plato silently rejects Plato's doctrine of a life after death.

Fārābī could go so far in the *Plato,* not merely because that treatise is the least exposed and the shortest part of a larger work, but also because it sets forth explicitly the views of another man. As has been mentioned, he treats differently the two kinds of happiness in *On the Attainment of Happiness* and in the *Plato;* and he treats religious knowledge somewhat differently in the *Enumeration of the Sciences* and in the *Plato.* Proceeding in accordance with the same rule, he pronounces more or less orthodox views concerning the life after death in *The Virtuous Religious Community* and *The Political Governments,* i.e., in works in which he speaks in his own name. More precisely, in *The Virtuous Religious Community,* he pronounces simply orthodox views, and in *The Political Governments* he pronounces views which, if heretical, could nonetheless still be considered tolerable. But in his commentary on the *Nicomachean Ethics* he declares that there is only the happiness of this life, and that all divergent statements are based on "ravings and old women's tales."[9]

Fārābī avails himself then of the specific immunity of the commentator or of the historian in order to speak his mind concerning grave matters in his "historical" works, rather than in the works in which he speaks in his own name. Yet could not Fārābī, as a commentator, have expounded, without a muttering of dissent, such views as he rejected as a man? Could he not have been attracted, as a student of philosophy, by what he abhorred as a believer? Could his mind not have been of the type that is attributed to the Latin Averroists? It almost suffices to state this suspicion in order to see that it is unfounded. The Latin Averroists gave a most literal interpretation of extremely heretical teachings. But Fārābī did just the reverse: he gave an extremely unliteral interpretation of a relatively tolerable teaching. Precisely as a mere commentator of Plato, Fārābī was compelled to embrace the doctrine of a life after death. His flagrant deviation from the letter of Plato's teaching, or his refusal to succumb to

9 Ibn Tufail, *Hajj ibn Yaqdhān,* ed. by L. Gauthier, Beyrouth, 1936, 14. Compare the remarks of Averroes which are quoted by Steinschneider, *Al-Farabi,* 94 and 106 ("In libro enim de Nicomachia videtur [Alfarabius] negare continuationem esse cum intelligentiis abstractis: et dicit hanc esse opinionem Alexandri, et quod non est opinionandum quod finis humanus sit aliud quam perfectio speculativa"). Compare Thomas Aquinas, Commentary on *Eth. Nic.* X, lect. 13 *vers.fin.,* and *S.c.G.* III cap. 48 *vers.fin.*

Plato's charms, proves sufficiently that he rejected the belief in a happiness different from the happiness of this life, or the belief in another life. His silence about the immortality of the soul in a treatise designed to present the philosophy of Plato "from its beginning to its end" places beyond any reasonable doubt the inference that the statements asserting the immortality of the soul, which occur in some of his other writings, must be regarded as accommodations to the accepted views.

Fārābī's Plato identifies the philosopher with the king. He remains silent, however, about the precise relationship between the philosopher and the king on the one hand, and the legislator on the other; to say the least, he does not explicitly identify the legislator with the philosopher-king. Whatever this may mean,[10] Fārābī suggests in the *Plato* that philosophy is not simply identical with the royal art: philosophy is the highest theoretical art, and the royal art is the highest practical art; and the fundamental difference between theory and practice remains a major theme throughout the *Plato*. Since he contends that philosophy and the royal art together are required for producing happiness, he agrees in a way with the orthodox view according to which philosophy is insufficient for leading man to happiness. Yet the supplement to philosophy which, according to him, is required for the attainment of happiness is not religion or Revelation but politics, if Platonic politics. He substitutes politics for religion. He thus may be said to lay the foundation for the secular alliance between philosophers and princes friendly to philosophy, and to initiate the tradition whose most famous representatives in the West are Marsilius of Padua and Machiavelli.[11] He speaks of the need for the virtuous city which he calls "another city." He means to replace the other world or the other life by the other city. The other city stands midway between this world and the other world, since it is an earthly city indeed, yet a city existing not "in deed" but "in speech."

In fact, it is by no means certain that the purpose of Plato or of Aristotle, as Fārābī understood it, required the actualization

[10] The meaning is indicated by the fact that in the three last paragraphs of the *Plato*, "philosopher," "king," "perfect man" and "investigator" on the one hand, and "legislator" and "virtuous men" on the other, are treated as interchangeable.

[11] See below, p. 91, note 156.

of the best political order or of the virtuous city. Fārābī adumbrates the problem by making a distinction between Socrates' investigations and Plato's investigations, as well as between "the way of Socrates" and the way adopted eventually by Plato. "The science and the art of Socrates" which is to be found in Plato's *Laws,* is only a part of Plato's, the other part being "the science and the art of Timaeus" which is to be found in the *Timaeus.* "The way of Socrates" is characterized by the emphasis on "the scientific investigation of justice and the virtues," whereas the art of Plato is meant to supply "the science of the essence of every being" and hence especially the science of the divine and of the natural things. The difference between the way of Socrates and the way of Plato points back to the difference between the attitude of the two men toward the actual cities. The crucial difficulty was created by the political or social status of philosophy: in the nations and cities of Plato's time, there was no freedom of teaching and of investigation. Socrates was therefore confronted with the alternative, whether he should choose security and life, and thus conform with the false opinions and the wrong way of life of his fellow-citizens, or else non-conformity and death. Socrates chose non-conformity and death. Plato found a solution to the problem posed by the fate of Socrates, in founding the virtuous city in speech: only in that "other city" can man reach his perfection. Yet, according to Fārābī, Plato "repeated" his account of the way of Socrates and he "repeated" the mention of the vulgar of the cities and nations which existed in his time.[12] The repetition amounts to a considerable modification of the first statement, or to a correction of the Socratic way. The Platonic way, as distinguished from the Socratic way, is a combination of the way of Socrates with the way of Thrasymachus; for the intransigent way of Socrates is appropriate only for the philosopher's dealing with the elite, whereas the way of Thrasymachus, which is both more and less exacting than the former, is appropriate for his dealings with the vulgar. What Fārābī suggests is that by combining the way of Socrates with the way of Thrasymachus, Plato avoided the conflict with the vulgar and thus the fate of Socrates. Accordingly, the revolutionary quest for the other city ceased to be necessary:

[12] As regards the precise meaning of "repetition," see below, pp. 62-64.

Plato substituted for it a more conservative way of action, namely, the gradual replacement of the accepted opinions by the truth or an approximation to the truth. The replacement of the accepted opinions could not be gradual, if it were not accompanied by a provisional acceptance of the accepted opinions: as Fārābī elsewhere declares, conformity with the opinions of the religious community in which one is brought up, is a necessary qualification for the future philosopher.[13] The replacement of the accepted opinions could not be gradual if it were not accompanied by the suggestion of opinions which, while pointing toward the truth, do not too flagrantly contradict the accepted opinions. We may say that Fārābī's Plato eventually replaces the philosopher-king who rules openly in the virtuous city, by the secret kingship of the philosopher who, being "a perfect man" precisely because he is an "investigator," lives privately as a member of an imperfect society which he tries to humanize within the limits of the possible. Fārābī's remarks on Plato's policy define the general character of the activity of the *falāsifa.*

In the light of these considerations, it would appear to be rash to identify the teaching of the *falāsifa* with what they taught most frequently or most conspicuously. The attempt to establish their serious teaching is rendered still more difficult by the fact that some opponents of the *falāsifa* seem to have thought it necessary to help the *falāsifa* in concealing their teaching, because they feared the harm which its publication would cause to those of their fellow-believers whose faith was weak.

What Fārābī indicates in regard to the procedure of the true philosophers, is confirmed by a number of remarks about the philosophic distinction between the exoteric and the esoteric teaching which occur in the writings of his successors. Fārābī's *Plato* informs us about the most obvious and the crudest reason why this antiquated or forgotten distinction was needed. Philosophy and the philosophers were "in grave danger." Society did not recognize philosophy or the right of philosophizing. There was no harmony between philosophy and society. The

[13] *On the Attainment of Happiness (k.tahsīl as-sa'āda,* Hyderabad 1345, 45). Compare the first two maxims of Descartes' "morale par provision" (*Discours de la méthode,* III).

philosophers were very far from being exponents of society or of parties. They defended the interests of philosophy and of nothing else. In doing this, they believed indeed that they were defending the highest interests of mankind.[14] The exoteric teaching was needed for protecting philosophy. It was the armor in which philosophy had to appear. It was needed for political reasons. It was the form in which philosophy became visible to the political community. It was the political aspect of philosophy. It was "political" philosophy. From here we shall perhaps understand sometime why Fārābī presented the whole of philosophy within a political framework, or why his most comprehensive writings are "political books." It is not impossible that the title "the two philosophies" by which his treatise *On the Purposes of Plato and of Aristotle* was known, intimated the difference between "the two philosophies" or "the two doctrines": the exterior and the interior. This possibility cannot be neglected in any serious evaluation of the Platonism or rather Neo-Platonism of the *falāsifa,* and in particular of the use which they sometimes made of the Neo-Platonic *Theology of Aristotle.* It suffices here to remark that Fārābī's *Plato* shows no trace whatever of Neo-Platonic influence.

In most of the current reflections on the relation between philosophy and society, it is somehow taken for granted that philosophy always possessed political or social status. According to Fārābī, philosophy was not recognized in the cities and nations of Plato's time. He shows by his whole procedure that there was even less freedom of philosophizing in the cities and nations of his own time, i.e., "after philosophy had been blurred or destroyed." The fact that "philosophy" and "the philosophers" came to mean in the Islamic world a suspect pursuit and a suspect group of men, not to say simply unbelief and unbelievers, shows sufficiently how precarious the status of philosophy was: the legitimacy of philosophy was not recognized.[15] Here, we are touching on what, from the point of view of the sociology of philosophy, is the most important difference between Christianity on the one hand, and Islam as well as Judaism on the

---

[14] Fārābī, *Plato,* §17.
[15] Compare Gardet-Anawati, *op. cit.,* 78, 225, and 236.

Introduction   19

other. For the Christian, the sacred doctrine is revealed theology; for the Jew and the Muslim, the sacred doctrine is, at least
primarily, the legal interpretation of the Divine Law (*talmud*
or *fiqh*). The sacred doctrine in the latter sense has, to say the
least, much less in common with philosophy than the sacred
doctrine in the former sense. It is ultimately for this reason that
the status of philosophy was, as a matter of principle, much more
precarious in Judaism and in Islam than in Christianity: in
Christianity philosophy became an integral part of the officially
recognized and even required training of the student of the
sacred doctrine. This difference explains partly the eventual
collapse of philosophic inquiry in the Islamic and in the Jewish
world, a collapse which has no parallel in the Western Christian
world.

Owing to the position which "the science of *kalām*" acquired
in Islam, the status of philosophy in Islam was intermediate between its status in Christianity and in Judaism. To turn therefore to the status of philosophy within Judaism, it is obvious that
while no one can be learned in the sacred doctrine of Christianity without having had considerable philosophic training, one
can be a perfectly competent talmudist without having had any
philosophic training. Jews of the philosophic competence of
Halevi and Maimonides took it for granted that being a Jew and
being a philosopher are mutually exclusive. At first glance,
Maimonides' *Guide for the Perplexed* is the Jewish counterpart
of Thomas Aquinas' *Summa Theologica;* but the *Guide* never
acquired within Judaism even a part of the authority which the
Summa enjoyed within Christianity; not Maimonides' *Guide,*
but his *Mishne Torah,* i.e., his codification of the Jewish law,
could be described as the Jewish counterpart to the *Summa.*
Nothing is more revealing than the difference between the beginnings of the *Guide* and of the *Summa.* The first article of the
Summa deals with the question as to whether the sacred doctrine is required besides the philosophic disciplines: Thomas as
it were justifies the sacred doctrine before the tribunal of philosophy. One cannot even imagine Maimonides opening the
Guide, or any other work, with a discussion of the question as to
whether the Halakha (the sacred Law) is required besides the

philosophic disciplines. The first chapters of the *Guide* look like a somewhat diffuse commentary on a Biblical verse (Genesis 1, 27) rather than like the opening of a philosophic or theological work. Maimonides, just as Averroes, needed much more urgently a legal justification of philosophy, i.e., a discussion in legal terms of the question whether the Divine Law permits or forbids or commands the study of philosophy, than a philosophic justification of the Divine Law or of its study. The reasons which Maimonides adduces in order to prove that certain rational truths about divine things must be kept secret, were used by Thomas in order to prove that the rational truth about the divine things was in need of being divinely revealed.[16] In accordance with his occasional remark that the Jewish tradition emphasized God's justice rather than God's wisdom, Maimonides discerned the Jewish equivalent to philosophy or theology in certain elements of the Aggadah (or Legend), i.e., of that part of the Jewish lore which was generally regarded as much less authoritative than the Halakhah.[17] Spinoza bluntly said that the Jews despise philosophy.[18] As late as 1765, Moses Mendelssohn felt it necessary to apologize for recommending the study of logic, and to show why the prohibition against the reading of extraneous or profane books does not apply to works on logic.[19] The issue of traditional Judaism versus philosophy is identical with the issue of Jerusalem versus Athens. It is difficult not to see the connection between the depreciation of the primary object of philosophy—the heavens and the heavenly bodies—in the first chapter of Genesis, the prohibition against eating of the tree of knowledge of good and evil in the second chapter, the divine name "I shall be what I shall be," the admonition that the Law is not in heaven nor beyond the sea, the saying of the prophet Micah about what the Lord requires of man, and such Talmudic utterances as these: "for him who reflects about four things—about what is above, what is below, what is before, what is behind—it would be better not to have come into the world,"

[16] Compare *Guide* I 34 with Thomas, *S.c.G.* I 4 and *Quaest. disput. De Veritate* q. 14 a. 10.

[17] Compare the passages indicated below, p. 39 n. 5 with *Guide* III 17 (35 a Munk).

[18] *Tr. Theol.-pol.* XI *vers.fin.* Cf. ib. I (§41 Bruder). See also Georges Vajda, *Introduction à la Pensée Juive du Moyen Age*, Paris, 1947, 43.

[19] *Gesammelte Schriften*, Jubilaeums-Ausgabe, II, 202-207.

and "God owns nothing in His World except the four.cubits of the Halakhah."[20]

The precarious status of philosophy in Judaism as well as in Islam was not in every respect a misfortune for philosophy. The official recognition of philosophy in the Christian world made philosophy subject to ecclesiastical supervision. The precarious position of philosophy in the Islamic-Jewish world guaranteed its private character and therewith its inner freedom from supervision. The status of philosophy in the Islamic-Jewish world resembled in this respect its status in classical Greece. It is often said that the Greek city was a totalitarian society. It embraced and regulated morals, divine worship, tragedy and comedy. There was however one activity which was essentially private and trans-political: philosophy. Even the philosophic schools were founded by men without authority, by private men. The Islamic and Jewish philosophers recognized the similarity between this state of things and the one prevailing in their own time. Elaborating on some remarks of Aristotle, they compared the philosophic life to the life of the hermit.

Fārābī ascribed to Plato the view that in the Greek city the philosopher was in grave danger. In making this statement, he merely repeated what Plato himself had said. To a considerable extent, the danger was averted by the art of Plato, as Fārābī likewise noted. But the success of Plato must not blind us to the existence of a danger which, however much its forms may vary, is coeval with philosophy. The understanding of this danger and of the various forms which it has taken, and which it may take, is the foremost task, and indeed the sole task, of the sociology of philosophy.

[20] Compare Maimonides, *Guide* I 32 (36 b Munk) and his Introduction to his commentary on the Mishna (*Porta Mosis*, ed. E. Pococke, Oxford, 1655, 90).

2

PERSECUTION AND THE ART OF WRITING

> "That vice has often proved an eman-
> cipator of the mind, is one of the
> most humiliating, but, at the same
> time, one of the most unquestionable,
> facts in history."
>
> —W. E. H. Lecky

I

In a considerable number of countries which, for about a hundred years, have enjoyed a practically complete freedom of public discussion, that freedom is now suppressed and replaced by
a compulsion to coordinate speech with such views as the government believes to be expedient, or holds in all seriousness. It
may be worth our while to consider briefly the effect of that
compulsion, or persecution, on thoughts as well as actions.[1]

A large section of the people, probably the great majority of
the younger generation,[2] accepts the government-sponsored
views as true, if not at once at least after a time. How have they
been convinced? And where does the time factor enter? They
have not been convinced by compulsion, for compulsion does

[1] *Scribere est agere.* See Sir William Blackstone, *Commentaries*, Book IV, chap.
6. Compare Machiavelli, *Discorsi*, III, 6 (*I Classici del Giglio*, pp. 424-26) and
Descartes, *Discours de la méthode*, VI, beginning.

[2] "*Socrates:* Do you know by what means they might be persuaded to accept
this story? *Glauco:* By no means, as far as they themselves are concerned, but I
know how it could be done as regards their sons and their descendants and the
people of a later age generally speaking. *Socrates:* . . . I understand, more or less,
what you mean." Plato, *Republic*, 415 c6-d5.

not produce conviction. It merely paves the way for conviction by silencing contradiction. What is called freedom of thought in a large number of cases amounts to—and even for all practical purposes consists of—the ability to choose between two or more different views presented by the small minority of people who are public speakers or writers.[3] If this choice is prevented, the only kind of intellectual independence of which many people are capable is destroyed, and that is the only freedom of thought which is of political importance. Persecution is therefore the indispensable condition for the highest efficiency of what may be called *logica equina*. According to the horse-drawn Parmenides, or to Gulliver's Houyhnhnms, one cannot say, or one cannot reasonably say "the thing which is not": that is, lies are inconceivable. This logic is not peculiar to horses or horse-drawn philosophers, but determines, if in a somewhat modified manner, the thought of many ordinary human beings as well. They would admit, as a matter of course, that man can lie and does lie. But they would add that lies are short-lived and cannot stand the test of repetition—let alone of constant repetition—and that therefore a statement which is constantly repeated and never contradicted must be true. Another line of argument maintains that a statement made by an ordinary fellow may be a lie, but the truth of a statement made by a responsible and respected man, and therefore particularly by a man in a highly responsible or exalted position, is morally certain. These two enthymemes lead to the conclusion that the truth of a statement which is constantly repeated by the head of the government and never contradicted is absolutely certain.

This implies that in the countries concerned all those whose thinking does not follow the rules of *logica equina*, in other words, all those capable of truly independent thinking, cannot be brought to accept the government-sponsored views. Persecution, then, cannot prevent independent thinking. It cannot prevent even the expression of independent thought. For it is as true today as it was more than two thousand years ago that it is a safe venture to tell the truth one knows to benevolent and trustworthy acquaintances, or more precisely, to reasonable friends.[4]

[3] "Reason is but choosing" is the central thesis of Milton's *Areopagitica*.
[4] Plato, *Republic*, 450 d3-e1.

Persecution cannot prevent even public expression of the heterodox truth, for a man of independent thought can utter his views in public and remain unharmed, provided he moves with circumspection. He can even utter them in print without incurring any danger, provided he is capable of writing between the lines.

The expression "writing between the lines" indicates the subject of this article. For the influence of persecution on literature is precisely that it compels all writers who hold heterodox views to develop a peculiar technique of writing, the technique which we have in mind when speaking of writing between the lines. This expression is clearly metaphoric. Any attempt to express its meaning in unmetaphoric language would lead to the discovery of a terra incognita, a field whose very dimensions are as yet unexplored and which offers ample scope for highly intriguing and even important investigations. One may say without fear of being presently convicted of grave exaggeration that almost the only preparatory work to guide the explorer in this field is buried in the writings of the rhetoricians of antiquity.

To return to our present subject, let us look at a simple example which, I have reason to believe, is not so remote from reality as it might first seem. We can easily imagine that a historian living in a totalitarian country, a generally respected and unsuspected member of the only party in existence, might be led by his investigations to doubt the soundness of the government-sponsored interpretation of the history of religion. Nobody would prevent him from publishing a passionate attack on what he would call the liberal view. He would of course have to state the liberal view before attacking it; he would make that statement in the quiet, unspectacular and somewhat boring manner which would seem to be but natural; he would use many technical terms, give many quotations and attach undue importance to insignificant details; he would seem to forget the holy war of mankind in the petty squabbles of pedants. Only when he reached the core of the argument would he write three or four sentences in that terse and lively style which is apt to arrest the attention of young men who love to think. That central passage would state the case of the adversaries more clearly, compellingly and mercilessly than it had ever been stated in the heyday of liberalism, for he would silently drop all the foolish excrescences of the liberal creed which were allowed to grow up during the time when liberalism had succeeded and therefore was approaching dormancy. His reasonable young reader would for the first time catch a glimpse of the forbidden fruit. The attack, the bulk of the work, would consist of virulent expansions of the most virulent utterances in the holy book or books of the ruling party. The intelligent young man who, being young, had until then been somehow attracted by those immoderate utterances, would now be merely disgusted and, after having tasted the forbidden fruit, even bored by them. Reading the book for the second and third time, he would detect in the very arrangement of the quotations from the authoritative books significant additions to those few terse statements which occur in the center of the rather short first part.

Persecution, then, gives rise to a peculiar technique of writing, and therewith to a peculiar type of literature, in which the truth about all crucial things is presented exclusively between the lines. That literature is addressed, not to all readers, but to trustworthy and intelligent readers only. It has all the advantages of private communication without having its greatest disadvantage—that it reaches only the writer's acquaintances. It has all the advantages of public communication without having its greatest disadvantage—capital punishment for the author. But how can a man perform the miracle of speaking in a publication to a minority, while being silent to the majority of his readers? The fact which makes this literature possible can be expressed in the axiom that thoughtless men are careless readers, and only thoughtful men are careful readers. Therefore an author who wishes to address only thoughtful men has but to write in such a way that only a very careful reader can detect the meaning of his book. But, it will be objected, there may be clever men, careful readers, who are not trustworthy, and who, after having found the author out, would denounce him to the authorities. As a matter of fact, this literature would be impossible if the Socratic dictum that virtue is knowledge, and therefore that thoughtful men as such are trustworthy and not cruel, were entirely wrong.

Another axiom, but one which is meaningful only so long as

persecution remains within the bounds of legal procedure, is that a careful writer of normal intelligence is more intelligent than the most intelligent censor, as such. For the burden of proof rests with the censor. It is he, or the public prosecutor, who must prove that the author holds or has uttered heterodox views. In order to do so he must show that certain literary deficiencies of the work are not due to chance, but that the author used a given ambiguous expression deliberately, or that he constructed a certain sentence badly on purpose. That is to say, the censor must prove not only that the author is intelligent and a good writer in general, for a man who intentionally blunders in writing must possess the art of writing, but above all that he was on the usual level of his abilities when writing the incriminating words. But how can that be proved, if even Homer nods from time to time?

II

SUPPRESSION of independent thought has occurred fairly frequently in the past. It is reasonable to assume that earlier ages produced proportionately as many men capable of independent thought as we find today, and that at least some of these men combined understanding with caution. Thus, one may wonder whether some of the greatest writers of the past have not adapted their literary technique to the requirements of persecution, by presenting their views on all the then crucial questions exclusively between the lines.

We are prevented from considering this possibility, and still more from considering the questions connected with it, by some habits produced by, or related to, a comparatively recent progress in historical research. This progress was due, at first glance, to the general acceptance and occasional application of the following principles. Each period of the past, it was demanded, must be understood by itself, and must not be judged by standards alien to it. Each author must, as far as possible, be interpreted by himself; no term of any consequence must be used in the interpretation of an author which cannot be literally translated into his language, and which was not used by him or was not in fairly common use in his time. The only presentations of an author's views which can be accepted as true are those ultimately borne out by his own explicit statements. The last of these principles is decisive: it seems to exclude a priori from the sphere of human knowledge such views of earlier writers as are indicated exclusively between the lines. For if an author does not tire of asserting explicitly on every page of his book that *a* is *b*, but indicates between the lines that *a* is not *b*, the modern historian will still demand explicit evidence showing that the author believed *a* not to be *b*. Such evidence cannot possibly be forthcoming, and the modern historian wins his argument: he can dismiss any reading between the lines as arbitrary guesswork, or, if he is lazy, he will accept it as intuitive knowledge.

The application of these principles has had important consequences. Up to a time within the memory of men still living, many people, bearing in mind famous statements of Bodin, Hobbes, Burke, Condorcet and others, believed that there is a difference in fundamental conceptions between modern political thought and the political thought of the Middle Ages and of antiquity. The present generation of scholars has been taught by one of the most famous historians of our time that "at least from the lawyers of the second century to the theorists of the French Revolution, the history of political thought is continuous, changing in form, modified in content, but still the same in its fundamental conceptions."[5] Until the middle of the nineteenth century, Averroes was thought to have been hostile to all religion. After Renan's successful attack on what is now called a medieval legend, present-day scholars consider Averroes a loyal, and even a believing, Muslim.[6] Previous writers had believed that "the abrogation of religious and magical thought" was characteristic of the attitude of the Greek physicians. A more recent writer

[5] A. J. Carlyle, *A History of Mediaeval Political Theory in the West*, I (2nd ed., London, 1927), 2.
[6] Ernest Renan, *Averroès et l'Averroïsme* (3rd ed., Paris, 1866), 292 ff. Léon Gauthier, *La théorie d'Ibn Rochd (Averroès) sur les rapports de la religion et de la philosophie* (Paris, 1909), 126 ff. and 177 ff. Compare the same author's "Scolastique musulmane et scolastique chrétienne," *Revue d'Histoire de la Philosophie*, II (1928), 221 ff. and 333 ff.

asserts that "the Hippocratic physicians . . . as scientists embraced a supernatural dogma."[7] Lessing, who was one of the most profound humanists of all times, with an exceedingly rare combination of scholarship, taste and philosophy, and who was convinced that there are truths which should not or cannot be pronounced, believed that "all ancient philosophers" had distinguished between their exoteric and their esoteric teaching. After the great theologian Schleiermacher asserted, with an unusually able argument, the view that there is only one Platonic teaching, the question of the esotericism of the ancient philosophers was narrowed down, for all practical purposes, to the meaning of Aristotle's "exoteric speeches"; and in this regard one of the greatest humanists of the present day asserts that the attribution of a secret teaching to Aristotle is "obviously a late invention originating in the spirit of Neo-Pythagoreanism."[8] According to Gibbon, Eusebius "indirectly confesses that he has related whatever might redound to the glory, and that he has suppressed all that could tend to the disgrace of religion." According to a present-day historian, "the judgment of Gibbon, that the *Ecclesiastical History* was grossly unfair, is itself a prejudiced verdict."[9] Up to the end of the nineteenth century many philosophers and theologians believed that Hobbes was an atheist. At present many historians tacitly or explicitly reject that view; a contemporary thinker, while feeling that Hobbes was not exactly a religious man, has descried in his writings the outlines of a neo-Kantian philosophy of religion.[10] Montesquieu himself, as well as some of his contemporaries, believed that *De l'esprit des lois* had a good and

[7] Ludwig Edelstein, "Greek Medicine in its Relation to Religion and Magic," *Bulletin of the Institute of the History of Medicine*, V (1937), 201 and 211.

[8] Lessing, *Ernst und Falk*, 2nd dialogue; and "Leibniz von den ewigen Strafen," *Werke* (Petersen and v. Olshausen edition), XXI, 147. Friedrich Schleiermacher, *Platons Werke* (Berlin, 1804), vol. I, 1, pp. 12-20. Werner Jaeger, *Aristotle* (Oxford, 1934), 33. See also Sir Alexander Grant, *The Ethics of Aristotle* (London, 1874) I, 398 ff. and Eduard Zeller, *Aristotle and the Earlier Peripatetics* (London, 1897), I, 120 ff.

[9] James T. Shotwell, *The History of History*, I (New York, 1939), 356 ff.

[10] Ferdinand Tönnies, *Thomas Hobbes* (3rd ed., Stuttgart, 1925), 148. George E. G. Catlin, *Thomas Hobbes* (Oxford, 1922), 25. Richard Hönigswald, *Hobbes und die Staatsphilosophie* (Munich, 1924), 176 ff. Leo Strauss, *Die Religionskritik Spinozas* (Berlin, 1930), 80. Z. Lubienski, *Die Grundlagen des ethisch-politischen Systems von Hobbes* (Munich, 1932), 213 ff.

even a wonderful plan; Laboulaye still believed that the apparent obscurity of its plan as well as its other apparent literary deficiencies were due to censorship or persecution. One of the most outstanding present-day historians of political thought, however, asserts that "there is not in truth much concatenation of subject-matter, and the amount of irrelevance is extraordinary," and that "it cannot be said that Montesquieu's *Spirit of the Laws* has any arrangement."[11]

This selection of examples, which is not wholly arbitrary, shows that the typical difference between older views and more recent views is due not entirely to progress in historical exactness, but also to a more basic change in the intellectual climate. During the last few decades the rationalist tradition, which was the common denominator of the older views, and which was still rather influential in nineteenth-century positivism, has been either still further transformed or altogether rejected by an ever-increasing number of people. Whether and to what extent this change is to be considered a progress or a decline is a question which only the philosopher can answer.

A more modest duty is imposed on the historian. He will merely, and rightly, demand that in spite of all changes which have occurred or which will occur in the intellectual climate, the tradition of historical exactness shall be continued. Accord-

---

[11] George H. Sabine, *A History of Political Theory* (New York, 1937), 556 and 551. Friedrich Meinecke, *Die Entstehung des Historismus* (Munich, 1936), 139 ff. and 151, footnote 1. Édouard Laboulaye, "Introduction à l'Esprit des Lois," *Oeuvres complètes de Montesquieu* (Paris, 1876) vol. 3, pp. xviii ff. Laboulaye quotes in that context an important passage from d'Alembert's "Éloge de Montesquieu." See also Bertolini's "Analyse raisonnée de l'Esprit des Lois," *ibid.*, pp. 6, 14, 23 ff., 34 and 60 ff. The remarks of d'Alembert, Bertolini and Laboulaye are merely explanations of what Montesquieu himself indicates for example when he says in the preface: "Si l'on veut chercher le dessein de l'auteur, on ne le peut bien découvrir que dans le dessein de l'ouvrage." (See also the end of the eleventh book and two letters from Helvétius, *ibid.*, vol. 6, pp. 314, 320). D'Alembert says: "Nous disons de l'*obscurité* que l'on peut se permettre dans un tel ouvrage, la même chose que du *défaut d'ordre*. Ce qui seroit obscur pour les lecteurs vulgaires, ne l'est pas pour ceux que l'auteur a eus en vue; d'ailleurs l'obscurité volontaire n'en est pas une. M. de Montesquieu ayant à présenter quelquefois des vérités importantes, dont l'énoncé absolu et direct auroit pu blesser sans fruit, a eu la prudence de les envelopper; et, par cet innocent artifice, les a voilées à ceux à qui elles seroient nuisibles, sans qu'elles fussent perdues pour les sages." Similarly, certain contemporaries of the "rhetor" Xenophon believed that "what is beautifully and methodically written, is not beautifully and methodically written" (*Cynegeticus*, 13. 6).

ingly, he will not accept an arbitrary standard of exactness which might exclude a priori the most important facts of the past from human knowledge, but will adapt the rules of certainty which guide his research to the nature of his subject. He will then follow such rules as these: Reading between the lines is strictly prohibited in all cases where it would be less exact than not doing so. Only such reading between the lines as starts from an exact consideration of the explicit statements of the author is legitimate. The context in which a statement occurs, and the literary character of the whole work as well as its plan, must be perfectly understood before an interpretation of the statement can reasonably claim to be adequate or even correct. One is not entitled to delete a passage, nor to emend its text, before one has fully considered all reasonable possibilities of understanding the passage as it stands—one of these possibilities being that the passage may be ironic. If a master of the art of writing commits such blunders as would shame an intelligent high school boy, it is reasonable to assume that they are intentional, especially if the author discusses, however incidentally, the possibility of intentional blunders in writing. The views of the author of a drama or dialogue must not, without previous proof, be identified with the views expressed by one or more of his characters, or with those agreed upon by all his characters or by his attractive characters. The real opinion of an author is not necessarily identical with that which he expresses in the largest number of passages. In short, exactness is not to be confused with refusal, or inability, to see the wood for the trees. The truly exact historian will reconcile himself to the fact that there is a difference between winning an argument, or proving to practically everyone that he is right, and understanding the thought of the great writers of the past.

It must, then, be considered possible that reading between the lines will not lead to complete agreement among all scholars. If this is an objection to reading between the lines as such, there is the counter-objection that neither have the methods generally used at present led to universal or even wide agreement in regard to very important points. Scholars of the last century were inclined to solve literary problems by having recourse to the genesis of the author's work, or even of his thought. Contradictions or divergences within one book, or between two books by the same author, were supposed to prove that his thought had changed. If the contradictions exceeded a certain limit it was sometimes decided without any external evidence that one of the works must be spurious. That procedure has lately come into some disrepute, and at present many scholars are inclined to be rather more conservative about the literary tradition, and less impressed by merely internal evidence. The conflict between the traditionalists and the higher critics is, however, far from being settled. The traditionalists could show in important cases that the higher critics have not proved their hypotheses at all; but even if all the answers suggested by the higher critics should ultimately prove to be wrong, the questions which led them away from the tradition and tempted them to try a new approach often show an awareness of difficulties which do not disturb the slumber of the typical traditionalist. An adequate answer to the most serious of these questions requires methodical reflection on the literary technique of the great writers of earlier ages, because of the typical character of the literary problems involved— obscurity of the plan, contradictions within one work or between two or more works of the same author, omission of important links of the argument, and so on. Such reflection necessarily transcends the boundaries of modern aesthetics and even of traditional poetics, and will, I believe, compel students sooner or later to take into account the phenomenon of persecution. To mention something which is hardly more than another aspect of the same fact, we sometimes observe a conflict between a traditional, superficial and doxographic interpretation of some great writer of the past, and a more intelligent, deeper and monographic interpretation. They are equally exact, so far as both are borne out by explicit statements of the writer concerned. Only a few people at present, however, consider the possibility that the traditional interpretation may reflect the exoteric teaching of the author, whereas the monographic interpretation stops halfway between the exoteric and esoteric teaching of the author.

Modern historical research, which emerged at a time when

persecution was a matter of feeble recollection rather than of forceful experience, has counteracted or even destroyed an earlier tendency to read between the lines of the great writers, or to attach more weight to their fundamental design than to those views which they have repeated most often. Any attempt to restore the earlier approach in this age of historicism is confronted by the problem of criteria for distinguishing between legitimate and illegitimate reading between the lines. If it is true that there is a necessary correlation between persecution and writing between the lines, then there is a necessary negative criterion: that the book in question must have been composed in an era of persecution, that is, at a time when some political or other orthodoxy was enforced by law or custom. One positive criterion is this: if an able writer who has a clear mind and a perfect knowledge of the orthodox view and all its ramifications, contradicts surreptitiously and as it were in passing one of its necessary presuppositions or consequences which he explicitly recognizes and maintains everywhere else, we can reasonably suspect that he was opposed to the orthodox system as such and —we must study his whole book all over again, with much greater care and much less naïveté than ever before. In some cases, we possess even explicit evidence proving that the author has indicated his views on the most important subjects only between the lines. Such statements, however, do not usually occur in the preface or other very conspicuous place. Some of them cannot even be noticed, let alone understood, so long as we confine ourselves to the view of persecution and the attitude toward freedom of speech and candor which have become prevalent during the last three hundred years.

III

THE TERM persecution covers a variety of phenomena, ranging from the most cruel type, as exemplified by the Spanish Inquisition, to the mildest, which is social ostracism. Between these extremes are the types which are most important from the point of view of literary or intellectual history. Examples of these are found in the Athens of the fifth and fourth centuries B.C., in some Muslim countries of the early Middle Ages, in seventeenth-century Holland and England, and in eighteenth-century France and Germany—all of them comparatively liberal periods. But a glance at the biographies of Anaxagoras, Protagoras, Socrates, Plato, Xenophon, Aristotle, Avicenna, Averroes, Maimonides, Grotius, Descartes, Hobbes, Spinoza, Locke, Bayle, Wolff, Montesquieu, Voltaire, Rousseau, Lessing and Kant,[12] and in some cases even a glance at the title pages of their books, is sufficient to show that they witnessed or suffered, during at least part of their lifetimes, a kind of persecution which was more tangible than social ostracism. Nor should we overlook the fact, not sufficiently stressed by all authorities, that religious persecution and persecution of free inquiry are not identical. There were times and countries in which all kinds, or at least a great variety of kinds, of worship were permitted, but free inquiry was not.[13]

What attitude people adopt toward freedom of public discussion, depends decisively on what they think about popular education and its limits. Generally speaking, premodern philosophers were more timid in this respect than modern philosophers. After about the middle of the seventeenth century an ever-increasing number of heterodox philosophers who had suffered from persecution published their books not only to communicate their thoughts but also because they desired to contribute to the abolition of persecution as such. They believed that suppression of free inquiry, and of publication of the results of free inquiry, was accidental, an outcome of the faulty construction of the body politic, and that the kingdom of general darkness could be replaced by the republic of universal light. They looked forward to a time when, as a result of the progress of popular education, practically complete freedom of speech would be

[12] In regard to Kant, whose case is in a class by itself, even a historian so little given to suspicion or any other sort of skepticism as C. E. Vaughan remarks: "We are almost led to suspect Kant of having trifled with his readers, and of nursing an esoteric sympathy with Revolution." (*Studies in the History of Political Philosophy*, Manchester, 1939, II, 83.)

[13] See the "fragment" by H. S. Reimarus, "Von Duldung der Deisten," in Lessing's *Werke* (Petersen and v. Olshausen edition) XXII, 38 ff.

possible, or—to exaggerate for purposes of clarification—to a time
when no one would suffer any harm from hearing any truth.[14]
They concealed their views only far enough to protect themselves as well as possible from persecution; had they been more
subtle than that, they would have defeated their purpose, which
was to enlighten an ever-increasing number of people who were
not potential philosophers. It is therefore comparatively easy
to read between the lines of their books.[15] The attitude of an
earlier type of writers was fundamentally different. They believed that the gulf separating "the wise" and "the vulgar" was
a basic fact of human nature which could not be influenced by
any progress of popular education: philosophy, or science, was
essentially a privilege of "the few." They were convinced that
philosophy as such was suspect to, and hated by, the majority of
men.[16] Even if they had had nothing to fear from any particular
political quarter, those who started from that assumption would
have been driven to the conclusion that public communication
of the philosophic or scientific truth was impossible or unde-
sirable, not only for the time being but for all times. They must
conceal their opinions from all but philosophers, either by limiting themselves to oral instruction of a carefully selected group

[14] The question whether that extreme goal is attainable in any but the most
halcyon conditions has been raised in our time by Archibald MacLeish in "Post-
War Writers and Pre-War Readers," *Journal of Adult Education*, vol. 12 (June,
1940) in the following terms: "Perhaps the luxury of the complete confession,
the uttermost despair, the farthest doubt should be denied themselves by writers
living in any but the most orderly and settled times. I do not know."

[15] I am thinking of Hobbes in particular, whose significance for the development outlined above can hardly be overestimated. This was clearly recognized by
Tönnies, who emphasized especially these two sayings of his hero: "Paulatim
eruditur vulgus" and "Philosophia ut crescat libera esse debet nec metu nec
pudore coercenda." (Tönnies, *op. cit.*, pp. iv, 195.) Hobbes also says: "Suppression
of doctrines does but unite and exasperate, that is, increase both the malice and
power of them that have already believed them." (*English Works*, Molesworth
edition, VI, 242.) In his *Of Liberty and Necessity* (London 1654, 35 ff.) he writes
to the Marquess of Newcastle: "I must confess, if we consider the greatest part of
Mankinde, not as they should be, but as they are . . . I must, I say, confess that
the dispute of this question will rather hurt than help their piety, and therefore
if his Lordship [Bishop Bramhall] had not desired this answer, I should not
have written it, nor do I write it but in hopes your Lordship and his, will keep
it private."

[16] Cicero, *Tusculanae Disputationes*, II, 4. Plato, *Phaedo*, 64 b; *Republic*, 520
b2-3 and 494 a4-10.

of pupils, or by writing about the most important subject by means of "brief indication."[17]

Writings are naturally accessible to all who can read. Therefore a philosopher who chose the second way could expound only such opinions as were suitable for the nonphilosophic majority: all of his writings would have to be, strictly speaking, exoteric. These opinions would not be in all respects consonant with truth. Being a philosopher, that is, hating "the lie in the soul" more than anything else, he would not deceive himself about the fact that such opinions are merely "likely tales," or "noble lies," or "probable opinions," and would leave it to his philosophic readers to disentangle the truth from its poetic or dialectic presentation. But he would defeat his purpose if he indicated clearly which of his statements expressed a noble lie, and which the still more noble truth. For philosophic readers he would do almost more than enough by drawing their attention to the fact that he did not object to telling lies which were noble, or tales which were merely similar to truth. From the point of view of the literary historian at least, there is no more noteworthy difference between the typical premodern philosopher (who is hard to distinguish from the premodern poet) and the typical modern philosopher than that of their attitudes toward "noble (or just) lies," "pious frauds," the "ductus obliquus"[18] or "economy of the truth." Every decent modern reader is bound to be shocked by the mere suggestion that a great man might have deliberately deceived the large majority of his readers.[19] And yet, as a liberal theologian once remarked, these imitators of the resourceful Odysseus were perhaps merely more sin-

---

[17] Plato, *Timaeus*, 28 c3-5, and *Seventh Letter*, 332 d6-7, 341 c4-e3, and 344 d4-e2. That the view mentioned above is reconcilable with the democratic creed is shown most clearly by Spinoza, who was a champion not only of liberalism but also of democracy (*Tractatus politicus*, XI, 2, Bruder edition). See his *Tractatus de intellectus emendatione*, 14 and 17, as well as *Tractatus theologico-politicus*, V 35-39, XIV 20 and XV end.

[18] Sir Thomas More, *Utopia*, latter part of first book.

[19] A rather extensive discussion of the "magna quaestio, latebrosa tractatio, disputatio inter doctos alternans," as Augustinus called it, is to be found in Grotius' *De Jure Belli ac Pacis*, III, chap. I, §7 ff., and in particular §17, 3. See also *inter alia* Pascal's ninth and tenth *Provinciales* and Jeremy Taylor, *Ductor Dubitantium*, Book III, chap. 2, rule 5.

cere than we when they called "lying nobly" what we would call "considering one's social responsibilities."

An exoteric book contains then two teachings: a popular teaching of an edifying character, which is in the foreground; and a philosophic teaching concerning the most important subject, which is indicated only between the lines. This is not to deny that some great writers might have stated certain important truths quite openly by using as mouthpiece some disreputable character: they would thus show how much they disapproved of pronouncing the truths in question. There would then be good reason for our finding in the greatest literature of the past so many interesting devils, madmen, beggars, sophists, drunkards, epicureans and buffoons. Those to whom such books are truly addressed are, however, neither the unphilosophic majority nor the perfect philosopher as such, but the young men who might become philosophers: the potential philosophers are to be led step by step from the popular views which are indispensable for all practical and political purposes to the truth which is merely and purely theoretical, guided by certain obtrusively enigmatic features in the presentation of the popular teaching—obscurity of the plan, contradictions, pseudonyms, inexact repetitions of earlier statements, strange expressions, etc. Such features do not disturb the slumber of those who cannot see the wood for the trees, but act as awakening stumbling blocks for those who can. All books of that kind owe their existence to the love of the mature philosopher for the puppies[20] of his race, by whom he wants to be loved in turn: all exoteric books are "written speeches caused by love."

Exoteric literature presupposes that there are basic truths which would not be pronounced in public by any decent man, because they would do harm to many people who, having been hurt, would naturally be inclined to hurt in turn him who pronounces the unpleasant truths. It presupposes, in other words, that freedom of inquiry, and of publication of all results of inquiry, is not guaranteed as a basic right. This literature is then essentially related to a society which is not liberal. Thus one may very well raise the question of what use it could be in a truly liberal society. The answer is simple. In Plato's *Banquet*,

[20] Compare Plato, *Republic*, 539 a5-d1, with *Apology of Socrates*, 23 c2-8.

Alcibiades—that outspoken son of outspoken Athens—compares Socrates and his speeches to certain sculptures which are very ugly from the outside, but within have most beautiful images of things divine. The works of the great writers of the past are very beautiful even from without. And yet their visible beauty is sheer ugliness, compared with the beauty of those hidden treasures which disclose themselves only after very long, never easy, but always pleasant work. This always difficult but always pleasant work is, I believe, what the philosophers had in mind when they recommended education. Education, they felt, is the only answer to the always pressing question, to the political question par excellence, of how to reconcile order which is not oppression with freedom which is not license.

3

THE LITERARY CHARACTER OF THE
GUIDE FOR THE PERPLEXED

ἡ γὰρ ὕστερον εὐπορία λύσις τῶν
πρότερον ἀπορουμένων ἐστί, λύειν
δ᾽ οὐκ ἔστιν ἀγνοοῦντας τὸν δεσμόν.
—Aristotle

Among the many historians who have interpreted Maimonides'
teaching, or who are making efforts to interpret it, there is
scarcely one who would not agree to the principle that that
teaching, being essentially medieval, cannot be understood by
starting from modern presuppositions. The differences of view
between students of Maimonides have thus to be traced back,
not necessarily to a disagreement concerning the principle itself,
but rather to its different interpretation, or to a difference of
attitude in its application. The present essay is based on the
assumption that only through its most thoroughgoing application can we arrive at our goal, the true and exact understanding
of Maimonides' teaching.[1]

I. THE SUBJECT MATTER

THE interpreter of the *Guide for the Perplexed* ought to raise,
to begin with, the following question: To which science or sci-

---

[1] In the footnotes Roman and Arabic figures before the parentheses indicate the
part and chapter of the *Guide*, respectively. The figures in the parentheses before
the semicolon indicate the page in Munk's edition, and figures following the
semicolon indicate pages and lines in Joel's edition. For the first book of the
Mishneh Torah, I have used M. Hyamson's edition (New York, 1937).

ences does the subject matter of the work belong? Maimonides answers it almost at the very beginning of his work by saying that it is devoted to the true science of the law.

The true science of the law is distinguished from the science of the law in the usual sense, i.e., the *fiqh*.[2] While the term *fiqh* naturally occurs in the *Guide* on more than one occasion, the explanation of its meaning has been reserved for almost the very end of the work. *Fiqh* is the exact determination, by way of "deduction" from the authoritative statements of the law, of those actions by means of which man's life becomes noble, and especially of the actions of worship.[3] Its most scientific treatment would consist in a coherent and lucid codification of the law, such as achieved by Maimonides in his *Mishneh Torah,* which he calls "our great work on the *fiqh.*" In contradistinction to the legalistic study of the law, which is concerned with what man ought to do, the true science of the law is concerned with what man ought to think and to believe.[4] One may say that the science of the law in general is divided into two parts: a practical part which is treated in the *Mishneh Torah,* and a theoretical part which is treated in the *Guide.* This view is confirmed by the fact that the former work deals with beliefs and opinions only insofar as they are implied in prohibitions and commands, whereas the *Guide* deals with commands and prohibitions only in order to explain their reasons.

The relation between the two parts, or kinds, of the science of the law, may be described in a somewhat different way by saying that, whereas science of the law in the usual sense is the study of the halakah, the true science of the law corresponds to the aggadah. As a matter of fact, the *Guide* is a substitute for two books, planned by Maimonides, on the nonlegal sections of the Bible and the Talmud. But, above all, its most important feature, which distinguishes it from all philosophic as well as halakic books, is also characteristic of a part of the aggadic literature.[5]

Since Maimonides, however, uses an Islamic term to designate

[2] I, Introd. (3a; 2, 14 f., 26 f.).
[3] III, 54 (132b; 467, 20-25); cf. III, 27 (59b; 371, 29); 51 (123b; 455, 21-22).
[4] II, 10 (22b; 190, 14); I, Introd. (11a-b; 13, 3-5). Cf. the passages quoted in note 3.
[5] I, Introd. (5b and 11b; 5, 18 ff. and 13, 12-15). Cf. I, 70 (92b; 120, 4-8); 71 (94a; 121, 25-28).

the ordinary science of the law, it may be worth while to consider what Islamic term would supply the most proper designation for that science of the law which is the subject of the *Guide*. Students of the *fiqh* deal with the actions prescribed by the law, but do not deal with the "roots of religion," i.e., they do not attempt to prove the opinions or beliefs taught by the law. There seems to be little doubt that the science dealing with those roots is identical with the true science of the law.[6] Since the students of the roots are identified by Maimonides with the *Mutakallimûn*, the students of the *kalâm*, we shall say that the true science of the law is the *kalâm*.[7] It is true that Maimonides vigorously attacks the *kalâm;* yet in spite of his ruthless opposition to the assumptions and methods of the *Mutakallimûn*, he professes to be in perfect harmony with their intention.[8] The intention of the science of *kalâm* is to defend the law, especially against the opinions of philosophers.[9] And the central section of the *Guide* is admittedly devoted to the defense of the principal root of the law, the belief in creation, against the contention of the philosophers that the visible world is eternal.[10] What distinguishes Maimonides' *kalâm* from the *kalâm* proper is his insistence on the fundamental difference between intelligence and imagination, whereas, as he asserts, the *Mutakallimûn* mistake imagination for intelligence. In other words, Maimonides insists on the necessity of starting from evident presuppositions, which are in accordance with the nature of things, whereas the *kalâm* proper starts from arbitrary presuppositions, which are chosen not because they are true but because they make it easy to prove the beliefs taught by the law. Maimonides' true science of the law and the *kalâm* thus belong to the same genus,[11] the specific

---

[6] III, 51 (123b-124a; 455, 21-23). Cf. III, 54 (132a-b; 467, 7-9) with I, Introd. (3a; 2, 12-14).

[7] I, 71 (96b-97a; 125, 12). Cf. I, 73 (105b; 136, 2). Maimonides was called a שריש by Messer Leon; see Steinschneider, *Jewish Literature*, 310.

[8] II, 19 (40a; 211, 24-25); I, 71 (97b; 126, 4-5). Cf. also I, 73 (111b; 143, 6).

[9] Farabi, *'Ihṣâ al-'ulûm*, chap. 5. (See the Hebrew translation in Falakera's *Reshit Hokmah*, ed. David, 59 ff.) Farabi's discussion of the *kalâm*, and the framework of that discussion, are of decisive importance for the understanding of the *Guide*. Cf. also Plato's *Laws*, X, 887b8 and 890d4-6. I, 71 (94b, 95a; 122, 19-22; 123, 2-3).

[10] I, 71 (96a; 124, 18-19); II, 17 (37a; 207, 27-28).

[11] Cf. Aristotle, *Eth. Nic.*, 1098a8-10.

difference between them being that the *kalâm* proper is imaginative, whereas that of Maimonides is an intelligent, or enlightened *kalâm*.

The tentative descriptions of the true science of the law which have been set forth thus far are useful, and even indispensable, for the purpose of counteracting certain views more commonly held of the character of the *Guide*. In order to arrive at a more definitive description of the subject matter of that work, we have to make a fresh start by reminding ourselves again of the authoritative statements with which it opens.

Maimonides states that the intention of his work is to explain the meaning of Biblical words of various kinds, as well as of Biblical parables. Such an explanation is necessary, because the external meaning of both lends itself to grave misunderstanding. Since the internal meaning, being hidden, is a secret, the explanation of each such word or parable is the revelation of a secret. The *Guide* as a whole is thus devoted to the revelation of the secrets of the Bible.[12] *Secret*, however, has manifold meanings. It may refer to the secret hidden by a parable or word, but it also may mean the parable or word itself which hides a secret. With reference to the second meaning, the *Guide* may more conveniently be said to be devoted to the explanation of the secrets of the Bible. Thus the true science of the law is nothing other than the explanation of the secrets of the Bible, and in particular of the Torah.

There are as many secrets of the Torah as there are passages in it requiring explanation.[13] Nevertheless, it is possible to enumerate at least the most momentous secret topics. According to one enumeration, these topics are: divine attributes, creation, providence, divine will and knowledge, prophecy, names of God. Another enumeration, which seems to be more lucid, presents the following order: *Ma'aseh bereshit* (the account of creation), *ma'aseh merkabah* (the account of the chariot, Ezekiel 1 and 10), prophecy, and the knowledge of God.[14] However those two enumerations may be related to each other, it is certain that

[12] I, Introd. (2b-3b, 6a, 6b-7a; 2, 6-29; 6, 12-19; 7, 10-8, 3). Cf. *ibid.* (2a, 8a; 1, 14; 9, 6).
[13] See in particular III, 50 *in princ.*
[14] I, 35 (42a; 54, 20-26); II, 2 (11a-b; 176, 18-23).

ma'aseh bereshit and *ma'aseh merkabah* occupy the highest rank among the secrets of the Bible. Therefore, Maimonides can say that the first intention, or the chief intention of the *Guide* is the explanation of *ma'aseh bereshit* and *ma'aseh merkabah*. The true science of the law is concerned with the explanation of the secrets of the Bible, and especially with the explanation of *ma'aseh bereshit* and of *ma'aseh merkabah*.[15]

II. A PHILOSOPHIC WORK?

THE finding that the *Guide* is devoted to the explanation of the secret teaching of the Bible seems to be a truism. Yet it is pregnant with the consequence that the *Guide* is not a philosophic book.

The fact that we are inclined to call it a philosophic book is derived from the circumstance that we use the word "philosophy" in a rather broad sense. We commonly do not hesitate, for example, to count the Greek Sophists among the philosophers and we even speak of philosophies underlying mass movements. The present usage may be traced back to the separation of philosophy from science—a separation which has taken place during the modern centuries. For Maimonides, who knew nothing of "systems of philosophy" and consequently nothing of the emancipation of sober science from those lofty systems, philosophy has a much narrower, or a much more exact meaning than it has at the present time. It is not an exaggeration to say that for him philosophy is practically identical with the teaching as well as the methods of Aristotle, "the prince of the philosophers," and of the Aristotelians.[16] And he is an adversary of philosophy thus

---

[15] II, 29 (65b; 243, 17-19); III, Introd. (2a; 297, 5-7). Cf. the distinction between *fiqh* and secrets of the Torah in I, 71 (93b; 121, 20-22) with the distinction between *fiqh* and the true science of the law at the beginning of the work. For an interpretation, see A. Altmann, "Das Verhältnis Maimunis zur jüdischen Mystik," *Monatsschrift für Geschichte und Wissenschaft des Judentums*, LXXX (1936), 305-30.

[16] I, 5 *in princ.*; II, 23 (51a; 225, 4). I. Heinemann goes too far, however, in stating (*Die Lehre von der Zweckbestimmung des Menschen im griechisch-römischen Altertum und im jüdischen Mittelalter* [Breslau, 1926], 99, n. 1) that "*Failasûf* heisst nicht Philosoph, sondern steht für Aristoteles oder Aristoteliker." Cf. I, 17, 71 (94b; 122, 26-28); II, 21 (47b; 220, 20); III, 16 (31a; 334, 22-24), where *falsafa* or *falásifa* other than Aristotelian are mentioned.

understood. It is against the opinions of *"the* philosophers"[17] that he defends the Jewish creed. And what he opposes to the wrong opinions of *the* philosophers is not a true philosophy, and in particular not a religious philosophy, or a philosophy of religion, but "our opinion, i.e., the opinion of our law," or the opinion of "us, the community of the adherents of the law," or the opinion of the "followers of the law of our teacher Moses."[18] He obviously assumes that the philosophers form a group[19] distinguished from the group of adherents of the law and that both groups are mutually exclusive. Since he himself is an adherent of the law, he cannot possibly be a philosopher, and consequently a book of his in which he explains his views concerning all important topics cannot possibly be a philosophic book. This is not to deny that he acknowledges, and even stresses, the accordance which exists between the philosophers and the adherents of the law in every respect except as regards the question (which, however, is the decisive question) of the creation of the world. For certainly such an accordance between two groups proves their nonidentity.

There is, perhaps, no greater service that the historian can render to the philosopher of our time than to supply the latter with the materials necessary for the reconstruction of an adequate terminology. Consequently, the historian is likely to deprive himself of the greatest benefit which he can grant both to others and to himself, if he is ashamed to be a micrologist. We shall, then, not hesitate to refrain from calling the *Guide* a philosophic book. To justify fully our procedure we only have to consider Maimonides' division of philosophy. According to him, philosophy consists of two parts, theoretical philosophy and practical philosophy; theoretical philosophy in its turn is subdivided into mathematics, physics, and metaphysics; and practical philosophy consists of ethics, economics, "government of the

[17] Cf., for instance, III, 16 *in princ.*

[18] Cf., for instance, II, 21 (47a; 220, 17 f.); II, 26 (56a; 230, 30); III, 17 (34b; 338, 21), 21 (44b; 351, 17-18).

[19] That kind of group, one individual case of which is the group of the philosophers, is called by Maimonides פרקה or פריק (Ibn Tibbon: כת. The Greek equivalent is αἱρεσις; cf. G. Bergsträsser, *Hunain ibn Ishâq über die syrischen und arabischen Galen-Uebersetzungen*, Leipzig, 1925, p. 3 of the Arabic text); cf. II, 15 (33a; 203, 17 f.); III, 20 (42a; 348, 16).

city," and "government of the great nation or of the nations."[20]
It is obvious that the *Guide* is not a work on mathematics or
economics; and there is practically complete agreement among
the students of Maimonides that it is not devoted to political
science of either kind. Nor is it an ethical treatise, since Maimonides expressly excludes ethical topics from the *Guide*.[21] The
only sciences, then, to which that work could possibly be devoted
are physics and metaphysics, which occupy the highest rank
among the sciences.[22] This view seems to be confirmed by Maimonides' professions (1) that the chief intention of the *Guide*
is to explain *ma'aseh bereshit* and *ma'aseh merkabah*, and (2)
that *ma'aseh bereshit* is identical with physics, and *ma'aseh
merkabah* with metaphysics.[23] For these two statements seem to
lead to the inference that the chief intention of the *Guide* is to
treat of physics and metaphysics. This inference is contradicted,
however, by another express statement of Maimonides, according to which all physics and an unlimited number of metaphysical topics are excluded from the *Guide*. He mentions in this
connection particularly the doctrine of separate intelligences.[24]
Thus the only philosophic subject treated, as such, in the *Guide*
seems to be the doctrine of God.[25] But Maimonides excludes
further all subjects proved, or otherwise satisfactorily treated by
the philosophers and leaves no doubt that the philosophers succeeded in proving the existence of God as well as his unity and
incorporeity.[26] In accordance with this, Maimonides clearly
states that these three doctrines do not belong to the secrets of
the Torah,[27] and hence neither to *ma'aseh bereshit* nor to

[20] *Millot ha-higgayon*, ch. 14. Cf. H. A. Wolfson, "The Classification of the Sciences in Mediaeval Jewish Philosophy," *Hebrew Union College Jubilee Volume*, 1925, 263-315.
[21] III, 8 *in fine*. Cf. I, Introd. (11a-b; 13, 3-5).
[22] III, 51 (124a; 456, 1-4).
[23] I, Introd. (3b; 3, 8-9). Cf. n. 15.
[24] II, 2 (11a-12a; 176, 3-27). Cf. also I, 71 (97b; 126, 13-15). As regards the philosophic doctrine of the sublunary world, cf. II, 22 (49b-50a; 223, 15-17); for that of the soul, cf., I, 68 *in princ.*
[25] Notice the identification of *ma'aseh merkabah*, or metaphysics, with the doctrine of God in I, 34 (40b; 52, 24-25).
[26] I, 71 (96b; 124, 29-125, 6); II, 2 (11a-12a; 176, 3-27). Cf. II, 33 (75a; 256, 21-25).
[27] I, 35.

ma'aseh merkabah, the principal subjects of the *Guide.* Thus
we are led to the conclusion that no philosophic topic of any
kind is, as such, the subject matter of the *Guide.*

We are then confronted with the perplexing contradiction
that Maimonides, on the one hand, identifies the main subjects
of the *Guide* with physics and metaphysics, the most exalted
topics of philosophy, while on the other hand he excludes from
the field of his investigation every subject satisfactorily treated
by the philosophers. To solve that contradiction one might suggest that the *Guide* is devoted to the discussion of such "physical" and "metaphysical" topics as are not satisfactorily treated by
the philosophers. This would amount to saying that the subjects
of the *Guide* are "physics" and "metaphysics," insofar as these
transcend philosophy, and consequently that the *Guide* is not a
philosophic book.

Yet the objection may be raised that this suggestion disregards
Maimonides' explicit and unqualified identification of *ma'aseh
bereshit* with physics and of *ma'aseh merkabah* with metaphysics. If we assume for the time being that this objection is sound,
we seem to have no choice but to admit that the question of the
subject matter of the *Guide* does not allow of any answer whatsoever. But, as a matter of fact, the very obviousness of the only
possible answer[28] is the reason why that answer could escape our
notice. The apparently contradictory facts that (1) the subject
matter of the *Guide* are *ma'aseh bereshit* and *ma'aseh merkabah,*
and that (2) Maimonides, in spite of his identifying *ma'aseh
bereshit* with physics and *ma'aseh merkabah* with metaphysics,
excludes physics and metaphysics from the *Guide,* may be reconciled by the formula that the intention of the *Guide* is to prove
the identity, which to begin with was asserted only, of *ma'aseh
bereshit* with physics and of *ma'aseh merkabah* with metaphysics. Physics and metaphysics are indeed philosophic disciplines, and a book devoted to them is indeed a philosophic book.
But Maimonides does not intend to treat physics and metaphysics; his intention is to show that the teaching of these philosophic disciplines, which is presupposed, is identical with the

---

[28] That is to say, the only answer which could be given if the suggestion made
in the foregoing paragraph is ruled out. Cf., however, pp. 56 ff., below.

secret teaching of the Bible.[29] The demonstration of such identity is no longer the duty of the philosopher, but is incumbent upon the student of the true science of the law. The *Guide* is then under no circumstances a philosophic book.[30]

As a corollary we have to add that the *Guide* cannot be called a theological work, for Maimonides does not know of theology as a discipline distinct from metaphysics. Nor is it a book of religion, for he expressly excludes religious, together with ethical topics from the subject matter of his work.[31] Until we shall have rediscovered a body of terms which are flexible enough to fit Maimonides' thought, the safest course will be to limit the description of the *Guide* to the statement that it is a book devoted to the explanation of the secret teaching of the Bible.

III. THE CONFLICT BETWEEN LAW AND NECESSITY

WHEN Maimonides embarked upon the explanation of the secrets of the Torah, he was confronted with the apparently overwhelming difficulty created by the "legal prohibition"[32] against explaining those secrets. The very same law, the secrets of which Maimonides attempted to explain, forbids their explanation. According to the ordinance of the talmudic sages, *ma'aseh merkabah* ought not to be taught even to one man, except if he be wise and able to understand by himself, and even to such a one only the "chapter headings" may be transmitted. As regards the other secrets of the Bible, their revelation to many people met with scarcely less definite disapproval in the Talmud.[33] Explaining secrets in a book is tantamount to transmitting those secrets to thousands of men. Consequently, the talmudic prohibition mentioned implies the prohibition against writing a book devoted to their explanation.[34]

This prohibition was accepted by Maimonides not only as

---

[29] As regards the identification of the teaching of revelation with the teaching of reason in medieval Jewish philosophy, cf. Julius Guttmann, *Die Philosophie des Judentums* (Munich, 1933), 71 f.

[30] Cf. also above p. 39 (and n. 5), and below pp. 54 (and n. 60), 57 (and n. 64).

[31] III, 8 *in fine*.

[32] III, Introd. (2a and b; 297, 16 and 25).

[33] I, Introd. (3b-4a; 3, 9-19); 33 (36a; 48, 19-21); 34 (40b; 52, 24-53,3); III, Introd.

[34] I, Introd. (4a; 3, 19-20); III, Introd. (2a; 297, 15-16).

legally binding, but also as evidently wise; it was in full accordance with his own considered judgment that oral teaching in general is superior to teaching by writing. This view may be traced back to an old philosophic tradition.[35] The works of Aristotle, which were known to Maimonides, are "acroamatic" and not "exoteric," and his method of expounding things betrays more often than not its provenance from Platonic or Socratic dialectics. Even *the* classical statement about the danger inherent in all writing may have been known to Maimonides, for the famous doctrine of Plato's *Phaedrus* had been summarized by Fārābī in his treatise on Plato's philosophy.[36] Be this as it may, not the ambiguous advice of the philosophers but the unequivocal command of the law was of primary importance to Maimonides.[37]

If a book devoted to the explanation of the secrets of the Bible is prohibited by law, how then can the *Guide*, being the work of an observant Jew, be a book? It is noteworthy that Maimonides himself in the *Guide* never calls it a book, but consistently refers to it as a *maqâla (ma'amar)*.[38] *Maqâla* (just as *ma'amar*) has several meanings. It may mean a treatise; it is used in that sense when Maimonides speaks, for instance, of the *Treatise on Government* by Alexander of Aphrodisias. But it may also mean— and this is its original connotation—a speech. Maimonides, by refraining from calling the *Guide* a book and by calling it a *maqâla*, hints at the essentially oral character of its teaching. Since, in a book such as the *Guide*, hints are more important than explicit statements, Maimonides' contentions concerning the superiority of oral teaching very probably have to be taken quite literally.

If the *Guide* is, in a sense, not a book at all, if it is merely a substitute for conversations or speeches, then it cannot be read

---

[35] I, 71 (93b; 121, 14-24); III, Introd. (2b; 297, 25-26). Cf. I, 17 and Introd. (4a; 3, 19-20).

[36] Cf. Falakera's Hebrew translation of Fārābī's treatise in *Reshit hokmah*, ed. David, p. 75 bottom.

[37] The inferiority of writing is also indicated by the designation of those Biblical works which had not been composed by prophets proper as "writings." Cf. II, 45 (94a, 95b; 283, 1-5; 284, 21-285, 3).

[38] This fact is pointed out by Abravanel in his *Ma'amar ḳaṣer bebi'ur sod ha-moreh*. Ibn Tibbon, in his preface to his translation of the *Guide*, calls it הספר הנכבד הזה מאמר מורה נבוכים.

in the way we may read, for instance, Ibn Sina's *Al-Shifâ,* or Thomas Aquinas's *Summa theologica.* To begin with, we may assume rather that the proper way of studying it is somehow similar to the way in which traditional Judaism studies the law.[39] This would mean that if we wish to know what Maimonides thinks, say, about the prophecy of Moses, it would not be sufficient to look up that chapter of his work which is explicitly devoted to that subject, and in which we might find perfectly clear and apparently final statements about it; nor would it be sufficient to contrast the latter with divergent statements unexpectedly occurring in other chapters. We would also have to take into account analogous "decisions" given by Maimonides with regard to entirely different "cases," and to make ourselves familiar with the general rules of analogy which obtain in oral discussions of that kind. Producing a clear statement of the author, in the case of a book like the *Guide,* is tantamount to raising a question; his answer can be ascertained only by a lengthy discussion, the result of which may again be open, and intended to be open, to new "difficulties." If it is true that the *Mishneh Torah* is but the greatest post-talmudic contribution to the oral discussions of the halakah, then it may be asserted with equal right that Maimonides, while writing the *Guide,* continued the aggadic discussions of the Talmud. And just as the *Mishneh Torah,* far from terminating the halakic discussions, actually served as a new starting point for them, in the same way the *Guide,* far from offering a final interpretation of the secret teaching of the Bible,[40] may actually have been an attempt to revive the oral discussion thereof by raising difficulties which intentionally were left unsolved.

But although the method employed by Maimonides in the *Guide* may come as near as is humanly possible to the method of oral teaching, the *Guide* does not for that reason cease to be a book. Consequently the very existence of the *Guide* implies a conscious transgression of an unambiguous prohibition. It seems that Maimonides for a while intended to steer a middle course

[39] Cf. H. A. Wolfson, *Crescas' Critique of Aristotle* (Cambridge, 1929), 22 ff. Maimonides indicates the similarity between the prohibition against writing down the oral law and that against writing down the secret teaching of the law; see I, 71 *in princ.*

[40] Cf., for instance, III, Introd. (2b; 298, 1-2); I, 21 (26b; 34, 10-12).

between oral and confidential teaching, which is permitted, and teaching in writing, which is forbidden. That kind of writing which comes nearest to confidential conversation is private correspondence with a close friend. As a matter of fact, the *Guide* is written in the form of letters addressed to a friend and favorite pupil, Joseph.[41] By addressing his book to one man, Maimonides made sure that he did not transgress the prohibition against explaining *ma'aseh merkabah* to more than one man. Moreover, in the *Epistula dedicatoria* addressed to Joseph, he mentions, as it were in passing and quite unintentionally, that Joseph possessed all the qualities required of a student of the secret lore and explains the necessity of written communication by his pupil's departure.[42] This justification would have held good if Maimonides had refrained from making public these private "letters to a friend." In spite of this inconsistency and in spite of his evident determination to write the *Guide* even if he had never met Joseph, or if Joseph had never left him,[43] it would be a mistake to assume that the dedicatory epistle is wholly ironical. For we need only ask ourselves: what was the ultimate reason for Joseph's premature departure, and we are going over from the sphere of private and playful things to the sphere of public and serious matters. Joseph's departure, we may say, was the consequence of his being a Jew in the Diaspora. Not a private need but only an urgent necessity of nation-wide bearing can have driven Maimonides to transgressing an explicit prohibition. Only the necessity of saving the law can have caused him to break the law.[44]

---

[41] Cf. in particular II, 24.

[42] These observations on the *Ep. ded.* cannot furnish a sufficient interpretation of that remarkable piece of literature, but deal merely with its more superficial meaning. Maimonides mentions Joseph's poems in order to show that the latter possessed the indispensable ability of expressing himself beautifully; cf. I, 34 (41a; 53, 14) with I, Introd. (7a-b; 8, 7-8). As regards the other qualities of Joseph, see Shem Tob's commentary on the *Ep. ded.*

[43] It is controversial whether Maimonides finished the *Guide* before he made the acquaintance of Joseph or thereafter. According to Z. Diesendruck, "On the Date of the Completion of the Moreh Nebukim," *Hebrew Union College Annual*, XII-XIII, 496, the *Guide* was finished in 1185, i.e., at about the time when Joseph's sojourn with Maimonides began. Even if the *Guide* was not finished before the year 1190, which is the latest possible date (see *ibid.*, pp. 461, 470), it certainly had been conceived and partly elaborated before Joseph's arrival.

[44] I, Introd. (9b; 10, 28-29) in the interpretation of Fürstenthal and Munk.

The necessity of taking such an extraordinary measure was a consequence of the long duration of the Diaspora. The secrets of the Torah, "the fountainhead of ancient Greek, and, consequently, also of Arabian wisdom,"[45] had been handed down from time immemorial by oral tradition. Even when the oral law, which likewise ought not to have been written down, was finally compiled in written form, the talmudic sages wisely insisted on the secret teaching being transmitted to posterity only by word of mouth from one scholar to another. Their command was obeyed; there is not a single book extant which contains the secret teaching in whole or in part. What had come down to Maimonides were only slight intimations and allusions in Talmud and Midrash.[46] However, continuity of oral tradition presupposes a certain normality of political conditions. That is why the secrets of the Torah were perfectly understood only as long as Israel lived in its own country in freedom, not subjugated by the ignorant nations of the world.[47] Particularly happy was the period when the supreme political authority rested in the hands of King Solomon who had an almost complete understanding of the secret reasons of the commandments.[48] After Solomon, wisdom and political power were no longer united; decline and finally loss of freedom followed. When the nation was led into captivity, it sustained further loss in the perfect knowledge of the secrets. Whereas Isaiah's contemporaries understood his brief hints, the contemporaries of Ezekiel required many more details in order to grasp the sacred doctrine. The decline of knowledge became even more marked with the discontinuation of prophecy itself.[49] Still more disastrous was the victory of the Romans, since the new Diaspora was to last so much longer than the first.[50] As time went on, the external con-

[45] Baron, *Outlook*, 105, with reference to I, 71 *in princ.* Cf. also II, 11 (24a-b; 192, 17-29).

[46] I, Introd. (9b; 10, 26-27); 71 (93b-94a; 121, 9-26) [the words *tanbîhât yasîra wa-ishârât* recall the title of Ibn Sînâ's book *Ishârât wa-tanbîhât;* cf. also II, 29 (46a; 244, 8)]; III, Introd. (2a-b; 297, 15-20). Maimonides here tacitly denies any authenticity or value to books such as the *Sefer ha-Yeṣirah* or *She'ur ḳomah;* cf. Baron, *Outlook*, 89.

[47] I, 71 (93b; 121, 10-11).

[48] III, 26 (58a; 369, 14-16). Cf. Baron, *Outlook*, 51-54.

[49] III, 6 (9b; 307, 12-15); II, 32 (73b; 254, 23-24), 36 (80a; 263, 19-26).

[50] Cf. I, 71 (93b; 121, 10). Cf. also M.T., Introd.

ditions for oral communication of the secrets of the Torah became increasingly precarious. The moment seemed imminent when it would become altogether impossible. Confronted with that prospect, Maimonides decided to write down the secret teaching.

The question naturally arises as to how Maimonides came into its possession. Once, in suggesting a date for the coming of the Messiah (in *Iggeret Teiman*), he refers to a tradition, obviously oral, which he had received from his father, who in turn had received it from his father and grandfather, and which in that way went back to the very beginning of the Diaspora. If we were to generalize from this remark, we would have to assume that he owed his entire knowledge of the secrets of the Torah to an uninterrupted oral tradition going back to the time of the second temple. We would then not only have to accept the legend of his conversion to the Kabbalah in his old age, but we would be forced to admit that he was a Kabbalist throughout his mature life, since the content of the *Guide* would be nothing but a secret teaching based on (oral) tradition. Indeed, as it seems that there had existed no Kabbalah, strictly speaking, before the completion of the *Guide*,[51] one might suggest that Maimonides was the first Kabbalist.

Such venturesome hypotheses are, however, ruled out by his express statements. He not only disclaims the privilege of having had a special revelation about the hidden meaning of *ma'aseh merkabah*, but also disavows his indebtedness to any (human) teacher for his knowledge of the secret doctrine.[52] He apparently believed that the oral tradition of the secret teaching had been interrupted long before his time. That is also why he could not find any traces of a genuine Jewish secret tradition in the Gaonic literature, whereas he claims to have found such traces in the Talmud and in the Midrash. Neither was he able to detect any remnant of the holy doctrine still living in the nation.[53] He was, then, not the last heir of an age-old tradition, but rather its first

[51] "Zur Bezeichnung der Mystik wurde der Terminus [Kabbala] erst sehr spät verwandt, und ist zuerst bei Isaak dem Blinden (ca. 1200) nachweisbar." G. Scholem, *Encyclopaedia Judaica*, IX, 632.

[52] III, Introd. (2b; 297, 27-28). Cf., however, III, 22 (46a; 353, 21-22). Cf. also the allusion to a spurious "mystical" tradition in I, 62 (80b; 104, 26).

[53] I, 71 (94a; 121, 25-122, 3); III, Introd. (2b; 297, 17-18).

rediscoverer after it had been lost for a long time. He rediscovered the secret teaching by following the indications which are met with in the Bible and in the words of the sages but also by making use of speculative premises.[54] Since the Bible and the Talmud had been studied no less thoroughly by his predecessors than by him, his rediscovery must have been due to a particularly deep understanding of the "speculative premises," i.e., of philosophy. He did not feel conscious of thereby introducing a foreign element into Judaism, for long before his time the "Andalusian" Jews had accepted the teachings of the philosophers as far as these were consonant with the basis of the Torah.[55] Philosophic teachings thus belonged, in a sense, to the tradition of Maimonides' family. Perhaps he even believed that the resurgence of philosophic studies in the Middle Ages more or less coincided with the disappearance of the secret teaching of Judaism and that thus the chain of tradition never was interrupted. After all, the defensible part of the philosophic teaching appeared to him as but a last residue of Israel's own lost inheritance.[56]

The philosophic tradition of enlightened Andalusia thus gave Maimonides the first impulse to search the Bible for its secrets. Owing to his exertions during the greater part of his life, he succeeded in detecting a great many of them. At the same time he clearly realized that his achievement was not likely to be repeated by many others, if by any. For the age of philosophy in Muslim countries was drawing to its close. Fearing, therefore, that the precious doctrine might again be lost for centuries, he decided to commit it to writing, notwithstanding the talmudic prohibition. But he did not act imprudently. He insisted on taking a middle course[57] between impossible obedience and flagrant transgression. He thought it his duty to give such a written explanation of the Biblical secrets as would meet all the conditions required from an oral explanation. In other words, he had to become a master of the art of revealing by not revealing and of not revealing by revealing.

---

[54] III, Introd. (2b; 297, 28-29).
[55] I, 71 (94a; 122, 9-10).
[56] See above p. 50. Cf. Altmann, *op. cit.*, 315 ff.
[57] Cf. III, Introd. (3a; 298, 8-9).

The law requires that only the "chapter headings" be transmitted. Maimonides decided to abide by that precept. But the law goes further: it requires that even those "chapter headings" be not transmitted even to one, except he be wise and able to understand by himself. As long as the secret teaching was transmitted by oral instruction, that requirement was easily complied with: if the teacher had not known the pupil for a long time beforehand, as probably was almost always the case, he could test the pupil's intellectual capacities by having a talk with him on indifferent subjects before he started to explain to him some of the secrets of the Bible. But how can the author of a book examine his readers, by far the greater part of whom may not yet be born when the book is published? Or does there exist some sort of examination by proxy which would allow the author to prevent incompetent readers not only from understanding his book—this does not require any human effort—but even from finding out the very formulation of the "chapter headings"? To see that such a device does exist, we have only to remind ourselves of how a superior man proceeds if he wishes to impart a truth, which he thinks not to be fit for everybody's use, to another man who may or may not be able to become reconciled to it. He will give him a hint by casting some doubt on a remote and apparently insignificant consequence or premise of the accepted opinion. If the listener understands the hint, the teacher may explain his doubts more fully and thus gradually lead him to a view which is of necessity nearer the truth (since it presupposes a certain reflection) than is the current opinion. But how does he proceed, if the pupil fails to understand the hint? He will simply stop. This does not mean that he will stop talking. On the contrary, since by suddenly becoming silent he would only perplex the pupil without being of any help to him, he will continue talking by giving the first, rather revealing sentence a more conventional meaning and thus gradually lead him back to the safe region of accepted views. Now this method of stopping can be practiced in writing as well as in speech, the only difference being that the writer must stop in any case, since certainly the majority of readers must be prevented from finding out the "chapter headings." That is to say, the writer has to interrupt his short hints by long stretches of silence, i.e., of insignificant talk. But a good author will never submit to the ordeal of indulging in insignificant talk. Consequently, after having given a hint which refers to a certain chapter of the secret teaching, he will write some sentences which at first glance seem to be conventional, but which on closer examination prove to contain a new hint, referring to another chapter of the secret teaching. By thus proceeding, he will prevent the secret teaching being prematurely perceived and therefore inadequately understood; even those readers who not only noticed but even understood the first hint and might understand further hints directly connected with it, would experience considerable difficulty even in suspecting the second hint, which refers to a different section of the argument. It is hardly necessary to add that there are as many groups of hints as there are chapters, or subdivisions of chapters, of the secret teaching, and that in consequence an ingenious author has at his disposal almost infinite possibilities of alternatively using hints of different groups.

We are now in a position to appreciate the bearing of the following statement of Maimonides: "You will not demand from me here [in the *Guide*] anything except chapter headings; and even those headings are, in this treatise, not arranged according to their intrinsic order or according to any sequence whatsoever, but they are scattered and intermingled with other subjects, the explanation of which is intended."[58] It is true Maimonides makes this statement with regard to his explanation of *maʿaseh merkabah* only. But there can be no doubt that he has followed the same method in his explanation of *maʿaseh bereshit* and, indeed, of all the secrets of the Torah.[59] It is for this reason that the whole work has to be read with particular care, with a care, that is, which would not be required for the understanding of a scientific book.[60] Since the whole teaching characteristic of the *Guide* is of a secret nature, we are not surprised to observe Maimonides entreating the reader in the most emphatic manner not to explain any part of it to others, unless the particular doctrine had already been clearly elucidated by famous teachers of the

[58] I, Introd. (3b; 3, 11-14).
[59] II, 29 (46a; 244, 10 f.). Cf. I, Introd. (3b-4b; 3, 17-4, 22), 17, 35 (42a; 54, 20-28). See also III, 41 (88b; 409, 16).
[60] I, Introd. (8b; 9, 26-10, 2), *ibid.* (3b; 3, 11-14); *ibid.* (4b; 4, 12-15).

law,[61] i.e., unless it is a popular topic, a topic only occasionally mentioned in the *Guide*.

The *Guide* is devoted to the explanation of an esoteric doctrine. But this explanation is itself of an esoteric character. The *Guide* is, then, devoted to the esoteric explanation of an esoteric doctrine. Consequently it is a book with seven seals. How can we unseal it?

IV. A MORAL DILEMMA

No historian who has a sense of decency and therefore a sense of respect for a superior man such as Maimonides will disregard light-heartedly the latter's emphatic entreaty not to explain the secret teaching of the *Guide*. It may fairly be said that an interpreter who does not feel pangs of conscience when attempting to explain that secret teaching and perhaps when perceiving for the first time its existence and bearing lacks that closeness to the subject which is indispensable for the true understanding of any book. Thus the question of adequate interpretation of the *Guide* is primarily a moral question.

We are, however, entitled to object to raising that moral question because the historical situation in which we find ourselves is fundamentally different from that of the twelfth century, and therefore we ought to be justified in not taking too personally, so to speak, Maimonides' will. It is true, at first glance, that objection seems to beg the question: it is based on the assumption that it is possible to have a sufficient knowledge of the historical situation of the twelfth century without having a true and adequate knowledge of the secret teaching of Maimonides. Yet, if one looks more closely, one sees that by the historical situation no historian understands the secret thoughts of an individual, but rather the obvious facts or opinions which, being common to a period, give that period its specific coloring. We happen to be excellently informed by competent historians about the opinions prevalent in the twelfth century, and each of us can see that they are fundamentally different from those prevalent in our time. Public opinion was then ruled by the belief in the revealed character of the Torah or the existence of

[61] I, Introd. (9a; 10, 4-8).

an eternal and unchangeable law, whereas public opinion today is ruled by historic consciousness. Maimonides himself justified his transgression of the talmudic injunction against writing on the esoteric teaching of the Bible by the necessity of saving the law. In the same way we may justify our disregard of Maimonides' entreaty not to explain the esoteric teaching of the *Guide* by appealing to the requirements of historic research. For both the history of Judaism and the history of medieval philosophy remain deplorably incomplete, as long as the secret teaching of Maimonides has not been brought to light. The force of this argument will become even stronger if we take into consideration that basic condition of historic research, namely, freedom of thought. Freedom of thought, too, seems to be incomplete as long as we recognize the validity of any prohibition to explain any teaching whatsoever. Freedom of thought being menaced in our time more than for several centuries, we have not only the right but even the duty to explain the teaching of Maimonides, in order to contribute to a better understanding of what freedom of thought means, i.e., what attitude it presupposes and what sacrifices it requires.

The position of Maimonides' interpreter is, then, to some extent, identical with that of Maimonides himself. Both are confronted with a prohibition against explaining a secret teaching and with the necessity of explaining it. Consequently, one might think it advisable for the interpreter to imitate Maimonides also with regard to the solution of the dilemma, i.e., to steer a middle course between impossible obedience and flagrant transgression by attempting an esoteric interpretation of the esoteric teaching of the *Guide*. Since the *Guide* contains an esoteric interpretation of an esoteric teaching, an adequate interpretation of the *Guide* would thus have to take the form of an esoteric interpretation of an esoteric interpretation of an esoteric teaching.

This suggestion may sound paradoxical and even ridiculous. Yet it would not have appeared absurd to such a competent reader of the *Guide* as Joseph ibn Kaspi, who did write an esoteric commentary on it. Above all, an esoteric interpretation of the *Guide* seems to be not only advisable, but even necessary.

When Maimonides, through his work, exposed the secret teaching of the Bible to a larger number of men, some of whom might not be as obedient to the talmudic ordinance nor as wise as he was, he did not rely entirely on those readers' compliance with the law or with his own emphatic entreaty. For the explanation of secrets is, as he asserts, not only forbidden by law, but also impossible by nature:[62] the very nature of the secrets prevents their being divulged. We are then confronted with a third meaning of the word "secret": secret may mean not only the Biblical word or parable which has an inner meaning, and the hidden meaning itself, but also, and perhaps primarily, the thing to which that hidden meaning refers.[63] The things spoken of by the prophets are secret, since they are not constantly accessible, as are the things described by the ordinary sciences,[64] but only during more or less short and rare intervals of spiritual daylight which interrupt an almost continuous spiritual darkness; indeed they are accessible not to natural reason, but only to prophetic vision. Consequently, ordinary language is utterly insufficient for their description; the only possible way of describing them is by parabolic and enigmatic speech.[65] Even the interpretation of prophetic teaching cannot but be parabolic and enigmatic, which is equally true of the interpretation of such an interpretation, since both the secondary and the primary interpretation deal with the same secret subject matter. Hence the interpretation of the *Guide* cannot be given in ordinary language, but only in parabolic and enigmatic speech. That is why, according to Maimonides, the student of those secrets is required not only to be of mature age, to have a sagacious and subtle mind, to possess perfect command of the art of political government and the speculative sciences, and to be able to understand

---

[62] I, Introd. (3b; 3, 15). Cf. I, 31 *in princ.*

[63] "Secrets of the being and secrets of the Torah," II, 26 (56b; 232, 5). For the distinction between various meanings of "secret," cf. Bacon, *Advancement of Learning*, ed. G. W. Kitchin, 205.

[64] I, Introd. (4b; 4, 15). This passage implies a fundamental distinction between esoteric and exoteric sciences. As regards such distinctions, cf. I. Goldziher, *Kitāb ma'āni al-nafs* (Berlin, 1907), pp. 28*-31.* According to a usual distinction, "the exterior science" *(al-'ilm al-barrāni)* is identical with Aristotelian philosophy and also with the *Kalām;* "the interior philosophy" *(al-falsafa al-dāḫila* or *al-falsafa al-ḫāṣṣa),* treated by the *muḥakkikūn,* deals with "the secrets of nature." The teaching of esoteric science is the knowledge *al-maḍnūn bihi.* Cf. I, 17 *in princ.,* 35 (41b; 54, 4), 71 (93b; 121, 20).

[65] I, Introd. (4a; 4, 4-7). See the commentaries of Ephodi and Shem Tob on the passage. I, Introd. (4a-b; 3, 23-4, 20).

the allusive speech of others, but also to be capable of presenting things allusively himself.[66]

If each student actually had to meet all these conditions, we should have to admit at once, i.e., before any serious attempt has been made to elucidate the esoteric teaching of the *Guide*, that the interpretation of that work is wholly impossible for the modern historian. The very intention of interpreting the *Guide* would imply an unbearable degree of presumption on the part of the would-be interpreter; for he would implicitly claim to be endowed with all the qualities of a Platonic philosopher-king. Yet, while a modest man, confronted with the requirements which we have indicated, will be inclined to give up the attempt to understand the whole *Guide*, he may hope to make some contribution to its understanding by becoming a subservient part of the community of scholars who devote themselves to the interpretation of the *Guide*. If that book cannot be understood by the exertions of one man, it may be understood by the collaboration of many, in particular of Arabists, Judaists, and students of the history of philosophy. It is true that when speaking of the conditions to be fulfilled by students of the secret teaching, Maimonides does not mention disciplines such as those just alluded to; as a matter of fact, he thought very slightly of history in general.[67] But in all justice it may be said that he did not know, and could not know history in the modern sense of the word, a discipline which, in a sense, provides the synthesis, indispensable for the adequate understanding of the secret doctrine, of philosophy and politics. Yet, however greatly we may think of the qualities of the modern historian, he certainly is neither per se able to understand esoteric texts nor is he an esoteric writer. Indeed the rise of modern historic consciousness came simultaneously with the interruption of the tradition of esotericism. Hence all present-day students of Maimonides necessarily lack the specific training required for understanding, to say nothing of writing, an esoteric book or commentary. Is, then, an interpretation of the *Guide* altogether impossible under the present circumstances?

Let us examine somewhat more closely the basic assumption

---

[66] I, 34 (41a; 53, 12-19), 33 (37b; 48, 22-25).
[67] Cf. Baron, *Outlook*, 3-4.

underlying the conclusion at which we have just arrived, or rather upon which we have just come to grief. Maimonides, it is true, states in unambiguous terms that direct and plain communication of the secrets of the things, or of the secrets of the Torah, is impossible by nature. But he also asserts in no less unambiguous terms that such a communication is forbidden by law. Now a rational law does not forbid things which are impossible in themselves and which therefore are not subject to human deliberation or action; and the Torah is the rational law par excellence.[68] Consequently the two statements appear to be contradictory. Since we are not yet in a position to decide which of them is to be discarded as merely exoteric, it will be wise to leave the question open for the time being and not to go beyond briefly discussing the possibilities of an answer. There are three possible solutions: (1) Maimonides may actually have believed in the unavoidable necessity of speaking enigmatically of secrets; (2) he may have conceded the possibility of plainly discussing them; (3) he may have approved some unknown intermediary position. There is, then, certainly a prima facie probability in the ratio of two to three that the first solution, which is wholly incompatible with our desire to understand the *Guide,* has to be ruled out. But even if the first solution had to be ultimately accepted, we need not be altogether despondent, since we may very well reject that view as erroneous. Esotericism, one might say, is based on the assumption that there is a rigid division of mankind into an inspired or intelligent minority and an uninspired or foolish majority. But are there no transitions of various kinds between the two groups? Has not each man been given freedom of will, so that he may become wise or foolish according to his exertions?[69] However important may be the natural faculty of understanding, is not the use of this faculty or, in other words, method, equally important? And method, almost by its very definition, bridges the gulf which separates the two unequal groups. Indeed, the methods of modern historical research, which have proved to be sufficient for the deciphering of hieroglyphs and cuneiforms, ought certainly to be sufficient also for the deciphering of a book such as the *Guide,* to which access

[68] III, 26. Cf. III, 17 (33a-b; 337, 8-15).
[69] M.T. Teshubah 5, 2.

could be had in an excellent translation into a modern language. Our problem reduces itself, therefore, to detecting the specific method which will enable us to decipher the *Guide*. What are, then, the general rules and the most important special rules according to which this book is to be read?

V. SECRETS AND CONTRADICTIONS

THE clue to the true understanding of the *Guide* is provided by the very feature of that book which, at first glance, seems to make it for all modern generations a book sealed with seven seals. I am referring to the fact that it is devoted to the esoteric explanation of an esoteric text. For it is merely a popular fallacy to assume that such an explanation is an esoteric work of the second power, or at least twice as esoteric, and consequently twice as difficult to understand as is the esoteric text itself. Actually, any explanation, however esoteric, of a text is intended to be helpful for its understanding; and, provided the author is not a man of exceptional inability, the explanation is bound to be helpful. Now, if by the help of Maimonides, we understand the esoteric teaching of the Bible, we understand at the same time the esoteric teaching of the *Guide,* since Maimonides must have accepted the esoteric teaching of the law as the true teaching. Or, to put it somewhat differently, we may say that, thanks to Maimonides, the secret teaching is accessible to us in two different versions: in the original Biblical version, and in the derivative version of the *Guide.* Each version by itself might be wholly incomprehensible; but we may become able to decipher both by using the light which one sheds on the other. Our position resembles then that of an archeologist confronted with an inscription in an unknown language, who subsequently discovers another inscription reproducing the translation of that text into another unknown language. It matters little whether or not we accept Maimonides' two assumptions, rejected by modern criticism, that the Bible is an esoteric text, and that its esoteric teaching is closely akin to that of Aristotle. As far as Maimonides is concerned, the Bible *is* an esoteric book, and even the most perfect esoteric book ever written. Consequently, when setting out to write an esoteric book himself, he had no choice but to take the

Bible as his model. That is to say, he wrote the *Guide* according to the rules which he was wont to follow in reading the Bible. Therefore, if we wish to understand the *Guide*, we must read it according to the rules which Maimonides applies in that work to the explanation of the Bible.

How did Maimonides read the Bible, or rather the Torah? He read it as the work of a single author, that author being not so much Moses as God himself. Consequently, the Torah was for him the most perfect book ever written as regards both content and form. In particular, he did not believe (as we are told to believe by modern Biblical criticism) that its formal deficiencies —for instance, the abrupt changes of subject matter, or repetitions with greater or slighter variations—were due to its having been compiled by unknown redactors from divergent sources. These deficiencies were for him purposeful irregularities, intended to hide and betray a deeper order, a deep, nay, divine meaning. It was precisely this intentional disorder which he took as his model when writing the *Guide*. Or, if we accept the thesis of modern Biblical criticism, we have to say that he took as his model a book which unintentionally lacks order and that by so doing he wrote a book which intentionally lacks order. At any rate the *Guide* certainly and admittedly is a book which intentionally lacks order. The "chapter headings" of the secret teaching which it transmits "are not arranged according to their intrinsic order or according to any sequence whatsoever, but they are scattered and intermingled with other subjects."[70] Instances of apparently bad composition are so numerous in the *Guide* and so familiar to its students that we need not mention here more than one example. Maimonides interrupts his explanation of Biblical expressions attributing to God place, local movement, and so on (I, 8-26) by an exposition of the meaning of *man* (I,14) and by a discussion of the necessity of teaching *maʿaseh bereshit* esoterically (I, 17), just as the Bible itself interrupts the story of Joseph by inserting into it the story of Judah and Tamar. Consequently, whenever we are confronted in the *Guide* with an abrupt change of subject matter, we have to follow the same rule of interpretation which Maimonides was wont to follow whenever he had to face a similar apparent

[70] I, Introd. (3b; 3, 11-14).

deficiency of the Bible: we have to find out, by guessing, the hidden reason of the apparent deficiency. For it is precisely that hidden reason, accessible only to guesswork, which furnishes a link between the scattered "chapter headings," if not a "chapter heading" itself. Certainly the chains of reasoning connecting the scattered "chapter headings," and possibly even some "chapter headings" themselves, are not stated within the chapters, but are written with invisible ink in the empty spaces between the chapters, between the sentences, or between the parts of the *Guide*.

Another kind of irregularity occurs, for example, in his explanation of the various groups of Biblical commandments (III, 36-49). At the beginning of each chapter reference is made to the book or books of the *Mishneh Torah* in which the laws under review had been codified. Maimonides deviates from that rule in the case of one chapter only (Chapter 41). That this is not a matter of chance can easily be seen from the context. There he points out with unusual clarity the difference between the text of the Biblical commands and their traditional interpretation; his intention is, as he expressly states, to explain the "texts," and not the *fiqh*.[71] The *Mishneh Torah* is devoted to the *fiqh*. Consequently, it would have been most misleading if he had referred, at the beginning of that chapter, to the corresponding "book" of the *Mishneh Torah*, i.e., to the "Book of Judges." It may be added in passing that a full discussion of this irregularity, which space does not here permit, would help explain the scarcely less perplexing difficulty of the inclusion in the "Book of Judges" of the laws concerning mourning.

As a last instance of those devices, which may be called intentional perplexities, suggested to Maimonides by his model, we may mention here repetitions of the same subject with apparently no, or only insignificant variations. He observes that Ezekiel had twice the same vision of the celestial chariot, the most secret subject, and that both visions, in their turn, were but repetitions of the corresponding vision of Isaiah.[72] Hardly less important was for him the realization that in the Book of Job all interlocutors apparently repeat continually one another's

---

[71] III, 41 (88b; 409, 15-16).
[72] III, 3 *in princ.*, 6.

statements; in particular Elihu, supposedly superior in wisdom to Job, Eliphaz, Bildad, and Zophar, does not seem to add anything of weight to what the others had said before him.[73] Maimonides naturally asserts that these repetitions are apparent rather than real, and that closer examination will reveal that the opinions of Job, Eliphaz, Bildad, and Zophar, as well as Elihu, differ materially from one another, and that the report of Ezekiel's second vision makes important additions to that of the first.[74] This method of repeating the same thing with apparently insignificant, but actually highly important variations was extremely helpful for Maimonides' purposes. An outstanding example may be found in his repeating in the *Guide,* with certain variations, the division of the Biblical laws into 14 groups, an arrangement which had determined the whole plan of the *Mishneh Torah.*[75] He thus created the impression of merely repeating the division made in the code, whereas actually the two divisions greatly differ from each other. As further obvious examples of the application of the same method, one may cite the differences between the arrangement of the 248 affirmative precepts in the enumeration at the beginning of *Mishneh Torah* (or in *Sefer ha-miṣvot)* on the one hand, and that in the body of that code on the other; the differences between the enumeration of the 5 opinions concerning providence in the *Guide,* III, 17, on the one hand, and that in the same work, III, 23, on the other;[76] and the differences between the enumeration of the 3 opinions concerning creation in the *Guide,* II, 13, on the one hand, and that in the same work, II, 32, on the other. In all these cases Maimonides apparently merely repeats himself by speaking twice of the same number, but actually he introduces in the repetitions new points of view which had not even been hinted at in the first statements. His aim in so doing is clearly revealed by his explanation of the method employed by the first 4 interlocutors in the Book of Job

---

[73] III, 23 (50a; 359, 4-9 and 14-15). Cf. also III, 24 (52b; 362, 22-23).

[74] III, 23 (50a; 359, 9-15); 1 (3a; 298, 23-24), 3 (6b and 7a; 303, 5, 19; 304, 4-5). Cf. M.T. Introd., 186th and 187th prohibition.

[75] Cf. also the fourteen principles in S.M.

[76] Notice also the three opinions on providence indicated in III, 17 (37b; 342, 20 f.), as well as the two opinions indicated in III, 21 (44b; 351, 17-18).

(Job, Eliphaz, Bildad, and Zophar): "Each one of them repeats the subject of which the other had spoken . . . in order to hide the subject peculiar to the opinion of each, so that it should appear to the vulgar that the opinion of all of them is one opinion generally agreed upon."[77] That is to say, the purpose of repeating conventional statements is to hide the disclosure, in the repetition, of unconventional views. What matters is, then, not the conventional view, constantly repeated, which may or may not be true, but the slight additions to, or omissions from the conventional view which occur in the repetition and which transmit "chapter headings" of the secret and true teaching. This is what Maimonides rather clearly intimates by saying that closer examination of Elihu's repetitious speech brings to light "the additional subject which he introduced, and this subject was the intention."[78] The question as to whether and to what extent Maimonides has generally employed this method of making hardly discernible additions to the "first statement" par excellence, i.e., to the Biblical text itself, must remain unanswered in the present discussion.[79]

Since these rules of interpretation seem to confer excessive importance on every word used by Maimonides, we must have recourse again to our initial assumption that the *Guide* is an imitation of the Bible, and in particular of the Torah. Maimonides read the Torah as a book, every word of which was of divine origin and, consequently, of the greatest importance.[80] How conscientiously he strove to detect the full significance of each Biblical term, however indifferent it might seem to be in its context, is known to every reader of the *Guide*, the first intention of which was to explain certain groups of Biblical words.[81] He

[77] III, 23 (50a; 359, 11-14).
[78] III, 23 (50a; 359, 9-10).
[79] Cf. III, Introd. (2b-3a; 298, 3-9). The method of "repetition" was certainly not invented by Maimonides; it was applied before him on a large scale by Fārābī, who "repeated" the same teaching by making additions to it or omissions from it, in *Al-siyâsât al-madaniyya*, in *Al-madina al-fâdila*, and in *Al-milla al-fâdila*. And let us not forget Plato who (to mention only two examples) "repeated" the teachings of the *Republic* in the *Laws*, and in the *Apology* "reiterated" the defense of Socrates as well as the charge brought against him three times.
[80] M.T. *Teshubah* 3, 17.
[81] I, Introd. (2b; 2, 6 ff.).

expressly applied the same principle of reading, or writing, to his own work:

> if you wish to grasp the totality of what this treatise contains, so that nothing of it will escape you, then you must connect its chapters one with another;[82] and when reading a given chapter, your intention must be not only to understand the totality of the subject of that chapter, but also to grasp each word which occurs in it in the course of the speech, even if that word does not belong to the intention of the chapter. For the diction of this treatise has not been chosen by haphazard, but with great exactness and exceeding precision.[83]

Maimonides naturally read the Torah as a book which is in no way frivolous. Since he considered histories and poems to be frivolous writings, he was compelled to conceive of the Biblical stories as of "secrets of the Torah."[84] As he had such a contempt for stories, it is most unlikely that the few stories which he inserted into the *Guide* have to be accepted at their face value: some necessity must have driven him to tell those stories in order to instill either some true opinion or some good moral habit into the minds of his readers.[85] In one case he tells us the story of how, "many years ago," a scientist had put to him a certain question, and how he had answered it.[86] Since the *Guide* is written "with great exactness and exceeding precision," it is safe to say that the framework of the story conveys some teaching which is not transmitted by the content of the discussion with the scientist. We find in the *Guide* more stories of things which happened "many years ago," such as the history of the science of *kalâm* and the story of the two books which Maimonides had begun to write on the parables of the prophets and of the Midrashim.[87] We do not hesitate to call also the "dedicatory

[82] That is to say, you must do with the chapters of the *Guide* what Solomon did with the words and parables of the Bible; just as Solomon found out the secret teaching of the Bible by connecting word with word, and parable with parable, in the same way we may find out the secret teaching of the *Guide* by connecting chapter with chapter, and, indeed, secret word with secret word. Cf. I, Introd. (6b; 6, 26-7, 2).

[83] I, Introd. (8b; 9, 26-30).

[84] I, 2 (13b; 16, 9-11); III, 50. Cf. Baron, *Outlook*, 8, n. 4.

[85] Cf. III, 50 (120a; 451, 1-3).

[86] I, 2.

[87] I, 71. I, Introd. (5b; 5, 17 ff.); III, 19 (40a; 346, 3 ff.). Cf. III, 32 (70a-b; 385, 13-20).

epistle" a story, i.e., to assume that it, too, is one of the "secrets" of the *Guide*. Quotations from Maimonides' Commentary on the Mishnah and his code, indeed all quotations in the *Guide*, belong to the same class of hints.

After these preliminary remarks, we must try to place the method of reading the *Guide* on a firmer basis. In order to arrive at rules which would relieve us of the burdensome necessity of guessing Maimonides' secret thoughts, we must make a fresh start by discussing more exactly the relation between the model, the Bible, and its imitation or repetition, the *Guide*. What is the literary genus including the Bible and the *Guide*, and what is the specific difference giving the *Guide* its peculiar character?

Both the Bible, as Maimonides was wont to understand it, and the *Guide* are esoteric books. To cite but one other assertion of the author, his intention in writing the *Guide* was that the truths should flash up and then disappear again.[88] The purpose of the *Guide* is, then, not only to reveal the truth, but also to hide it. Or, to express the same thing in terms of quantity, a considerable number of statements are made in order to hide the truth rather than to teach it.

But what is the difference between the esoteric method of the Bible and that of the *Guide?* The authors of the Bible chose, in order to reveal the truth by not revealing it, and not to reveal it by revealing it, the use of words of certain kinds and of parables and enigmas.[89] Parables seem to be the more important vehicle, for Maimonides speaks of them much more fully than he does of the kinds of words in question.[90] Thus the suspicion arises that the species of esoteric books to which the Bible belongs is parabolic literature. That suspicion leads us to raise the question whether parables and enigmas are indispensable for esoteric teaching. As a matter of fact, that question is raised by Maimonides himself. After asserting that nobody is capable of completely explaining the secrets and that therefore every teacher speaks of them by using parables and enigmas, he goes on to say that, if someone wishes to teach the secrets without

[88] I, Introd. (3b; 3, 14).
[89] I, Introd. (5a; 5, 11 and 16).
[90] Cf. the index to Munk's *Guide, s.vv.* "allégories" and "noms."

using parables and enigmas, he cannot help substituting for them obscurity and briefness of speech.[91] This remark may refer to an extreme case which is not likely to occur, but it also may suggest a possible innovation. Whether or not that case is likely and whether Maimonides is willing to make the innovation,[92] the substitution indicated by him is certainly possible. Thus his remark implies the admission that there exists a species of unparabolic esoteric literature and, consequently, that the species of esoteric books to which the Bible belongs may rightly be described as parabolic literature.

The question of how to avoid parables and enigmas when speaking of the secrets is taken up again by Maimonides a little further on in the general introduction to his work, in his discussion of the explanation of parables. He discusses that question by telling us a story. He narrates that once upon a time he had intended to write two books in order to explain the parables of the Bible and those of the Midrashim, but that when attempting to write these books he was faced by a dilemma. Either he could give the explanation in the form of parables, which procedure would merely exchange one individual for another of the same species, or he could explain the parables in unparabolic speech, in which case the explanation would not be suitable for the vulgar. Since the explanations given in the *Guide* are not addressed to the vulgar, but to scholars,[93] we may expect from the outset that they would be of an unparabolic character. Moreover, we know from Maimonides' earlier statement that parabolic and enigmatic representation of the secret teaching can be avoided: it can be replaced by obscurity and briefness of speech, i.e., by ways of expression which are suitable exclusively to scholars who, besides, are able to understand of themselves. Above all, in the case of an explanation of parabolic texts, it is not only possible, but even necessary to avoid parabolic speech: a parabolic explanation would be open to the objection, so aptly made by Maimonides himself, that it merely replaces one individual by another individual of the same species, or,

[91] I, Introd. (4b-5a; 4, 11-13, 17-19, 26-28).

[92] I, Introd. (9b; 10, 24-28).

[93] Cf. I, Introd. (5b; 5, 18-25) with *ibid.* (3a and 4b; 2, 11 ff. and 4, 8-12).

in other words, that it is no explanation at all. What is then, the species of speech, different from that of parabolic speech, the use of which Maimonides had to learn after he had decided to write the *Guide* instead of the two popular books? What is the species, of which all expositions of the truth, given in the *Guide*, are individuals? To answer this question, we must first raise the more general question as to what is the genus which includes the species, hitherto unknown, of the expositions of the truth characteristic of the *Guide*, as well as of the species of parabolic expositions? The answer to this question, which no careful student of the *Guide* can help raising, is given by Maimonides in the last section of the general introduction to his work, where he quite abruptly and unexpectedly introduces a new subject: the various reasons for contradictions occurring in various kinds of books. We already know the hidden motive underlying this sudden change of subject matter; that hidden motive is the somewhat disguised question of the method characteristic of the *Guide* or, to speak more generally and vaguely, the question of the genus including the esoteric methods of both the Bible and the *Guide*. To the latter question, Maimonides gives here the rather undisguised answer that the genus looked for is contradictory speech. To the former question, he answers with equal clarity that the contradictions met with in the *Guide* are to be traced back to two reasons: to the requirements of teaching obscure matters, i.e., of making them understood, and to the requirements of speaking, or writing, of such matters. The contradictions caused by the former are bound to be known to the teacher (provided he did not make them deliberately), and they escape the pupil until he has reached an advanced stage of training; that is to say, they certainly escape the vulgar. But as regards the contradictions caused by the latter requirements, they always are deliberately made, and the author must take the utmost care to hide them completely from the vulgar.[94] Those disclosures of Maimonides enable us to describe the form of the esoteric teaching of the *Guide:* Maimonides teaches the truth not by inventing parables (or by using contradictions between parabolic statements), but by using conscious and inten-

[94] I, Introd. (10a, 10b, 11b; 11, 19-26 and 12, 7-12 and 13, 13-15).

tional contradictions, hidden from the vulgar, between unparabolic and unenigmatic statements.[95]

From this result the inference must be drawn that no interpreter of the *Guide* is entitled to attempt a "personal" explanation of its contradictions. For example, he must not try to trace them back to the fact, or assumption, that the two traditions which Maimonides intended to reconcile, i.e., the Biblical tradition and the philosophic tradition, are actually irreconcilable; or, more philosophically but scarcely more adequately, to explain them by assuming that Maimonides was on the track of philosophic problems transcending the horizon of the philosophic tradition, but was unable to free himself sufficiently from its shackles. Such attempts would serve a useful purpose if meant to explain highly complicated and artificial reconciliations of contradictions. They are both erroneous and superfluous if they are destined to explain contradictions which, if unintentional, would betray not the failure of a superior intellect in the face of problems either insoluble or very difficult to solve, but rather scandalous incompetence.[96] All these attempts would tacitly or expressly presuppose that the contradictions had escaped Maimonides' notice, an assumption which is refuted by his unequivocal statements. Therefore, until the contrary has been proved, it must be maintained that he was fully aware of every contradiction in the *Guide,* at the very time of writing the contradictory sentences. And if the objection is made that we ought to allow for the possibility that unconscious and unintentional contradictions have crept into the *Guide,* since philosophers hardly inferior to Maimonides have been found guilty of such contradictions, we answer by referring to Maimonides' emphatic declaration concerning the extreme care with which he had written every single word of his book and by asking the objectors to produce similar declarations from those books of other philosophers which they may have in mind. Therefore the duty of the interpreter is not to explain the contradictions, but to find out in each case which of the two statements was con-

[95] Cf. I, Introd. (10a; 11, 13-16). Cf. the somewhat different interpretation followed by Altmann, *op. cit.,* 310 f.
[96] Cf. I, Introd. (10b; 12, 4-7).

sidered by Maimonides to be true and which he merely used as a means of hiding the truth.

Maimonides has raised the question whether contradictions caused by the requirements of speaking, or writing, of obscure matters are also to be found in the Bible: he demands that this question be very carefully studied.[97] In fact, it reveals itself as being the decisive question, once one has looked beneath the surface of the teaching of the *Guide*. Since he does not answer it explicitly, it must here be left open. Neither can we discuss here the related questions as to whether the Maimonidean method of teaching the truth was influenced by a philosophic tradition; whether it is characteristic of a particular kind of philosophic literature; and whether, in accordance with the terminology of the philosophic tradition, the *Guide* ought not to be described rather as an exoteric work. If this description should ultimately prove correct, the meaning of the term "addition" would have to undergo a profound change: it would not mean the decisively important secret teaching which is added to the conventional view, but rather the imaginative representation which is added to the undisguised truth.[98]

Since the contradictions in the *Guide* are concealed, we must briefly consider at least some of the ways of hiding contradictions. (1) The most obvious method is to speak of the same subject in a contradictory manner on pages far apart from each other. The symbol of this method is: $a = b$ (page 15) — $a \neq b$ (page 379). Considering, however, the carelessness with which we usually read, one may reduce the distance between the pages to any positive number. (2) A variation of this method is to make one of the two contradictory statements in passing, as it were. A good example is Maimonides' incidental denial of the obligatory character of the entire sacrificial legislation.[99] (3) A third method is to contradict the first statement not directly, but by contra-

[97] I, Introd. (11b; 13, 6-8).

[98] For the two meanings of *addition*, cf. I, Introd. (7a-b; 8, 6, 15), on the one hand, and *ibid.* (8a; 9, 8), on the other. Cf. also in the *Treatise on Resurrection* the beginning of the treatise proper. The importance of the term "addition," for instance, for the doctrine of attributes may be indicated here in passing.

[99] III, 46 (102a-b; 427, 14-16). Cf. Munk, *Guide*, III, 364, n. 5. An allusion to this statement is implied in Joseph ibn Kaspi's commentaries on Deut. 17:14 f. and I Sam. 8:6.

dicting its implications. The symbol of this method is: $a = b -$
$b = c - [a = c] - a \neq c - [a \neq b]$, the brackets indicating propositions which are not to be pronounced. It may be illustrated
by the contradiction between the statements that "one of the
main subjects of the *Guide* is *ma'aseh bereshit*" and that
"*ma'aseh bereshit* is physics" on the one hand, and that "physics
is not a subject of the *Guide*" on the other; or by the contradiction between the contentions that "explanation of the secrets is
impossible by nature" and that "explanation of the secrets is
forbidden by the law." (4) Another method is to contradict the
first statement not directly, but by seemingly repeating it while
actually adding to it, or omitting from it, an apparently negligible expression. The symbol of that method is: $a = b - [b = \beta +$
$\varepsilon] - a = \beta - [a \neq b]$. (5) Another method is to introduce between the two contradictory statements an intermediary assertion, which, by itself not contradictory to the first statement, becomes contradictory to it by the addition, or the omission, of an
apparently negligible expression; the contradictory statement
creeps in as a repetition of the intermediary statement. The
symbol of this method is: $a = b - a \neq \beta - [b = \beta + \varepsilon] - a \neq b$.
(6) To use ambiguous words. The symbol is:
$a = c - \left[c \genfrac{}{}{0pt}{}{=}{\neq} b \genfrac{<}{}{0pt}{}{a = b}{a \neq b} \right]$. For example, the sentence, "a certain statement is an addition," may mean a true addition to an
untruth, or an untrue addition to the truth.

While on the subject of ambiguous words, we may indicate
their great importance for the reader of the *Guide*. According
to Maimonides, the Bible teaches the truth by using certain
kinds of words, as well as by parables. While excluding the latter
from his own work, he nowhere indicates his intention of avoid-
ing the former, and in particular ambiguous words. The expression "ambiguous word" is itself ambiguous. Used as a technical
term, it means a word which is applied to "two objects between
which there is a similarity with regard to some thing which is
accidental to both and which does not constitute the essence of
either of them."[100] In another less technical, but scarcely less

---

[100] I, 56 (68b; 89, 18-20). Cf. H. A. Wolfson, "The Amphibolous Terms in
Aristotle, Arabic Philosophy and Maimonides," *The Harvard Theological Review*
XXXI (1938), 164.

important sense, it means "a word fitly spoken" (Proverbs 25:11). For, according to Maimonides, this Biblical expression describes "a speech spoken according to its two faces," or "a speech which has two faces, i.e., which has an exterior and an inner" face; an exterior useful, for instance, for the proper condition of human societies, and an inner useful for the knowledge of the truth.[101] An ambiguous speech in the second sense would, then, be a speech with one face toward the vulgar, and with another face toward the man who understands by himself. Not only speeches, or sentences, but also words with two faces were indispensable to Maimonides, when he attempted to reveal the truth to the latter while hiding it from the former. For a secret is much less perfectly concealed by a sentence than by a word, since a word is much smaller in extent, and consequently *ceteris paribus* a much better hiding place than a whole sentence. This is especially true of common words, placed unobtrusively within an unobtrusive sentence. It is just such common words of hidden ambiguity which Maimonides has primarily in mind when he asks the reader to pay very close attention to every word which he happens (or rather seems to happen) to use; and when he emphatically entreats him not to explain anything in the *Guide*, not even a single word, unless it expressed something which had already been accepted and openly taught by earlier Jewish authorities.[102] Evidently the explanation of a single word cannot be so grave a matter unless that word is filled with high explosive which can destroy all beliefs not firmly grounded in reason; i.e., unless its actual and hidden meaning lends to some important statement a sense totally different from, or even diametrically opposed to the sense which it would have, if this particular word were to be accepted in its apparent or conventional meaning. Is such a word not to be called an ambiguous word, "a word fitly spoken"? Apart from all general considerations, one may cite a number of individual examples of ambiguous terms intentionally used by Maimonides. Such terms are: "the wise" or "the

---

[101] I, Introd. (6b-7a; 7, 15-8, 3). The fact that the whole passage (6a-8b; 6, 19-9, 25), which apparently deals with parables only, actually has still another meaning, is indicated by the seeming clumsiness with which the apparent subject is introduced.

[102] I, Introd. (9a; 10, 4-7).

learned," "the men of speculation,"[103] "the virtuous," "the community of the believers in [God's] unity," "government," and
"providence," "addition," "secret," "belief," "action," "possible."

Returning to Maimonides' use of contradictions, one may
assume that all important contradictions in the *Guide* may be
reduced to the single fundamental contradiction between the
true teaching, based on reason, and the untrue teaching, ema-
nating from imagination. But whether this be the case or not,
we are certainly in need of a general answer to the general question: which of the two contradictory statements is in each instance considered by Maimonides as the true statement? That
answer would be *the* guide for the understanding of Maimonides' work. It is provided by his identification of the true
teaching with some secret teaching. Consequently, of two contradictory statements made by him, that statement which is most
secret must have been considered by him to be true. Secrecy is
to a certain extent identical with rarity; what all people say all
the time is the opposite of a secret. We may therefore establish
the rule that of two contradictory statements in the *Guide* or in
any other work of Maimonides that statement which occurs least
frequently, or even which occurs only once, was considered by
him to be true. He himself alludes to this rule in his *Treatise
on Resurrection,* the most authentic commentary on the *Guide,*
when he stresses the fact that resurrection, though a basic principle of the law, is contradicted by many scriptural passages, and
asserted only in two verses of the Book of Daniel. He almost
pronounces that rule by declaring, in the treatise mentioned,
that the truth of a statement is not increased by repetition nor
is it diminished by the author's failure to repeat it: "you know
that the mention of the basic principle of unity, i.e., His word
'The Lord is one,' is not repeated in the Torah."

To sum up: Maimonides teaches the truth not plainly, but
secretly; i.e., he reveals the truth to those learned men who are
able to understand by themselves and at the same time he hides
it from the vulgar. There probably is no better way of hiding
the truth than to contradict it. Consequently, Maimonides

[103] Cf., for instance, I, Introd. (9b; 10, 21); III, 15 (28b; 331, 27-29).

makes contradictory statements about all important subjects; he reveals the truth by stating it, and hides it by contradicting it. Now the truth must be stated in a more hidden way than it is contradicted, or else it would become accessible to the vulgar; and those who are able to understand by themselves are in a position to find out the concealed statement of the truth. That is why Maimonides repeats as frequently as possible the conventional views which are suitable to, or accepted by the vulgar, but pronounces as rarely as possible contradictory unconventional views. Now a statement contradictory to another statement is, in a sense, its repetition, agreeing with it in almost every respect and differing only by some addition or omission. Therefore we are able to recognize the contradiction only by a very close scrutiny of every single word, however small, in the two statements.

Contradictions are the axis of the *Guide*. They show in the most convincing manner that the actual teaching of that book is sealed and at the same time reveal the way of unsealing it. While the other devices used by Maimonides compel the reader to guess the true teaching, the contradictions offer him the true teaching quite openly in either of the two contradictory statements. Moreover, while the other devices do not by themselves force readers to look beneath the surface—for instance, an inappropriate expression or a clumsy transition, if noticed at all, may be considered to be merely an inappropriate expression or a clumsy transition, and not a stumbling block—the contradictions, once they are discovered, compel them to take pains to find out the actual teaching. To discover the contradictions or to find out which contradictory statement is considered by Maimonides to be true, we sometimes need the help of hints. Recognizing the meaning of hints requires a higher degree of understanding by oneself than does the recognition of an obvious contradiction. Hints are supplied by the application of the other Maimonidean devices.

To make our enumeration of those devices somewhat more complete, and not to mention intentional sophisms and ironical remarks, we shall first briefly clarify our foregoing remark on Maimonides' extensive use of words of certain kinds. We may call those words secret words. His secret terminology requires a special study, based upon a complete index of words which have, or may have, secret meaning. These words are partly ambiguous, as in the instances mentioned above, and partly unambiguous, such as *ádamiyyûn, fiqh, dunyâ*. In the second place we may mention various kinds of apostrophes to the reader and mottoes prefixed to the whole work or to individual parts. Another device consists in silence, i.e., the omission of something which only the learned, or the learned who are able to understand of themselves, would miss. Let us take the following example. Maimonides quotes in the *Guide* four times, if I am not mistaken, expressly as an utterance of Aristotle, and with express or tacit approval, the statement that the sense of touch is a disgrace to us.[104] Such fourfold repetition of an express quotation in a book so carefully worded as the *Guide* proves that the quotation is something like a *leitmotif*. Now, that quotation is incomplete. Maimonides omits two words which profoundly alter its meaning. Aristotle says: δόξειεν ἂν δικαίως (ἡ ἀφὴ) ἐπονείδιστος εἶναι.[105] Maimonides omits, then, those two words which characterize the utterance as an ἔνδοξον. Readers of the *Guide*, cognizant of the teachings of the "prince of philosophers," naturally noticed the omission and realized that the passages into which the quotation is inserted are of a merely popular, or exoteric character. If one examines the four quotations more closely, one notices that while in the second and third citation Maimonides mentions the name of Aristotle, but not the work from which it is taken, he expressly cites the *Ethics* in the first passage, thus intimating that its source is a book based mainly on ἔνδοξα. In the last quotation Maimonides adds the remark that the quotation is literal, but two or three lines further on, while speaking of the same subject, he refers to the *Ethics* and the *Rhetoric*, i.e., to books devoted to the analysis of ἔνδοξα. There can be no doubt that Maimonides was fully aware of the fact that his citation from Aristotle actually reflected popular rather than philosophic opinion. It is still less doubtful

---

[104] II, 36 (79a; 262, 11-12); 40 (86b; 272, 4-5); III, 8 (12b; 311, 9-10); 49 (117a; 447, 1-2). Cf. also III, 8 (14a; 313, 18-19).

[105] *Eth., Nic.* 1118b2. I am naturally following that interpretation of the passage cited, on which is based the Arabic translation as quoted by Maimonides. Cf. Averroes *ad loc.:* "et iustum est nos opinari a nobis [sic] quod sensus iste opprobriosus est nobis." Cf. *De anima*, 421a 19-26.

that Maimonides, while agreeing with the complete statement of
Aristotle, viz., that the sense of touch is popularly considered
disgraceful, by no means believed in the soundness of this popular judgment. As a matter of fact, he contradicted it quite openly
by denying any difference in dignity between the senses and
by ascribing to the imagination of the vulgar the distinction
between senses which are supposed to be perfections and those
believed to be imperfections.[106] The reader of the *Guide*,
familiar with the main controversial topics of the Middle Ages,
will at once realize the bearing of Maimonides' misquotation:
the statement of Aristotle, as cited by Maimonides, would afford
an excellent justification of ascetic morality—for what Maimonides would call "exaggeration"—and in particular for an
ascetic attitude toward sexuality.[107] And the reader who looks
up the passages in question in the *Guide* will notice that one of
these misquotations is inserted into what Munk calls the "défi-
nition générale de la prophétie." Another characteristic omission is Maimonides' failure to mention the immortality of the
soul or the resurrection of the body, when he attempts explicitly
to answer the question of Divine Providence.[108] He begins his
discussion (III, 16-24) by reproducing the philosophic argument against individual providence, mainly based on the
observation that the virtuous are stricken with misery, while
the wicked enjoy apparent happiness. It is therefore all the
more perplexing that he pays no attention to what Leïbniz has
called[109] "le remède [qui] est tout prêt dans l'autre vie." Neither
does he mention that remedy in his express recapitulation of the
view of Providence characteristic of the literal sense of the
Torah.[110] On the other hand, he elsewhere explains in the same
context the "good at thy latter end" alluded to in Deuteronomy

---

[106] I, 47, 46 (51b-52a; 68, 16-21); 2 (14a; 16, 22-17, 3).

[107] Cf., in this connection, III, 8 (14a-b; 313, 22-314, 14).

[108] This is not to deny that Maimonides mentions here the "other world," in
connection with such views of Providence as he rejects or the truth of which he
neither discusses nor asserts. The phrase in III, 22 (46a; 354, 3-4), "the thing
which remains of man after death," is naturally noncommittal with respect to
the immortality of the individual soul. Cf. I, 74 (121b; 155, 9-10).

[109] *Théodicée*, §17.

[110] III, 17 (34b-37b; 338, 21-343, 5).

8:16 as the fortitude acquired by the privations from which Israel had suffered while wandering through the desert.[111]

The fourth and last kind of hints to be indicated here are the *rashei perakim*. This expression, which we have hitherto rendered as "chapter headings," may also mean "beginnings of chapters." In some cases, indeed, Maimonides gives us important hints by the initial word or words of a chapter. The opening word of the section devoted to the rational explanation of Biblical commandments (III, 25-49) is the noun, *al-af'âl* ("the actions"). The *af'âl*, synonymously used with *a'mâl*, constitute the second half of the law, the first half consisting of *ârâ'*[112] ("opinions"). Thus this opening gives us a hint that all the preceding chapters of the *Guide* (I-III, 24) are devoted to the "opinions," as distinguished from "actions," which are taught or prescribed by the law. The initial words in the first chapter (III, 8) devoted to theodicy, or the question of providence, is the expression "All bodies which come into existence and perish." These words indicate that this whole group of chapters (III, 8-24) deals exclusively with bodies which come into existence and perish, and not with bodies or souls which do not come into existence or perish. That this guess is correct is shown by other remarks of Maimonides.[113] From this opening, moreover, we must draw the inference that all preceding chapters (I, 1-III, 7) are devoted to things which do not come into existence and perish, and in particular to souls or intelligences which do not come into existence and perish, i.e., to *ma'aseh merkabah*. This inference is confirmed by Maimonides' statement, made at the end of Book III, Chapter 7, that all the preceding chapters are indispensable for the right understanding of *ma'aseh merkabah*, whereas in the following chapters not a word will be said, either explicitly or allusively, about that most exalted topic. Equally important are the beginnings of Book III, Chapter 24, which opens with the ambiguous word *'amr*, which may mean "thing"

---

[111] III, 24 (52b-53a; 362, 10-363, 4). Cf. M.T. Teshubah 8, 1-2.

[112] Cf. in particular III, 52 (130b; 464, 26-465, 5) with Farabi, *'Ihṣâ al-'ulûm*, chap. 5 (or the Hebrew translation by Falakera, in *Reshit ḥokmah*, ed. by David, p. 59). For the two Arabic words for "actions," cf., for instance, III 25 (57a; 368, 8 and 10).

[113] III, 23 (50b-51a; 360, 1-14); 54 (135a; 470, 21-26).

as well as "command,"[114] and the beginning of the very first chapter of the whole work.

Necessity has led us to make such incoherent and fragmentary remarks about Maimonides' methods of presenting the truth that it will not be amiss if we conclude this chapter with a simile which may drive home its main content to those readers who are more interested in the literary than in the philosophic question. There are books the sentences of which resemble highways, or even motor roads. But there are also books the sentences of which resemble rather winding paths which lead along precipices concealed by thickets and sometimes even along well-hidden and spacious caves. These depths and caves are not noticed by the busy workmen hurrying to their fields, but they gradually become known and familiar to the leisured and attentive wayfarer. For is not every sentence rich in potential recesses? May not every noun be explained by a relative clause which may profoundly affect the meaning of the principal sentence and which, even if omitted by a careful writer, will be read by the careful reader?[115] Cannot miracles be wrought by such little words as "almost,"[116] "perhaps," "seemingly"? May not a statement assume a different shade of meaning by being cast in the form of a conditional sentence? And is it not possible to hide the conditional nature of such a sentence by turning it into a very long sentence and, in particular, by inserting into it a parenthesis of some length? It is to a conditional sentence of this kind that Maimonides confides his general definition of prophecy.[117]

VI. THE *GUIDE* AND THE CODE

As we have seen, the *Guide* is devoted to the true science of the law, as distinguished from the science of the law in the usual sense, the *fiqh*. It remains to be considered whether, according to Maimonides, the two kinds, or parts, of the science of the law

[114] Cf. III, 24 (54a; 364, 16 and 20 f.).
[115] Cf. in this connection I, 21 (26a; 33, 11-17), 27 *vers. fin.*
[116] Cf. III, 19 (39a; 345, 6).
[117] II, 36 (78b-79b; 262, 2-263, 1). Cf. Munk, *Guide*, II, 284, n. 1. Other examples of the same method occur in III, 51 (127b; 460, 27-461, 1) [cf. Munk, *Guide*, III, 445, n. 2] and III, 18 (39a; 344, 22).

are of equal dignity or whether one of them is superior to the other.

Several arguments tend to show that Maimonides attached a higher importance to the *fiqh,* or to use the Hebrew term, to the *talmud,*[118] than he did to the subject of the *Guide:* (1) He calls his talmudic code "our great work," whereas he describes the *Guide* as "my treatise." (2) The former exercised a great influence on traditional Juadaism, in which respect the *Guide,* already two or three centuries after its publication far surpassed by the *Zohar*[119] in deep and popular appeal, cannot possibly compete. (3) Even under the profoundly changed circumstances of the present time, the *Mishneh Torah* is able to elicit strong and deep emotions in modern readers, whereas the *Guide* is of hardly any interest to people who do not happen to be historians. (4) Whereas the subject matter of the *Mishneh Torah* is easily ascertainable, the question of the field to which the subjects of the *Guide* belong is highly perplexing; it is not a philosophic nor a theological work, nor a book of religion.[120] (5) The code is styled a "repetition of the Torah," whereas the "treatise" is a mere "guide for the perplexed." (6) The *fiqh's* precedence to the subject matter of the *Guide* (the *ma'aseh bereshit* and *ma'aseh merkabah*) is expressly stated by Maimonides when he says, as it were in defense of the *talmud* against the sages of the Talmud, that "although those things [the explanation of the precepts of the Torah] were called by the sages a small thing— for the sages have said 'a great thing is *ma'aseh merkabah,* and a small thing is the discussion of Abbaye and Raba'—yet they ought to have precedence."[121] (7) Having gone so far, one might be tempted to go even farther and assert that the subject of the *Guide* is subservient to and implied in the *talmud.* For Maimonides explicitly says that *pardes* (i.e., *ma'aseh merkabah* and *ma'aseh bereshit*) is included in the *talmud.*[122] This argument might be reinforced by (8) a hint which, as such, in a book such as the *Guide,* is incomparably more significant than an

---

[118] Cf. III, 54 (132b; 467, 19-22) with M.T. Talmud torah 1, 11.
[119] Cf. G. Scholem, *Die Geheimnisse der Schöpfung. Ein Kapitel aus dem Sohar* (Berlin, 1935), 6 f.
[120] See above, p. 46.
[121] M. T. Yesodei ha-torah, 4, 13.
[122] M. T. Talmud torah, 1, 12.

explicit statement. Maimonides explains the true science of the law at the very beginning of his work, whereas he explains the meaning of *fiqh* in the very last chapter. To understand this hint, we must make use of another hint contained in the "chapter headings" of the first and the last chapters. The first chapter begins with the word "Image," while the last chapter opens with the term "Wisdom." This indicates that readers of the *Guide* are to be led from "Image," the sphere of imagination, to "Wisdom," the realm of intelligence: the way which readers of the *Guide* go is an ascent from the lower to the higher, indeed, from the lowest to the highest knowledge. Now the last of the themes treated in the *Guide* is law proper, i.e., the commands and prohibitions of the Torah, and not *ma'aseh bereshit* and *ma'aseh merkabah*, which are dealt with in the preceding sections. Consequently, the precepts of the law, far from being "a small thing," are actually the highest subject, indeed, the end and purpose of the true science of the law. (9) This conclusion is confirmed by an express statement by Maimonides, which establishes the following ascending order of dignity: (a) knowledge of the truth, based on tradition only; (b) such knowledge, based on demonstration; (c) *fiqh*.[123] (10) This hierarchy is also in accordance with the saying of the sages that not study, but action is most important, and it is actions which are determined by the *fiqh*. That hierarchy is imitated by the whole plan of the *Guide*, inasmuch as Maimonides assigns the explanation of the laws to the last group of chapters of that work, and as he explains the meaning of *fiqh* in the last chapter of it: the end is the best.

We have marshaled here all the evidence in favor of the view that Maimonides attached greater importance to the *Mishneh Torah* than to the *Guide*, and hope not to have missed a single argument which has been or could plausibly be adduced in its support. Impressive as they may seem at first sight, however, these arguments possess no validity whatsoever. The second and third arguments are wholly immaterial, for they do not reflect Maimonides' own conviction, but deal exclusively with what other people thought, or think of the matter. Neither can the fourth argument claim serious consideration, for it, too, is neither based on a Maimonidean statement, nor does, in itself,

[123] III, 54 (132b; 467, 18-25).

the perplexing nature of the subject matter of a book necessarily prove its lower rank; the example of Aristotle's *Metaphysics* might be to the point. We shall, then, turn to the remaining seven arguments which are at least apparently based on explicit or implicit statements of Maimonides.

The inference drawn from the description of the *Mishneh Torah* as "our great work" and of the *Guide* as "my treatise" is of little weight. For it is based on a hint, and no evidence has thus far been forthcoming to prove the fact that, or to show the reason why, Maimonides was prevented from stating quite openly that the halakah is of higher dignity than the subject of the *Guide*. The description of the *Mishneh Torah* as a "great" work may very well refer to its length rather than to its dignity, for it is quite natural that a code should be lengthier than the discussion of "roots." Or are we to believe that Maimonides attached a higher value to the "great book" of the Sabean Isḥâq "on the laws of the Sabeans and the details of their religion and their feasts and their sacrifices and their prayers and the other subjects of their religion" than he did to the "book" of the same unknown author "on the defence of the religion of the Sabeans?"[124] Moreover, it is doubtful whether Maimonides actually called the *Guide* a "treatise," rather than a "speech," and whether he called the *Mishneh Torah* a "work." "Work" would be a synonym for "book."[125] While Maimonides, for the most part, uses the two terms interchangeably, yet in one instance at least he hints at a distinction between *kitâb* (*sefer,* "book") and *ta'lîf* (*hibbur,* usually translated by "work"). He does this when speaking of the contradictions which are to be found "in any book or in any *ta'lif.*"[126] Abravanel, in his commentary on this passage, suggests that Maimonides means by "books" the books par excellence, i.e., the Bible, while he means by *tawâlîf* (or, rather, *hibburim*) the talmudic and philosophic literature. However grateful we ought to be to Abravanel for his indicating the problem, we certainly cannot accept his solution. For in the same section of the *Guide* Maimonides mentions also

---

[124] Cf. III, 29 (66b; 380, 13-15).

[125] See Louis Ginzberg's note s.v. *hibbur,* in his appendix to I. Efros's *Philosophical Terms in the Moreh Nebukim,* New York, 1924. Cf. above, p. 47.

[126] I, Introd. (9b; 11, 7-8).

the "books" of the philosophers.[127] On the other hand, two lines below this distinction, Maimonides applies the word *ta'lîf* to such works as the Mishnah, the Baraitot, and the Gemara.[128] We shall then suggest that by occasionally distinguishing between "books" and *tawâlîf*, Maimonides intended to point out once for all the distinction between such writings as the Bible and the works of philosophers on the one hand, and other literature, as exemplified by the talmudic compilation on the other hand. In fact, "compilation" would be a more literal translation of *ta'lîf* or *ḥibbur* than is "work" or "book." We know from the example of *maqâla* that Maimonides, when using a word emphatically, uses it in its original sense, which, as such, is often more hidden, rather than in its derivative and more conventional meaning. Thus we ought to render *ta'lîf* or *ḥibbur*, when emphatically used by Maimonides, by "compilation," rather than by "work." Since he doubtless uses it emphatically when he regularly calls the *Mishneh Torah* a *ta'lîf* or a *ḥibbur*, we ought to substitute the translation "our great compilation," for the usual translation "our great work."[129] Maimonides does not, then, distinguish between the *Guide* and the *Mishneh Torah* as between a treatise and a sublime work, but rather as between a confidential communication and an extensive compilation.

It is likewise but a popular fallacy to assume that Maimonides attributes a higher dignity to the *Mishneh Torah* than to the *Guide*, because he calls the former *"our* great composition,"

---

[127] I, Introd. (11b; 13, 8). Abravanel's comment may have been suggested by a mistake of Ibn Tibbon (or of a copyist or printer), since we find, in our editions of Ibn Tibbon's translation, the words "the books of the philosophers" rendered by "the words of the philosophers." But it is also possible that that suggestion was caused by I, 8 (18b; 22, 26-27), where a distinction is drawn between the "books" of the prophets and the *tawâlif* (or *ḥibburim*) of the "men of science."

[128] Cf. I, Introd. (10a, 11, 10) with *ibid.* (10b-11a; 12, 12-19).

[129] The correctness of this translation becomes fully apparent when one examines the way in which Maimonides employs, in his introduction to M. T., the terms חבר and חבור as against כתב and ספר. The M. T. is a חבור, because he has composed it לחבר דברים המתחברים מכל אלו החבורין (i.e., from the talmudic and gaonic literatures). Cf. Teshubah 4, 7 (86b 11 Hyamson). For the original meaning of חבור, see also Yesodei ha-torah, 1, 11; 3, 7. L. Blau's suggestion (in MbM, II, 339 f.) that חבור corresponds to *summa*, as distinguished from *commentatio*, is ruled out by the fact that both M. T. and C. M. are called by Maimonides *ḥibburim* (or *tawâlîf*). See, for example, I, 71 (93b; 121, 19).

whereas he calls the latter *"my* treatise." For the plural is not
necessarily a *pluralis majestatis.* The significance of the singular
and the plural in Maimonidean usage comes out most clearly in
the discussion of Providence. There, he distinguishes, with an
unequivocalness which could hardly be surpassed, between *"our*
opinion" and *"my* opinion." He introduces "what I believe" as
one interpretation of "our opinion, i.e., the opinion of our law,"
and contrasts it with the interpretation accepted by "the general
run of our scholars." Somewhat later he distinguishes the opinion of "our religious community" about divine knowledge from
"my discourse" upon that subject.[130] Even more explicitly he
demarcates "what we say, viz., we, the community of the adherents of the law" and "our belief" from the opinion of the
philosophers and "what I say." Finally, he distinguishes between
"the opinion of our law," which he had identified before with
"our opinion," and the correct, or "my" opinion.[131] One may
explain this distinction in the following way: "our opinion" is
based on the literal sense of the Bible, whereas "my opinion" is
in accordance with the intention of the Bible, i.e., with its
hidden or secret meaning. For "my opinion" brings into harmony the intelligible view with the literal sense of the Bible.[132]
"My opinion" is distinguished from "our opinion" by including
some additional idea which reveals itself only after a careful
examination and which alone really matters. "Our opinion," on
the other hand, is the opinion to which all consent and which
all repeat and which does not contain any idea peculiar to any
individual, and especially not to "my opinion."[133] Although the
identity of the correct opinion with "my opinion" is yet to be
proved, and although in the present stage of research it would
be rash to exclude the possibility that "my opinion," too, is an
exoteric opinion, it is most important in the present connection
to realize that the distinction between "our opinion" and "my
opinion" is characteristic not only of Maimonides' discussion of
Providence, but also of the whole *Guide.* This is, indeed, the considered view of a medieval commentator, who sees in the distinc-

[130] III, 17 (34b; 338, 21-24). Cf. *ibid.* (35b; 340, 10 ff.). III, 18 *in fine.*
[131] III, 20 (41a-42a; 347, 21-348, 16); 23 (49b; 358, 26-359, 1).
[132] III, 17 (34b-35b; 338, 22; 339, 16; 340, 13 f.). Cf. *ibid.* (37b; 342, 26-27).
[133] Cf. III, 23 (50a; 359, 4-15).

tion here made between the opinion of "the general run of our scholars" and "my opinion" merely the application of a general principle which Maimonides pronounces at the beginning of his book by quoting Proverbs 22:17.[134] He understands this verse to signify "Bow down thine ear, and hearken to the words of the sages,[135] *but* apply thine heart unto mine opinion." This verse, then, establishes from the outset the principle of the *Guide* to reveal "my opinion" as an "addition" to "our opinion." Therefore the work is called "my speech." This conclusion is confirmed, rather than refuted by Maimonides' immediately preceding quotation from Proverbs 8:4, "Unto you, O men, I call; and my voice is to the sons of man," which, in Maimonides' interpretation, means to say that his call is addressed to the few elect individuals partaking of the angelic nature, while his articulate speech is addressed to the vulgar.[136] For, as has been shown, "my speech" is far from being identical with "my articulate speech"; "my speech" or perhaps "my opinion" is much more likely to be identical with "my call." Thus, we repeat, the *Guide* is "my speech" revealing "my opinion," as distinguished from "our opinion," expressed in "our compilation," the *Mishneh Torah*, where generally speaking, Maimonides appears as the mouthpiece of the Jewish community or of the Jewish tradition. Since Maimonides doubtless subordinated his own views to those of the Jewish tradition, one may object, his hint of calling the *Guide* "my" book and the *Mishneh Torah* "our" book would still prove that he attached a higher dignity to the latter work. We must therefore discuss the remaining six arguments.

The fifth argument is based on the hints supplied by the titles of the two books; a "repetition of the Torah" must be of a much higher order than a mere "guide for the perplexed." We shall not raise the objection that the former title ought not to be translated by "repetition of the Torah," but rather by "the second [book] after the Torah." It is true that the latter trans-

---

134 Shem Tob on III, 17 (34b; 338, 21-24): ועל זה ועל כיוצא בו נאמר הט אזנך ושמע דברי חכמים ולבך תשית לדעתי. See also *idem* on III, 18 *in fine*. Cf. also W. Bacher, MbM, II, 180.

135 Cf. II, 33 (76a; 257, 26-258, 1); M. T. Yesodei ha-torah 4, 13. See also C. M. on Sanhedrin X (Holzer, p. 9, or Pococke, p. 147).

136 I, 14; M. T. Yesodei ha-torah, 2, 7.

lation is based on the only explicit statement by which Maimonides justifies the title of his code.[137] But a book which is second to another book and which restates its only authentic interpretation may also rightly be called a repetition thereof.[138] The *Mishneh Torah* certainly is a repetition of the oral law, which, according to Maimonides, is the only authentic interpretation of the (written) Torah. It is hardly necessary to add that the allusion to Deuteronomy, is anything but unintentional. It should not be forgotten, however, that, some time before Maimonides, Abraham bar Hiyya had drawn the inference from the traditional designation of the fifth book of Moses as "Mishneh Torah" that a distinction is to be made between the Torah, i.e., the second, third, and fourth books of Moses, and the Mishneh Torah, i.e., the fifth book. According to Abraham, who, as it were, anticipated the most important result of modern Biblical criticism, the Torah regulates the "order of service" (i.e., of worship) to be followed by the "holy congregation," which cares little for earthly things and in particular not for national defense. This "order of service" is the rule of life which Israel followed while wandering through the desert, when it was protected in a miraculous way against any external menace, and which is also to be followed by Israel whenever it lives in exile and, unable to defend itself against its enemies, must place its reliance exclusively upon God's mercy. The Mishneh Torah, on the other hand, adds to the "order of service," which it presupposes or repeats, "the order of service to the kingdom"; it is addressed to the "just kingdom," a community undetached from earthly things and concerned about national defense. Mainly devoted to matters of jurisdiction, especially in agricultural life, and to laws concerning kings and wars, it establishes a rule of life which Israel followed as long as it lived in its

---

[137] See Blau, MbM, II, 338. From this fact, pointed out by him, Blau draws the inference that "das Wesen des Buches ist im Worte חבור ausgedrückt," viz., it is not expressed by the words *Mishneh Torah*. And he adds in italics: "Der Name *Mischne Torah* findet sich tatsächlich kein zweitesmal bei Maimuni." If this remark were correct, it certainly would deserve to be italicized, since it would show that Maimonides attached an extremely high and secret importance to the name *Mishneh Torah*. But as a matter of fact, that name occurs, I believe, ten times in the *Guide*.

[138] Cf. S. Zeitlin, *Maimonides* (New York, 1935), 86.

own land.[139] I venture to suggest that Maimonides remembered Abraham bar Hiyya's interpretation when he selected the name *Mishneh Torah* for his code, which contained not only the laws of exile but also those of the land; and that a certain reason, implied in Abraham's interpretation, led Maimonides to conclude his code so impressively with the laws regarding kings and their wars. In translating the title by "repetition of the Torah," we are also mindful of the peculiar significance with which the word *repetition* is used by Maimonides. But does the fact that the *Mishneh Torah* is a repetition of the Torah entitle us to assume that Maimonides judged that work, or its subject, to be more important than the *Guide* or its subject? "Repetition of the Torah" is an ambiguous expression: it may mean a repetition, reproducing the Torah in accordance with its external proportions, or one reproducing it with regard to the hidden and true proportions of its various subjects. There can be no doubt that the code reproduces the Torah according to its external proportions only. For the Torah consists of true "opinions" and of "actions," and whereas the "actions" are determined by it in great detail and with extreme precision, the true "opinions" are indicated only in bare outline. This proportion was preserved intact by the Talmud, since the sages of the Talmud spoke for the most part of precepts and manners, and not of opinions and beliefs.[140] In exactly the same way, the *Mishneh Torah* deals in the most detailed fashion with "actions," but speaks of the basic truths only briefly and allusively (though by allusions approximating clear pronouncements) and by haphazard.[141] The *Guide*, on the other hand, is devoted mainly, if not exclusively, to "opinions," as distinguished from "actions." Now "opinions" are as much superior in dignity to "actions" as is the perfection of the soul to that of the body. Therefore, the highest aim of the Torah is the regulation of our opinions, to which the order, prescribed by the Torah, of our actions is subservient.[142] Thus the true proportions of the subjects of the Torah are imitated not by the

[139] *Hegyon ha-nefesh*, ed. by Freimann, pp. 38a-39b.
[140] III, 27 (59b and 60a; 371, 29 f.; 372, 9 f.); 28 (60b-61a; 373, 7-17); I, Introd. (11a-b; 13, 2-5).
[141] I, Introd. (3b and 6a; 3, 7; 6, 8-9); I, 71 (97a; 125, 14).
[142] III, 27.

Mishneh Torah, which is devoted to the science of the law in its usual sense, but by the *Guide,* which is devoted to the true science of the law. We conclude, then, that whereas the *Mishneh Torah* is the "repetition of the Torah" *simpliciter* the *Guide* is the "repetition of the Torah" *par excellence.*[143] Should the objection be raised that the title of the *Guide* does not indicate its being a repetition of the Torah, we need only refer to the affinity between *guide* and *guidance (torah).*[144] The *Guide* is a repetition or imitation of the Torah particularly suitable to "perplexed" people, while the *Mishneh Torah* is such a repetition addressed primarily to people who are not "perplexed."

The sixth argument, referring to the explicit statement of Maimonides concerning the precedence of the *fiqh,* ignores his failure to contradict the talmudic saying that "the discussion of Abbaye and Raba is a small thing" as compared with *ma'aseh merkabah.* He merely explains that saying by adding to it the remark that knowledge of the precepts ought to precede concern with the secret topics. For knowledge of the precepts is indispensable for their execution, and their execution is indispensable for one's composure of mind, as well as for the establishment of peace and order; these, in turn, are indispensable for acquiring "the life of the coming world" or for acquiring true opinions.[145] That is to say, knowledge of the precepts is merely a means to an end, which, in its turn, is only a means to another, the ultimate end, i.e., to the understanding of *ma'aseh bereshit* and *ma'aseh*

---

[143] An allusion to that relation may be found in the fact that the M. T. consists of 14 (= 2 x 7) books, and that the precepts of the law are divided in the *Guide,* too, into 14 groups, whereas the explanation of the highest secret of the Torah, i.e., of *ma'aseh merkabah,* is given in 7 chapters of the *Guide.* Compare also the 49 (= 7 x 7) chapters which lead up from "Image" to "Angels," i.e., to a subject which is second to one subject only; and the 70 (= 10 x 7) chapters which lead up from "Image" to *rakab,* i.e., to the grammatical root of *merkabah.* To understand the number 70, one has to bear in mind that the word *ddamiyyûn* occurs, if I am not mistaken, 10 times in the *Guide,* and that the Torah speaks according to the language of *benei adam.* The word *adam* is explained in the fourteenth chapter of the *Guide;* the number of the chapter explaining the various meanings of man is the same as the number of the books of the M. T. or of parts of the law. See also above, n. 137.

[144] Compare the explanation of *torah* as *hiddya* in III, 13 (25a; 327, 10 f.); I, 2 (13b; 16, 9) with the synonymous use of *hadd* and *dalla* in II, 12 (26b; 195, 27). See also III, 45 (101a; 425, 17).

[145] M. T. Yesodei ha-torah, 4, 13. Cf. M. T. Teshubah 8, 5-6, 14; M. N. III, 27 (59b; 371, 25-28).

merkabah. Knowledge of the precepts precedes, then, knowledge of the secrets, as the means precedes the end. Maimonides adds yet another reason: the precepts can be known to everybody, to young and old, to unintelligent as well as intelligent, whereas the secret teaching, which is clear and manifest to the "men of speculation" only, was not fully grasped even by some of the greatest sages of the Talmud.[146] We conclude, therefore, that the precedence attributed by Maimonides to knowledge of the precepts is merely a priority in time, and not at all a superior dignity.

The seventh argument is based on Maimonides' statement that *maʿaseh bereshit* and *maʿaseh merkabah* belong to the *talmud.* Maimonides makes this statement in connection with his division of the study of the Torah into three parts: the study of the written Torah, that of the oral Torah, and the Talmud. The study of the prophetic writings and hagiographa belongs to that of the written Torah; the study of explanations thereof is part of the oral Torah; and the study of secret subjects is included in the *talmud.*[147] In order to understand this statement correctly, we must first bear in mind that *talmud* may be used ambiguously for a certain group of writings (the Babylonian and Jerusalem Talmuds), as well as for a peculiar kind of study. In the former sense, the statement that secret topics belong to the *talmud,* and not to the written or oral Torah, would mean that they are to be found in the Talmud rather than in the Bible,[148] but it would have no bearing upon the subordination of the secret teaching to the *fiqh.* If we take *talmud,* as we probably should, in its second meaning, it would indeed seem at first sight that Maimonides subordinates the study of the secret topics to the *fiqh,* just as he certainly subordinates the study of the prophetic writings and the hagiographa to that of the Pentateuch. But what does he actually say? Starting from the implicit assumption that all studies which are of any value are comprised within the study of the Torah, he raises the question: to which part of that

[146] III, Introd. (2a; 297, 6-8, 9-10). Cf. also I, 17. M. T. Yesodei ha-torah 4, 13.
[147] M. T. Talmud torah, 1, 12.
[148] Cf. I, 71 (93b and 94a; 121, 11 f., 25 f.) and the parallel passage in III, Introd. (2b; 297, 17 f.).

study does the study of that "great thing" (i.e., of the secret teaching) belong? And he answers: since the secret topics are the most difficult topics,[149] their study must belong to the most advanced part of the all-comprising study of the Torah, i.e., to the *talmud*. He does not preclude the possibility that this most advanced study be subdivided into two distinct parts, the *fiqh* and the true science of the law.[150] In fact, he alludes to this possibility when he says that men, after having reached a more advanced stage of wisdom, ought to devote their time almost exclusively to the *talmud*, according to the level of their intelligence.

The tenth argument is based on the saying of R. Simeon ben Gamaliel that not study, but action is most important, and on the assumption that Maimonides must have accepted this saying in its apparent meaning. But, according to his explanation,[151] it merely refers to speeches about laws and virtues and merely demands that man's actions be in accordance with his speeches expressing obedient and virtuous thoughts. Otherwise, he expressly recognizes in the *Mishneh Torah* that study of the Torah is superior in dignity to all other actions.[152] Above all, in the last chapter of the *Guide* he asserts that most precepts of the law are merely a means for the acquisition of moral virtue, which, in turn, is merely a means subservient to the true end, namely, speculative virtue, or the true knowledge of things divine.[153]

In the light of this Maimonidean assertion and of the place where it is found, the eighth argument cannot possibly be sound. If, indeed, the first "chapter heading" of the *Guide*, "Image," were contrasted with a last "chapter heading," "Wisdom," we certainly would have to conclude that all readers of the *Guide* are meant to ascend from the lowest to the highest knowledge. But, as it happens, the last "chapter heading" is not "Wisdom," but "The word wisdom." Now "The word wisdom" is not necessarily superior to "Image," as is shown by the fact, constantly present in Maimonides' mind, that many learned people living

---

[149] M. T. Yesodei ha-torah 2, 12; 4, 11, 13.

[150] I, Introd. (3a; 2, 12-14); III, 54 (132a-b; 467, 2-22).

[151] C. M. on Abot, I, 17.

[152] M. T. Talmud torah, 1, 3; 3, 3-5.

[153] III, 54 (133b-134b; 468, 22-470, 11).

in a world of imaginary and imaginative ideas call their possession and use of these ideas "wisdom" or "speculation." On the other hand, "wisdom," if rightly understood, indicates something absolutely superior to "image"; a man who understands the word wisdom according to its true meaning has overcome, or is on the way to overcoming, his imaginary views. The equivocal last "chapter heading," when contrasted with the unequivocal first "chapter heading," indicates the ambiguity inherent in the reading of the *Guide*. Its reader may ascend from imaginary views to true wisdom, but he also may not leave the world of imagination for a single moment, so that he finally arrives at the mere word "wisdom," which is but a shadow or image of wisdom itself. But let us apply to such readers the Maimonidean dictum that there is no reason for mentioning them in this place in this treatise.[154] Let us think of that reader only to whom the *Guide* is addressed and who, after having undergone training by the *Guide,* will certainly have substituted intelligent views for imaginary ones. For such a reader the study of the *Guide* is an ascent from the lowest to the highest knowledge. This is only tantamount to saying that by understanding the last chapter, or the last group of chapters, he will have attained to a knowledge more complete than that which he had acquired before reading these chapters. But it obviously does not of necessity indicate the superior dignity of the subjects treated in the last group of chapters.

In order to grasp the principle underlying the arrangement of the various subjects in the *Guide,* we must remind ourselves of its original purpose to repeat the Torah with regard to the hidden proportions of its subjects. The Torah having been given to man by an intermediary prophet, we may be permitted for a little while to replace Torah by prophecy. Maimonides asserts that the prophet's ascent to the highest knowledge is followed by his descent to the "people of the earth," i.e., to their government and instruction.[155] The prophet is, then, a man who not only has attained the greatest knowledge, indeed a degree of knowledge which is not attained by mere philosophers, but who is able also to perform the highest political functions.[156] A similar combination of theoretical and political excellence is required for the understanding of the secret teaching of the prophets.[157] Since the *Guide* is devoted to the interpretation of that secret teaching, Maimonides will also have imitated, in some manner or other, the way of the prophets. To be sure, the prophet is enabled to perform his political function of governing the "people of the earth" and of teaching them by the power of his imagination, i.e., by his capacity of representing the truth to the vulgar by means of images or parables, as Maimonides clearly intimates in the general definition of prophecy and in the chapter following it.[158] He himself, however, attempts to replace the parables by another method of representing the truth. Yet the fundamental similarity between the prophet, the bringer of the secret teaching, and the interpreter of the secret teaching remains unaltered by that change in the method. Therefore, we are from the outset entitled to expect that the sequence of topics in the *Guide* would imitate the way of the prophets, which is ascent, followed by descent. This expectation is proved to be correct by the actual structure of the *Guide*. Maimonides, or his reader, gradually and slowly climbs up from the depth of "image" to *ma'aseh merkabah,* the highest subject, which is fully treated in Book III, Chapters 1-7 only. At the end of this exposition, Maimonides declares that he will say no more about that subject. Accordingly, he begins the next

[156] That Maimonides conceived of the prophets as statesmen is shown also by the main division of the affirmative precepts in S. M. (or in the enumeration of the 613 commandments at the beginning of M. T.). There he lists first the precepts regulating the relations between man and God, and then those which order the relations among men. (See the remarks of Peritz in MbM, I, 445 ff.). The second class of these precepts (Nos. 172-248) opens with the commandments regarding the prophet, the king, and the high court; the prophet evidently is the head of the political organization. Cf. II, 40 (85b-86a; 270, 24-27). The question of the relation between king and priest is touched upon in III, 45 (98b; 422, 9-13). How far Maimonides accepted the teaching of the *Falāsifa*, according to which a "priestly city" is one of the bad regimes, must here remain an open question. See Ibn Bağğa, *k. tadbîr al-mutawahhid*, chap. 1, in the Hebrew extraction by Moses Narboni, ed. by D. Herzog, p. 8; and Averroes, *Paraphrasis in Rempubl. Plat.*, tr. 3, in *Opp. Aristotelis* (Venice 1550), III, 187c19-24.

[157] See above, p. 57 f.

[158] See also Falakera, *Reshit hokmah,* ed. David, p. 30.

chapter with the heading, "All bodies which come into existence
and perish." Finally, he descends one more step, from "opinion"
to "actions." The same prophetic way of ascent, followed by
descent, is evidently used as a model in his recommended order
of studies for unprophetic men, referred to in the ninth argument, namely, (1) knowledge of the truth, based on tradition
only; (2) such knowledge based on demonstration; (3) *fiqh*.
For the demonstrative knowledge of truth is the highest degree
attainable to unprophetic men.[159]

To sum up, according to Maimonides the *Mishneh Torah* is
devoted to *fiqh*, the essence of which is to deal with actions;
while the *Guide* deals with the secrets of the Torah, i.e., primarily opinions or beliefs, which it treats demonstratively, or at
least as demonstratively as possible. Demonstrated opinions or
beliefs are, according to Maimonides, absolutely superior in
dignity to good actions or to their exact determination. In other
words, the chief subject of the *Guide* is *ma'aseh merkabah*,
which is "a great thing," while the chief subject of the *Mishneh
Torah* is the precepts, which are "a small thing." Consequently,
the subject of the *Guide* is, according to Maimonides, absolutely
superior in dignity to the subject of the *Mishneh Torah*. Since
the dignity of a book, *caeteris paribus*, corresponds to the dignity of its subject, and since, as is shown by a comparison of
Maimonides' own introductory remarks to the two books, he
wrote the *Guide* with no less skill and care than his code, we
must conclude that he considered the *Guide* as absolutely
superior in dignity.

This conclusion, based on the general principle underlying
his entire work and nowhere contradicted by him, that knowledge of the truth is absolutely superior in dignity to any action,
is reinforced by some further statements or hints. We have
started from the distinction made by him at the very beginning
of the *Guide* between the true science of the law and the *fiqh*:
the former deals chiefly with the secrets of the Bible or, more
generally, with opinions and beliefs both secret and public;[160]
in other words, it demonstrates the beliefs taught by the law.
Maimonides repeats this distinction in the last chapter, in a

---

[159] III, 54 (132b; 467, 18-27). Cf. I, 33 (36b; 47, 25-26).
[160] Cf., for example, I, 1 (12a; 14, 14), 18 (24a; 30, 7) with I, 35.

somewhat modified manner; he there distinguishes three sciences: the science of the Torah, wisdom, and *fiqh*.[161] The science of the law, or the science of the Torah, does not demonstrate the basic principles taught by the law, since the law itself does not demonstrate them.[162] The *fiqh*, which at the beginning of the *Guide* had been identified with the science of the law, is now clearly distinguished from it or from the science of the Torah, as well as from wisdom.[163] Wisdom is the demonstration of the opinions taught by the law. Now the *Guide* is devoted to such demonstration; hence the true science of the law, mentioned at the beginning as the subject of the work, is identical with wisdom, as distinguished from both the science of the law and from the *fiqh*. Maimonides repeats, then, the distinction between the true science of the law and the science of the law; yet he no longer calls the former a science of the law, but wisdom, and no longer identifies the (ordinary) science of the law (or of the Torah) with the *fiqh*. The relation of wisdom to the *fiqh* is explained by a simile: the students of the *fiqh*, arriving at the divine palace, merely walk around it, whereas only speculation on the "roots," i.e., demonstration of the basic truths taught by the law, leads one unto the presence of God.[164]

Though Maimonides discloses his view at the end of his work only, he does not fail to give hints of it on previous suitable occasions. When he tells the story of his abandoned plan to write two books on the parables of the prophets and the Midrashim, he states that he had intended those books for the vulgar, but later realized that such an explanation would neither be suitable for, nor fill a need felt by the vulgar. That is why he has limited himself to that brief and allusive discussion of the basic truths of the law, which is to be found in his code. In the *Guide*, however, he goes on to say, he addresses himself to a man who has studied philosophy and who, while believing in the teachings of

[161] III, 54 (132b; 467, 18-20).

[162] III, 54 (132a-b; 467, 2-9, 13-14).

[163] III, 54 (132a-b; 467, 18-23 and 7 and 13-14). Cf. III, 41 (88b; 409, 15-16); M. T. Talmud torah, 1, 11-12.

[164] III, 51 (123b-124a; 455, 21-28). In his commentary on this chapter, Shem Tob relates that "many talmudic scholars have asserted that Maimonides had not written this chapter, and that, if he did write it, it ought to be suppressed, or rather, it would deserve to be burned."

the law, is perplexed in regard to them.[165] Those sentences, enigmatic and elusive as they are, show clearly that the *Guide* was not addressed to the vulgar, nor the *Mishneh Torah* to the perplexed. Are we, then, to believe that the latter was written for students of philosophy who had not become perplexed as regards the teachings of the law? Hardly, since Maimonides does not tire of repeating that the code is devoted to the *fiqh* and consequently is addressed to students of *fiqh,* who may or may not be familiar with philosophy. This is also shown by his failure to discuss in the *Mishneh Torah* the basic truths of the law, according to his primary and main intention and only, as it were, incidentally or haphazardly.[166] Evidently the *Mishneh Torah* was written also for people who had not studied philosophy at all and therefore were not perplexed; in other words, it was addressed to "all men."[167] This is quite clearly the meaning of the following passage in the *Guide:* "I have already explained to all men the four differences by which the prophecy of our teacher Moses is distinguished from the prophecy of the other prophets, and I have proved it and made it manifest in the Commentary on the Mishna and in the *Mishneh Torah.*" The meaning of "all men" *(al-nâs kâffa)* is incidentally explained in connection with a synonymous phrase *(ǧamî' al-nâs):* "all men, i.e., the vulgar."[168] This allusion to the exoteric character of the code and the commentary naturally has to be taken into account, not only in the interpretation of these two works but also for the adequate understanding of all quotations from them in the *Guide.*

We conclude: The *Mishneh Torah* is primarily addressed to the general run of men, while the *Guide* is addressed to the small number of people who are able to understand by themselves.

[165] I, Introd. (5b-6a; 5, 18-6, 11).
[166] I, Introd. (3a; 2, 13-16); 71 (97a; 125, 23-24).
[167] Cf. M.T. Yesodei ha-torah, 4, 13.
[168] II, 35 *in princ.;* III, 22 (45b; 353, 10). Cf. also M. T., Introd., 4b, 4-19 (Hyamson), and *Ḳobeṣ,* II, 15b.

4

THE LAW OF REASON IN THE *KUZARI*

חכמת לשונו הרבה

תפלטני מריבי עם.

—Halevi on R. Baruch

Every student of the history of philosophy assumes, tacitly or expressly, rightly or wrongly, that he knows what philosophy is or what a philosopher is. In attempting to transform the necessarily confused notion with which one starts one's investigations, into a clear notion of philosophy, one is confronted sooner or later with what appears to be the most serious implication of the question "what a philosopher is," viz., the relation of philosophy to social or political life. This relation is adumbrated by the term "Natural Law," a term which is as indispensable as it is open to grave objections. If we follow the advice of our great medieval teachers and ask first "*the* philosopher" for his view, we learn from him that there are things which are "by nature just." On the basis of Aristotle, the crucial question concerns then, not the existence of a *ius naturale*,[1] but the manner of its existence: "is" it in the sense in which numbers and figures "are," or "is" it in a different sense? The question can be reduced, to begin with, to this more common form: is the *ius naturale* a dictate of right reason, a set of essentially rational rules?

The issue was stated with a high degree of clarity by Marsilius of Padua. According to him, Aristotle understands by *ius*

---

[1] Cf. Thomas Aquinas' commentary on Aristotle's *Ethics,* V, lect. 12 *in princ.*: ". . . juristae . . . idem . . . nominant jus, quod Aristoteles justum nominat."

naturale a set of conventional rules, but of such conventional rules as are accepted in all countries, "so to speak by all men"; these rules, being dependent on human institution, can only metaphorically be called *iura naturalia.* "Yet there are people," he goes on to say, "who call *ius naturale* the dictate of right reason concerning objects of action." Over against this he remarks that the very rationality of the *ius naturale* thus understood prevents its being universally, or generally, accepted, and hence, we shall add, its being identical with that φυσικὸν δίκαιον, or that κοινὸς νόμος, which Aristotle had in mind.[2] By rejecting, in the name of Aristotle, the view that the *ius naturale* is a set of essentially rational rules, the Christian Aristotelian Marsilius opposes the Christian Aristotelian Thomas Aquinas in particular who had said that, according to Aristotle, the "justum naturale" is "rationi inditum," and who had defined the "lex naturalis" as "participatio legis aeternae in rationali creatura."[3]

To return to the Jewish Aristotelians, Maimonides did not choose to employ in his discussion of this fundamental question the term "Natural Law."[4] Whatever may have been his reason,[5]

[2] *Defensor pacis,* II, c. 12, sect. 7-8. See also *ibid.,* I. c. 19, sect. 13: "iure quodam *quasi* naturali." The question of the relation of the φυσικὸν δίκαιον as discussed in *Eth. Nic.* 1134b 18 ff. to the κοινὸς νόμος as discussed in *Rhetoric* I 13, 2 must here be left open. Cf. n. 5.

[3] Commentary on the *Ethics,* VIII, lect. 13 (and *ibid.,* V, lect. 15). *Summa theologica,* 12, quaest. 91., art. 2.—The promiscuous use of "lex naturalis" and "ius naturale" is unobjectionable in the present context, since it appears to have been customary in the period under consideration; cf. Suarez, *Tr. de legibus,* I, c. 3, §7: ". . . (subdivisionem) legis creatae in naturalem et positivam . . . omnes etiam Theologi agnoscunt, et est frequens apud Sanctos, sive sub nomine legis, sive sub nomine juris positivi, et naturalis." Cf. also Chr. Wolff, *Jus naturae,* P. I., §3, who states "vulgo jus naturae cum lege naturae confundi." Cf. above all, Hobbes, *Leviathan,* ch. 14 *in princ.* among other passages.

[4] Grotius seems to have taken it for granted that there is a genuinely Jewish doctrine of natural law, and since he defines "jus naturale" as "dictatum rectae rationis," he attributes by implication to Maimonides in particular the belief in a natural law as a dictate of right reason. He says: "Juris ita accepti optima partitio est, quae apud Aristotelem exstat, ut sit aliud jus naturale, aliud voluntarium . . . Idem discrimen apud Hebraeos est, qui . . . jus naturale vocant מצות, jus constitutum [= voluntarium] חקים . . ." (*De jure belli,* I, c. 1., §9.2-10.1). The only Jewish source referred to by Grotius is *Guide,* III, 26, where Maimonides certainly does not speak of natural law nor of rational laws. (See I. Husik, "The Law of Nature, Hugo Grotius and the Bible," *Hebrew Union College Annual,* II, 1925, 399 n. 10.—Husik asserts in addition that Grotius "made a slip. Maimonides uses משפטים for the שכליות." But Grotius makes the following remark in a note to the word מצות: משפט [ומצות. Sic Maimonides libro

he preferred to discuss the question in this form: are there rational laws in contradistinction to the revealed laws? His discussion and its result are implied in his statement that those who speak of rational laws, are suffering from the disease of the mutakallimûn (the students of the kalâm). Since the content of the rational laws in question seems to be identical with that of the Natural Law, the statement referred to seems to be tantamount to a denial of the rational character of the Natural Law.[6] That statement implies besides that the laws which are called by the mutakallimûn "rational," are called by the philosophers, the followers of Aristotle, "generally accepted" (ἔνδοξα).[7] Accordingly, we would have to describe Marsilius' interpretation of the *ius naturale* as *the* philosophic view, and Thomas' interpre-

III., ductoris dubitantium cap. XXVI." The source of what he says in the text, viz., that the *jus naturale* is called by the Hebrews מצות, may well be *Eight Chapters* VI, where Maimonides says that the so-called rational laws were called by the Sages מצוות.) The Noahidic commandments cannot be identified with the natural law, at least not according to Maimonides. For—to say nothing of אבר מן החי‎—the prohibition against incest or inchastity which occupies the central place in his enumeration of the Noahidic commandments (*Mishneh Torah*, H. Melakhim, IX 1), is considered by him to belong to the revealed laws as distinguished from the so-called rational laws (*Eight Chapters*, VI. See also Saadya, *K. al-amânât*, III, ed. by Landauer, 118. For an interpretation of this view, cf. Falkera, *Sefer ha-mebakkesh*, ed. Amsterdam 1779, 31a, and Grotius, *op. cit.*, II, c. 5, §12 and 13). This is not contradicted by Maimonides' statement that the דעת inclines man toward six of the seven Noahidic commandments (H. Melakhim IX 1), for דעת does not necessarily mean "reason" or "intelligence." As regards the Decalogue, Maimonides makes it clear that only the first two propositions are "rational," whereas the eight others belong to the class of generally accepted and of traditional opinions (*Guide*, II 33, 75a Munk).—Cf. below n. 107.

[5] The reason may have been that he held, just as Averroes and Marsilius, that the *ius naturale* can only metaphorically be called "natural." Cf. Averroes on *Eth. Nic.* 1134b 18 f., who interprets δίκαιον φυσικόν as "ius naturale legale" (יושר טבעי נימוסי‎) and δίκαιον νομικόν as "(ius) legale tantum, i.e. positivum" (נימוסי ר"ל הנחיי‎). (*Aristotelis Opera*, Venice 1560, III, 243a; cf. M. Schwab, "Les versions hébraiques d'Aristote," *Gedenkbuch zur Erinnerung an David Kaufmann*, Breslau 1900, 122 f.) The best translation of Averroes' interpretation of δίκαιον φυσικόν would be "ius naturale conventionale"; for נימוסי means מפאת ההסכמה‎ (cf. Moritz Steinschneider, *Die hebräischen Uebersetzungen des Mittelalters*, Berlin 1893, 309 n. 310.) For the understanding of Averroes' interpretation one has to consider *Magna Moralia* 1195a 6-7.

[6] *Eight Chapters*, VI. Cf. *Guide*, III 17 (35a-b Munk) and Munk's note to his translation of this passage in *Guide*, III, 127 n. 1.

[7] Cf. *Millot ha-higgayon*, c. 8, and Abraham ibn Daûd, *Emunah ramah*, ed. by Weil, 75. Cf. also Ibn Tibbon, *Ruah hēn*, c. 6.

tation as the view of the kalâm or, perhaps, as *the* theological view.[7a]

The impression that the philosophers rejected the view that there are rational laws distinguished from the positive laws (and in particular the revealed laws), or that they denied the rational character of the Natural Law, is apparently contradicted by Yehuda Halevi's discussion of this question. Distinguishing between rational laws and revealed laws, and using the terms "rational laws" and "rational *nomoi*" synonymously, he asserts that the philosophers have set up rational *nomoi*:[8] a philosopher whom he introduces as a character of his dramatic prose-work, the *Kuzari*, admits such rational *nomoi* as a matter of course. An analysis of Halevi's remarks on this subject may contribute toward a better understanding of the philosophic teaching concerning Natural Law and the Law of Reason.

I. THE LITERARY CHARACTER OF THE *KUZARI*

IT IS NOT safe to discuss any topic of the *Kuzari* before one has considered the literary character of the book. The book is devoted to the defence of the Jewish religion against its most important adversaries in general, and the philosophers in particular.[9] Since it is directed against the philosophers, the Muslims and so on, it is as impossible to call it a philosophic book, as it is to call it an Islamic book, provided one is not willing to use the term "philosophic" in a sense totally alien to the thought of the author, i.e., to transgress one of the most elementary rules of historical exactness. And since it is not a philosophic book, one cannot read it in the manner in which we are used to read philosophic books.

By "philosophers" Halevi understands chiefly, although by

[7a] Cf. H. A. Wolfson, 'The Kalam Arguments for Creation etc.,' *Saadya Memorial Volume,* New York 1943, note 126.

[8] The term employed by Halevi, אלנואמים אלעקלליה, means literally "the intellectual *nomoi*." I am not at all certain whether this literal translation is not the most adequate one. To justify the usual translation, one may refer to IV 3 (236, 16 f.) *inter alia.*—Figures in parentheses indicate pages and lines of Hirschfeld's edition.

[9] The title of the original is "Book of argument and proof in defence of the despised religion." See also the beginning of the work.

no means exclusively, the Aristotelians of his period. According to Fârâbî, the most outstanding of these philosophers,[10] the discussions contained in the *Kuzari* would belong, not to philosophy (or, more specifically, to metaphysics or theology), but to "the art of kalâm"; for it is that art, and not philosophy, which is designed to defend religion, or rather, since there are a variety of religions, to defend "the religions,"[11] i.e., in each case that religion to which the scholar in question happens to adhere. This view of the relation of philosophy and kalâm is shared by Halevi: whereas the aim of philosophy is knowledge of all beings, the aim of kalâm is to "refute the Epicurean," i.e., to establish by argument those beliefs which the privileged souls hold without argument.[12] It is evident that the explicit aim of the *Kuzari* is identical with the aim of the kalâm. It is true, Halevi defines the kalâm not merely by its aim, but by its method and assumptions as well. For all practical purposes, he identifies "kalâm" with a special type of kalâm, the mu'tazilite kalâm, and he is almost as little satisfied with this typical kalâm as he is with any philosophic school: to say the least, he insists much more strongly than this typical kalâm on the inferiority of any reasoning on behalf of faith to faith itself.[13] But this does not prevent his book from being devoted almost exclusively to such reasoning. Besides, he actually refuses to subscribe to one of the two main sections of the typical kalâm teaching only, to its doctrine of the unity of God; as regards the other main section, the doctrine of the justice of God, which is of a more practical character than the first, he sets it forth, not as the teaching of other people, but as his own teaching.[14] Halevi's teaching and that of the typical

---

[10] Fârâbî was considered the highest philosophic authority of the period by such authorities as Avicenna (cf. Paul Kraus, "Les *Controverses* de Fakhr Al-Dîn Râzî," *Bulletin de l'Institut d'Égypte*, XIX, 1936-7, 203) and Maimonides (see his letter to Ibn Tibbon). Cf. also S. Pines, "Études sur Abu'l Barakât," *Revue des Études Juives*, CIV, 1938-9, n. 308.

[11] *Ihsa al-'ulûm*, ch. 5. Fârâbî presents the kalâm as a corollary to political science.

[12] Cf. IV 13 and 19 with V 16 (330, 13 f. and 18-20).

[13] V 16.

[14] The doctrine of the unity of God is presented in V 18, that of the justice of God in V 20. In V 19, it is made clear that Halevi does not identify himself with the former doctrine, whereas he does identify himself with the latter. (Cf. M. Ventura, *Le Kalâm et le Péripatétisme d'après le Kuzari*, Paris 1934, 10 ff.). It appears from V 2 (296, 1-2) that the question of predestination which in V 19

kalâm may therefore be said to belong to the same genus, the specific difference between them being that the former is much more anti-theoretical, and much more in favor of simple faith, than is the latter. At any rate, while it is impossible to call Halevi a philosopher, it is by no means misleading to call the author of the *Kuzari* a mutakallim.[15]

Halevi presents his defence of Judaism, not in the form of a coherent exposition given in his own name, but in the form of a conversation, or rather a number of conversations, in which he himself does not participate: the *Kuzari* is largely an "imitative," not "narrative"[16] account of how a pagan king (the Kuzari) gradually becomes converted to Judaism by engaging in conversations first with a philosopher, then with a Christian scholar, thereafter with a Muslim scholar, and finally with a Jewish scholar; the conversations between the king and the Jewish scholar make up the bulk of the work (about 172 pages out of 180). To understand the *Kuzari,* one has to understand, not only the content, i.e., the statements made by the Jewish scholar in particular, but also the form, i.e., the conversational setting of all statements in general and of each statement in particular. To understand any significant thesis of the work, one has to understand the statements made by the characters in the light of the conversational situation in which they occur: one has to translate the "relative" statements of the characters, i.e.,

---

is designated as the topic of V 20, does not belong to "theology" (cf. *ibid.* 294, 18), i.e., to the only theoretical discipline to which it could possibly belong. That question is described in V 19 as a "practical question," if we accept the reading of the original, or as a "scientific question," according to Ibn Tibbon's translation. Both readings are acceptable considering that that description is given, not by Halevi's spokesman, but by a much less competent man who may, or may not, have understood the character of the question concerned: actually it is a practical question, as is intimated in V 2 (296, 1-2). Cf. also the type of questions whose treatment is recommended in V 21.—The view that the question of Divine justice, and the implications of that question do not belong to "theology" (or metaphysics) and hence not to theoretical knowledge altogether, is shared by Maimonides as is shown by the place where he discusses them in both the *Mishneh Torah* and the *Guide:* he discusses them in both works after having completed his treatment of physics and metaphysics. (Cf. H. Teshuba, the heading and V ff., with H. Yesode ha-torah II 11 and IV 13; and *Guide,* III 8-24 with III 7 end and II 30.)

[15] As regards the relation of kalâm and dialectics, cf. V 1 and V 15-16 beg.

[16] Cf. Plato, *Republic,* 394 b9-c3.

the statements made by them according to their peculiar moral
and intellectual qualities and their peculiar intentions in a
peculiar conversational situation and possibly with a view to that
situation, into "absolute" statements of the author, i.e., statements which express the author's views directly.[17]

In the case of an author of Halevi's rank, it is safe to assume
that the connection between the content of his work and its
form is as necessary as such a connection can possibly be: he
must have chosen[18] the peculiar form of the *Kuzari* because he
considered it the ideal setting for a defence of Judaism. To
defend Judaism before a Jewish audience—even before an audience of "perplexed" Jews as in Maimonides' *Guide*—is almost
as easy as it is to praise Athenians before an Athenian audience:[19]
hence Judaism has to be defended before a Gentile. Besides, a
Gentile who is a Christian or a Muslim, recognizes the Divine

[17] One cannot simply identify Halevi's views with the statements of his spokesman, the Jewish scholar. Halevi intimates near the beginning of I 1 (3, 13)
that not all arguments of the scholar convinced him. Or should he have omitted
from his account those arguments of the scholar with which he could not
identify himself? He certainly does not say that he did so. On the contrary, he
claims that he has put down in writing the disputation as it had taken place
(3, 14). But, it will be argued, that disputation evidently never took place in
the form described by Halevi. Very well; but exactly if this is the case, Halevi
asserts the truth of something which he knew not to be true, and hence we have
to take his statements (or the statements of the man with whom he identifies
himself) with a grain of salt; as matters stand, this means that we have to distinguish between the "relative" and the "absolute" statements. Not without
good reason does he conclude the prooemium with the admonition "And those
who understand will comprehend." This remark cannot possibly refer to the fact
that the conversations are fictitious; for this is evident even to those who do not
understand. Moscato *ad loc.* prefers the MS. readings נפשו and ירעתו to the other
MS. readings, at present generally adopted, נפשי and ירעתי (3, 13): according to
the former readings, Halevi merely says that some of the arguments of the
scholar convinced the king, thus leaving it entirely open whether and how far
any of these arguments convinced the author.—The distinction between "relative"
and "absolute" statements is akin to the distinction between arguments *ad
hominem* and demonstrative arguments as used by H. A. Wolfson, "Hallevi and
Maimonides on design, chance and necessity," *Proceedings of the American
Academy for Jewish Research*, XI, 1941, 160 f.
[18] We should have to speak of a choice, even if there were only one version
of the story of the conversion of the Khazares, and Halevi had adopted that
version without making any changes. For there is no immediately evident compelling reason why a defence of Judaism should be presented in the form of
an account of how the Kuzari became converted to Judaism.
[19] Plato, *Menexenus*, 236a.

origin of the Jewish religion; hence Judaism has to be defended
before a pagan. Moreover, there are pagans in a social position
similar to that of the Jews and therefore apt to be sympathetic
to things Jewish: hence Judaism, the "despised religion" of a
persecuted nation, has to be defended before a pagan occupy-
ing a most exalted position, before a pagan king. And finally,
we can imagine even a pagan king harboring some sympathy
with Judaism and therefore easy to convince of the truth of
Judaism: hence Judaism has to be defended before a pagan king
who is prejudiced against Judaism. The Kuzari is a pagan king
prejudiced against Judaism.[20] While it is fairly easy to defend
Judaism before a Jewish audience, to defend Judaism before
a pagan king prejudiced against Judaism—*hoc opus, hic labor
est.* Now, the Jewish scholar conversing with the Kuzari suc-
ceeds not merely in defending Judaism, but in converting the
king, and indirectly the king's nation, to Judaism. That conversion is the most striking testimony to the strength of the
argument of the scholar. Yet such a conversion can easily be
invented by any poet, and an invented conversion which takes
place in the empty spaces of one's wishes, is much less convincing than an actual conversion which did take place in
the resisting world. Hence, Halevi chooses an actual conversion
of a pagan king, and an actual conversation leading to that
conversion, between the king and a Jewish scholar: he points
out that the story of the conversion is taken from the histories,
and as regards the arguments advanced by the scholar, he asserts
that he had heard them.[21] If one adds to the points just mentioned the fact that Halevi had to show the superiority of Judaism to Islam in particular, one sees that he had to choose such
an actual conversion of a pagan king to Judaism as had taken
place after the rise of Islam, and thus, that his choice of the story
of the Kuzari was absolutely rational and hence perfect.

The necessity of the connection between content and form
of the work will become still more apparent if one considers
what seems to be at first sight the strongest objection to the thesis
that the setting of the *Kuzari* is the ideal setting for a defence

[20] I 4 (8, 21 f.) and 12. Cf. also I 27 f.
[21] I 1 (3, 4-6 and 15 ff.) and II 1 beg.

of Judaism. The ideal defence of Judaism would be one which would convince the most exacting adversary if he judged fairly. Is the Kuzari an exacting adversary? However prejudiced against Judaism he may be, he meets two conditions which make him, to exaggerate for purposes of clarification, an easy prey to the superior knowledge, and the superior conversational skill, of the Jewish scholar. Two important things are settled with him before he meets the scholar. First he knows that philosophy (to say nothing of his pagan religion) is insufficient to satisfy his needs, and that a revealed religion (i.e., information given by God immediately to human beings concerning the kind of action which is pleasing to Him) is desirable, if open to grave doubts.[22] Now, for all practical purposes, there were only three religions which could claim to be the true and final revealed religion: Christianity, Islam and Judaism. The second thing settled with the king prior to his meeting the scholar, is that the claims of Christianity and Islam are unfounded. That is to say: he has almost no choice apart from embracing Judaism; he is a potential Jew before he ever met a Jew, or at least before he ever talked to a competent Jew.

To make a first step toward understanding this feature of the work, we have to mention the fact that the adversary par excellence of Judaism from Halevi's point of view is, not Christianity and Islam, but philosophy.[23] Hence one is entitled to consider the *Kuzari* primarily as a defence of Judaism against philosophy, and to raise the question as to whether the setting of the disputations is fit for such a defence. Philosophy is discussed twice: once between the king and a philosopher,[24] and once between the king and the Jew. There is no discussion of philosophy, and indeed no discussion whatsoever, between the Jew and the phi-

---

[22] I 2, 4 beg., and 10.

[23] Five positions more or less inimical to (orthodox) Judaism are coherently discussed in the *Kuzari*: philosophy, Christianity, Islam, Karaism and kalâm; philosophy is the only one of these positions which is coherently discussed twice (in I 1-3 and V 2-14). Besides, the occasional polemical references to philosophy are more numerous, and much more significant, than the corresponding references to any other of the positions mentioned. Above all, only the philosopher denies the Mosaic revelation whereas the Christian and the Muslim admit it.

[24] As regards the meaning of dialogues between kings and philosophers, cf. Plato's *Second Letter*, 310e4-311b7.

losopher:[25] the king meets the Jew long after the philosopher
has left. The philosopher is thoroughly familiar with philosophy, and so is the scholar. But the king cannot be said to have
a more than superficial knowledge of philosophy.[26] This means:
there is no discussion of philosophy between intellectual
equals.[27] The whole discussion takes place on a level decidedly
lower than that of a genuine philosophic discussion. For a defence of Judaism against philosophy, the setting of the *Kusari*
appears therefore to be singularly unsatisfactory. This remark is
all the more justified, since the defect mentioned could easily
have been avoided. Nothing indeed would have been easier for
the poet Halevi than to arrange a disputation between the
scholar and the philosopher before the king and his court, or
preferably before the king alone, a disputation which would
culminate in the conversion, not merely of the king, but above
all of the philosopher himself: a greater triumph for the scholar,
for the author, for Judaism, for religion could not be imag-
ined.[28] The poet refused to take this easy way. What was his
reason?

  Halevi knew too well that a genuine philosopher can never

[25] The subterraneous relation between the Jewish scholar and the philosopher
is hinted at by the author's remark that both were asked by the king about
their "belief," whereas both the Christian and the Muslim are said to have
been asked by the king about their "knowledge and action"; see I 1 (2, 18), 4
(8, 23), 5 (12, 5 f.), and 10. The scholar himself says that the king had asked him
about his "faith": I 25 (18, 12).

[26] Cf. I 72 ff. and IV 25 end.

[27] In this most important respect the form of the *Kuzari* agrees with that of
the Platonic dialogues: all Platonic dialogues consist of conversations between
a superior man, usually Socrates, and one or more inferior men. In some
Platonic dialogues, two genuine and mature philosophers are present, but they
have no discussion with each other: Socrates silently observes how Timaeus
explains the universe, or how the stranger from Elea trains Theaetetus or the
younger Socrates. In the *Parmenides*, we are confronted with the paradoxical
situation that Socrates, being still very young, is in the position of the inferior
as compared with Parmenides and Zeno.—The fact that the *Kuzari* is written
"in the form of a Platonic dialogue," has been noted by S. W. Baron, "Yehudah
Halevi," *Jewish Social Studies*, 1941, 257.

[28] In both the letter of Joseph, the king of the Khazares, to Hasdai ibn
Shaprut, and in the Genizah document published by Schechter (*Jewish Quarterly
Review*, N. S., III, 1912-3, 204 ff.), disputations between the various scholars
before the king are mentioned. In neither document is there any mention of a
philosopher. The addition of a philosopher and the omission of a disputation
before the king are the most striking differences between Halevi's version of
the story and these two other versions.

become a genuine convert to Judaism or to any other revealed religion. For, according to him, a genuine philosopher is a man such as Socrates who possesses "human wisdom" and is invincibly ignorant of "Divine wisdom."[29] It is the impossibility of converting a philosopher to Judaism which he demonstrates *ad oculos* by omitting a disputation between the scholar and the philosopher. Such a disputation, we may say to begin with, is impossible: *contra negantem principia non est disputandum.* The philosopher denies as such the premises on which any demonstration of the truth of any revealed religion is based. That denial may be said to proceed from the fact that he, being a philosopher, is untouched by, or has never tasted, that "Divine thing" or "Divine command" *(amr ilâhî)* which is known from actual experience both to the actual believer, the Jewish scholar, and the potential believer, the king. For in contrast with the philosopher, the king was from the outset, by nature, a pious man: he had been observing the pagan religion of his country with great eagerness and all his heart; he had been a priest as well as a king. Then something happened to him which offers a striking similarity, and at the same time a striking contrast, to what happened to the philosopher Socrates. Socrates is said to have been set in motion by a single oracle which the priestess of the Delphian god had given to an inquiring friend of his;

[29] Halevi mostly identifies "philosopher" with "Aristotelian" or even Aristotle himself, since Aristotle is the philosopher par excellence. But, as is shown by the fact that the Aristotelian school is only one among a number of philosophic schools—cf. I 13, IV 25 end and V 14 (328, 24-26)—, "philosophy" designates primarily, not a set of dogmas, and in particular the dogmas of the Aristotelians, but a method, or an attitude. That attitude is described in IV 18 and III 1 (140, 11-16). Its classic representative is Socrates. In order to establish the primitive and precise meaning which "philosophy" has in Halevi's usage, one has to start from IV 13, that fairly short paragraph in which "the adherents of the law" and "the adherents of philosophy" are contrasted with each other in the clearest manner, and which has the unique feature that each of these two terms which do not occur too often in the *Kuzari*, occurs in it three times. (To be exact, מתפלסף occurs three times, מתפלספה two times and תפלספה once.) The center of that paragraph is a saying of Socrates which deals precisely with the problematic relation between philosophy and law (viz., Divine law), or between human wisdom and Divine wisdom. That saying, going back to Plato's *Apology of Socrates* (20d6-e2), is quoted again, with some modifications, in V 14 (328, 13-18). The possibility, alluded to in IV 3 (242, 26), of "adherents of philosophy who belong to the adherents of the religions" is, to begin with, unintelligible rather than that truism which it is supposed to be today.

the king was awakened out of his traditionalism[30] by a number of dreams in which an angel, apparently answering a prayer of his, addressed him directly. Socrates discovered the secret of the oracle by examining the representatives of various types of knowledge; the king discovered the secret of his dreams by examining the representatives of various beliefs, and, more directly, by being tutored by the Jewish scholar. Socrates' attempt to check the truth of the oracle led him to the philosophic life; the king's attempt to obey the angel who had spoken to him in his dreams, made him at once immune to philosophy and ultimately led him into the fold of Judaism.[31] By indicating the facts mentioned which adumbrate the character of the king, Halevi makes clear the natural limits of his explicit arguments: these arguments are convincing, and are meant to be convincing, to such naturally pious people only as have had some foretaste of Divine revelation by having experienced a revelation by an angel or at least a rudimentary revelation of one kind or another.[32]

This explanation is, however, not fully satisfactory. For it is not true that a discussion between the believer and the philosopher is impossible for the reason mentioned. If that reason were valid, the philosopher as such would have to acknowledge his utter incompetence with regard to that vast realm of specific experiences which is the domain of faith. Philosophy being a kind of knowledge accessible to man as man, the believer who

---

[30] Cf. I 5 (12, 4 f.).

[31] I 1 (3, 6-12 and 15-17), 2, 98; II 1 beg. Cf. *Apology* 21b3-4 and c1-2.— Compare the transition from "as if an angel were speaking to him" (3, 7) to "the angel came to him at night and said" (3, 10 f.) with the transition from the Pythia to the god in the *Apology* (21a6 and b3); and the transition from "this caused him to inquire" (3, 11 f.) to "he commanded him in the dream to seek" (3, 16 f.) with the transition from Socrates' own decision to examine the oracle to the view that this examination was an act of obedience to the god in the *Apology* (21c1 and 23c1; cf. 37e6). What I am pointing out, are parallels, not necessarily borrowings. As regards the Arabic translation of the *Apology*, see M. Steinschneider, *Die arabischen Uebersetzungen aus dem Griechischen*, Leipzig 1897, 22.—The "as if" (3, 7) is, of course, absent from the parallel, or the model, in the letter of the king Joseph to Hasdai ibn Shaprut. Cf. I 87 (38, 27 ff.).

[32] Cf. note 47 below.—The limitation of the bearing of Halevi's argument may be compared to the limitation, suggested by Aristotle, of the ethical teaching: the ethical teaching, as distinguished from the theoretical teaching, is addressed, not to all intelligent people, but to decent people only, and only the latter can truly accept it. Cf. *Eth. Nic.* 1095b4-6 and 1140b13-18.

has exerted his natural faculties in the proper way, would know everything the philosopher knows, and he would know more; hence the philosopher who admits his incompetence concerning the specific experiences of the believer, would acknowledge, considering the infinite importance of any genuine revelation, that his position in regard to the intelligent believer is, possibly, not merely unambiguously worse, but infinitely worse than that of a blind man as compared with that of a man who sees. A merely defensive attitude on the part of the philosopher is impossible: his alleged ignorance is actually doubt or distrust.[33] As a matter of fact, the philosophers whom Halevi knew, went so far as to deny the very possibility of the specific experiences of the believers as interpreted by the latter, or, more precisely, the very possibility of Divine revelation in the precise sense of the term.[34] That denial was presented by them in the form of what claimed to be a demonstrative refutation. The defender of religion had to refute the refutation by laying bare its fallacious character. On the level of the refutation and of the refutation of the refutation, i.e., on the level of "human wisdom," the disputation between believer and philosopher is not only possible, but without any question the most important fact of the whole past.[35] Halevi draws our attention most forcefully to the possibility of such a disputation by inserting on an occasion which, we can be sure, was the most appropriate one, into the actual dialogue between the king and the scholar what almost amounts to a fictitious dialogue between the scholar

[33] The saying of Socrates which is quoted twice in the *Kuzari* (cf. note 29 above), viz., that he does not grasp the Divine Wisdom of the people to whom he is talking, is evidently a polite expression of his rejection of that wisdom. Those who do not think that Halevi noticed Socrates' irony, are requested to disregard this paragraph which is based on the assumption, in itself as indemonstrable as theirs, that he did notice it. From the context of the first of the two quotations it appears that the attitude of the philosophers is not altered if the people of Socrates' time are replaced by the adherents of revealed religion.

[34] I 1 (2, 21 ff.), 6, 8, 87, II 54 (114, 5-9), IV 3 (228, 18-23). A comparison of IV 3 *vers.fin.* (244, 22 ff.) with III 17 (168, 2-3) among other passages shows that the philosopher as such is a "sindik," an "apikores."

[35] Cf. 6-8.—One cannot recall too often this remark of Goethe (in the *Noten und Abhandlungen zum besseren Verständnis der West-östlichen Divans*): "Das eigentliche, einzige und tiefste Thema der Welt- und Menschengeschichte, dem alle übrigen untergeordnet sind, bleibt der Konflikt des Unglaubens und Glaubens."

and the philosopher: the scholar refutes an objection of the philosophers by addressing the philosopher directly.[36] The philosopher addressed is naturally not present and hence in no position to answer. It is therefore exceedingly hard to tell whether in an actual dialogue between scholar and philosopher, the philosopher would have been reduced to silence by a refutation which evidently satisfies the king, but perhaps not every reader.[37] What has been observed with regard to this particular refutation, calls for a generalization. Since no philosopher is present in the *Kuzari* to examine the argument of the scholar, we cannot be certain whether and how far a philosopher would have been impressed by that argument. If Halevi were a philosopher, the absence of an actual conversation between scholar and philosopher could be accounted for precisely on the ground of the doubt just expressed. The purpose of that feature of the work would be to compel the reader to think constantly of the absent philosopher, i.e., to find out, by independent reflection, what the absent philosopher might have to say. This disturbing and invigorating thought would prevent the reader from falling asleep, from relaxing in his critical attention for a single moment. But Halevi is so much opposed to philosophy, he is so distrustful of the spirit of independent reflection, that we are obliged not to lay too strong an emphasis on this line of approach.

To return to safer ground, we start from the well-known fact that Halevi, in spite of his determined opposition to philosophy as such, underwent the influence of philosophy to no inconsiderable degree. What does influence mean? In the case of a superficial man, it means that he accepts this or that bit of the influencing teaching, that he cedes to the influencing force on the points where it appears to him, on the basis of his previous notions, to be strong, and that he resists it on the points where it appears to him, on the basis of his previous notions, to be weak. A confused or dogmatic mind, in other words, will not be induced by the influencing force to take a critical distance from his previous notions, to look at things, not from his habit-

[36] II 6. The "O philosopher" of the scholar recalls the almost identical expression with which the king took leave of the real philosopher in I 4 (8, 19). (No allocution of the kind occurs in the king's conversations with the Christian and the Muslim.) In a sense, the philosopher is always present in the *Kuzari*.

[37] See the judicious remarks of Wolfson, *op. cit.*, 116 and 124 f.

ual point of view, but from the point of view of the center, clearly grasped, of the influencing teaching, and hence he will be incapable of a serious, a radical and relentless, discussion of that teaching. In the case of a man such as Halevi, however, the influence of philosophy on him consists in a conversion to philosophy: for some time, we prefer to think for a very short time, he was a philosopher.[38] After that moment, a spiritual hell, he returned to the Jewish fold. But after what he had gone through, he could not help interpreting Judaism in a manner in which only a man who had once been a philosopher, could interpret it. For in that moment he had experienced the enormous temptation, the enormous danger of philosophy.[39] The manner in which he defends Judaism against philosophy, testifies to this experience. For if he had presented a disputation between the Jewish scholar and the philosopher, i.e., a discussion of the crucial issue between truly competent people, he would have been compelled to state the case for philosophy with utmost clarity and vigor, and thus to present an extremely able and ruthless attack on revealed religion by the philosopher. There can be no doubt, to repeat, that the arguments of the philosopher could have been answered by the scholar; but it is hard to tell whether one or the other of the readers would not have been more impressed by the argument of the philosopher than by the rejoinder of the scholar. The *Kuzari* would thus have become an instrument of seduction, or at least of confusion. Of the kalâm, the defence of religion by means of argument, the scholar who presents such a defence himself, says with so many words that it may become dangerous because it leads to, or implies the raising of, doubts.[40] But what is true of the kalâm, is of course infinitely truer of philosophy. Nothing is more revealing than the way in which Halevi demonstrates *ad oculos* the danger of philosophy. The king had been converted to Judaism, i.e., his resistance, based on the influence of philosophy, had been overcome; he had been given a detailed instruction

---

[38] Cf. Baron, *op. cit.*, 259 n. 33.

[39] The wisdom of the Greeks has either no fruit at all or else a pernicious fruit, viz., the doctrine of the eternity of the world—therefore it is extremely dangerous—; but it has blossoms (and evidently beautiful ones)—therefore it is extremely tempting. Cf. Halevi's *Divan*, ed. Brody, II, p. 166.—As regards the lacking "fruit" of philosophy, cf. V 14 (326, 6-8).

[40] V 16. Cf. Elia del Medigo, *Beḥinat ha-dat*, ed. by S. Reggio, 8.

in the Jewish faith; the errors of the philosophers had been pointed out to him on every suitable occasion; he had even begun to consider himself a normal Jew. Then, almost at the end of their intercourse, a question of his induces the scholar to give him a summary and very conventional sketch of the philosophic teaching. The consequence of this disclosure is contrary to all reasonable expectation: in spite of all that men and angels had done to protect him, the king is deeply impressed by that unimpressive sketch of philosophy, so much so, that the scholar has to repeat his refutation of philosophy all over again.[41] Only by elaborating the philosophic argument which Halevi, or rather his characters merely sketch, can one disinter his real and inexplicit objection to, and refutation of, that argument.[42]

The explanation suggested might seem to impute to Halevi a degree of timidity which does not become a great man. But the line of demarcation between timidity and responsibility is drawn differently in different ages. As most people today would readily admit, we have to judge an author according to the standards which prevailed in his age. In Halevi's age, the right, if not the duty, to suppress teachings, and books, which are detrimental to faith, was generally recognized. The philosophers themselves did not object to it. For the insight into the dangerous nature of philosophy was not a preserve of its orthodox adversaries, such as Halevi. The philosophers themselves had taken over the traditional distinction between exoteric and esoteric teachings, and they held therefore that it was dangerous, and hence forbidden, to communicate the esoteric teaching to the general public.[43] They composed their books in accordance with that view. The difficulties inherent in Halevi's presentation of philosophy[44] may very well reflect difficulties inherent in the presentation of philosophy by the philosophers them-

[41] V 13-14 beg.
[42] Cf. note 17 above.
[43] Cf. Averroes, *Philosophie und Theologie*, ed. by M. J. Müller, Munich 1859, 70 ff.
[44] To my mind, the most telling of these difficulties is the description of the various philosophic sects (those of Pythagoras, Empedocles, Plato, Aristotle, etc.), as sects of mutakallimûn; see V 14 (328, 23; cf. 330, 5). Cf. also V 1 where, at least apparently (cf. Ventura, *loc. cit.*, 11 n. 6: "Il y est incontestablement question des philosophes"), the account of the philosophic teaching is introduced as an account of the kalâm.

selves. Near the beginning of his *Hayy ibn Yukdhân,* Ibn Tufail
gives a remarkable account of the self-contradictions of Fârâbî
concerning the life after death, and of similar self-contradictions
of Ghazâlî. He also mentions the difference between Avicenna's
Aristotelianizing doctrine set forth in the *K.al-shifâ* and his real
doctrine set forth in his *Oriental Philosophy,* and he informs
us about Avicenna's distinction between the exterior and the
interior meaning of both the writings of Aristotle and his own
K.al-shifâ. Finally, he mentions Ghazâlî's enigmatic and elliptic
manner of writing in his exoteric works and the disappearance,
or practical inaccessibility, of his esoteric works.[45] The fact that
informations such as these are not at present considered basic
for the understanding of medieval philosophy, does not constitute a proof of their insignificance.[46]

To conclude: Halevi's defence of Judaism against its adversaries in general, and the philosophers in particular is addressed
to naturally pious people only, if to naturally pious people of
a certain type. A naturally pious man, as the Kuzari undoubt-
edly is, is by no means necessarily a naturally faithful man, i.e.,
a man who is naturally so immune to any false belief that he
does not need arguments in order to adhere to the true belief, to
Judaism: the Kuzari, the immediate and typical addressee of
the defence, offered in the *Kuzari,* of Judaism, is a naturally
pious man in a state of doubt.[47] Halevi refrained from refuting

[45] Ed. by L. Gauthier, 2nd ed., Beyrouth 1936, 13-18. Cf. Averroes, *op. cit.,*
17 f. and 70 ff., and Maimonides, *Treatise on Resurrection,* ed. by Finkel, 13.
Cf. also *Kuzari* V 14 (328, 24-26) on the two types of Aristotelians.—It is hardly
necessary to state explicitly that even the esoteric books are not esoteric strictly
speaking, but merely more esoteric than the exoteric books; consider Maimonides,
Guide, I Introd. (4a).

[46] The phenomenon in question is at present discussed under the title
"mysticism." But esotericism and mysticism are far from being identical. That
Fârâbî in particular has nothing in common with mysticism, is stated most
clearly by Paul Kraus, "Plotin chez les Arabes," *Bulletin de l'Institut d'Égypte,*
XXIII, 1940-1, 269 ff.

[47] As regards naturally faithful men, cf. V 2 (294, 15) and 16 (330, 26 ff.). As
regards the connection between natural faith and pure Jewish descent, one has
to consider I 95 and 115 (64, 8-10) and V 23 (356, 19 f.). In V 2 (294, 17) the
scholar admits the possibility that the Kuzari is naturally faithful, and not a
(pious) doubter. This would mean that his conversion has been effected decisively, not by argument, but by "slight intimations" and by "sayings" of the
pious" which kindled the spark in his heart. Since the scholar leaves it open
whether this is the case, we are entitled to stick, in the present article, to the
general impression derived from the *Kuzari,* that the king was converted by
argument, and hence that he is not naturally faithful.

the argument of the philosophers on its natural level out of a
sense of responsibility.[48] This explains also, as can easily be
inferred, why he addresses his defence of Judaism primarily to
a Gentile who, as such, is a doubter as regards Judaism. In
Halevi's age there unquestionably were doubting Jews,[49] those
"perplexed" men to whom Maimonides dedicated his *Guide*.
But is not a doubting Jew an anomaly? What is inscrutable
in everyday life, is made visible by the poet: the doubting Jew
to whom he addresses four fifths of his defence of Judaism, is
evidently not a descendant from the witnesses of the Sinaitic
revelation.

II. THE PHILOSOPHER AND HIS LAW OF REASON

THE Law of Reason is mentioned first by the philosopher, the
first interlocutor of the king. For the king, a pagan, approaches
first a spiritual descendant of the pagan Aristotle.[50] The philosopher reveals himself in two ways: by what he says and by the
manner in which he says it. By the content of his speech, he may
reveal himself as an adherent of one particular philosophic sect
among many, of one particular brand of Aristotelianism. But
philosophy is not identical with Aristotelianism. To recognize
the philosopher in the Aristotelian, one has to listen first to the
manner in which he speaks.

Whereas the Christian and the Jew open their expositions
with a "credo," the philosopher opens each of his two speeches
with a "non est." The philosopher's first word (לים) expresses a
denial: philosophy comes first into sight as a denial of something,
or, to make use of Hegel's interpretation of the *signum repro-
bationis* which an orthodox adversary had discovered on Spinoza's forehead, as a reprobation of something. The philosopher
does not start, as the Christian and the Jew do with an "I," nor,

---

[48] On the influence of this motive on the literary character of Maimonides'
Guide, cf. Isaak Heinemann, "Abravanels Lehre vom Niedergang der Mensch-
heit," *Monatschrift für Geschichte und Wissenschaft des Judentums*, LXXXII,
1938, 393.

[49] Halevi apparently denies this fact in IV 23 (266, 10-13); but, apart from
other considerations, the statement in question is supposed to have been made,
not in 1140, but in 740, i.e., prior to the emergence of philosophy in the Arabic-
speaking world; cf. I 1 (3, 5 f.) and 47.—Cf. also Baron, *op. cit.*, 252 f.

[50] Cf. I 63 and IV 3 (242, 23-26) with I 10 and V 20 (348, 25 ff. and 350, 2 ff.).

as the Muslim does with a "We."[51] In fact, apart from an exception to be mentioned immediately, he never speaks in the first person: he consistently speaks of "the philosophers," as if he did not belong to them. If the author and the king did not tell us that he is a philosopher, we could not be sure that he is one. He presents himself as an interpreter of, or as a messenger from, the philosophers rather than as a philosopher. The only exception to the rule mentioned are the three cases in which he uses the expression, never used by the Christian and the Muslim, "I mean to say";[52] he seems to be in the habit of expressing himself in a way which requires explanation; in three cases, he uses religious terms in a sense very different from their ordinary, religious meaning.

The angel had answered the king in his dream that while God liked his "intention," He disliked his "action." The philosopher answers the king who apparently had asked him about the kind of actions which God likes, that God has no likes or dislikes, no wish or will of any kind, and that God has no knowledge of changeable things, such as individual human beings and their actions and intentions.[53] The implication of the philosopher's answer is that the information which the king had received in his dream, is not true. He alludes to this implication by making it clear that prophecies, dreams and visions are not of the essence of the highest perfection of man.[54] There seems to be some connection between the form of the message which the king had received, and its content: between revelation and the emphasis on "action," and, on the other hand, between the philosopher's denial of revelation proper and his implied denial of the relevance of "action." By "action," both the angel and the king evidently understood ceremonial action: it was the king's manner of worship which was displeasing to God.[55] But "action" has more than one meaning: it may designate the most important and most venerable action, viz., ceremonial actions, but it may also designate of course any action and in particular

[51] I 1 (2, 18), 3, 4 (8, 23) and 11. Cf. I 5 (12, 6).
[52] אעני: I 1 (4, 23; 6, 24 and 25). Cf. *ib.* (4, 3 f. and 6, 9 f.). Cf. IV 13 (252, 28 ff.).
[53] I 1 (3, 1-21) and 2 (8, 1-2).
[54] I 1 end. Cf. I 4 (8, 14-18) and 87 (38, 27).
[55] See the context of במעשים ההם in I 1 (3, 10). Cf. Maimonides, *Guide*, III 38, 52 (130b) and 54 (134b).

moral action. The philosopher denies the relevance, not only of ceremonial actions, but of all actions; more precisely, he asserts the superiority of contemplation as such to action as such: from the philosopher's point of view, goodness of character and goodness of action is essentially not more than a means toward, or a by-product of, the life of contemplation.[56] The king who believes in revelation—to begin with, in revelation by angels, and later on in Divine revelation—, believes for the same reason in the superiority of action to contemplation; and the philosopher who denies revelation, believes for the same reason in the superiority of contemplation to action. It is only on the basis of the assumption of the superiority of practical life to contemplative life that the necessity of revelation in general, and hence the truth of a given revelation in particular can be demonstrated;[57] and this assumption is taken for granted by the king, who, as king, is the natural representative of the practical or political life.

From his theological assumptions, the philosopher is naturally led to the practical conclusion that a man who has become a philosopher, would choose one of these three alternatives: 1) to be indifferent as to manner of his worship and to his belonging to this or that religious, ethnic or political group; 2) to invent for himself a religion for the purpose of regulating his actions of worship as well as of his moral guidance and the guidance of his household and his city; 3) to take as his religion the rational *nomoi* composed by the philosophers and to make purity of the soul his purpose and aim. If one considers the context, it becomes apparent that the philosopher gives the king the conditional advice—conditional, that is, on the king's becoming a philosopher—to decide the religious question on grounds of expediency alone: the king may disregard his dream altogether and continue in his ancestral religion, or he may choose one of

[56] I 1 (6, 10-17). Cf. Fârâbî, *Al-madîna al-fâḍila*, ed. by Dieterici, 46, 16-19. As regards Maimonides, cf. the H. De'ot as a whole with *Guide* III 27 and I 2. Cf. also Julius Guttmann, "Zur Kritik der Offenbarungsreligion in der islamischen und jüdischen Philosophie," *Monatsschrift für Geschichte und Wissenschaft des Judentums*, LXXVIII, 1934, 459, and H. A. Wolfson, "Halevi and Maimonides on prophecy," *Jewish Quarterly Review, N. S.*, XXXII, 1942, 352.

[57] Cf. I 98, II 46 and III 23 (176, 18-20), and the scholar's attack on the contemplative religion in I 13. Cf. notes 14 and 32 above.

the other religions already in existence (Christianity or Islam e.g.), or he may invent a new religion, or he may adopt as his religion the rational *nomoi* of the philosophers.[58] This advice calls for some attention since it contains what may be said to be the only authentic declaration, occurring in the *Kuzari,* of the intentions of the philosophers; for that declaration is made by the philosopher in person, and not by the Jewish scholar who is an adversary of philosophy, nor by the king, who has only a superficial knowledge of philosophy. The religious in-difference of the philosopher knows no limits: he does not op-pose to the "errors" of the positive religions the religion of reason; he does not demand that a philosopher who as such no longer believes in the religion of his fathers, should reveal his religious indifference, proceeding from unbelief, by openly transgressing the laws of that religion; he does not by any means set up the behavior of Elisha ben Abuya,[59] or of Spinoza, as the model of philosophic behavior; he considers it perfectly legiti-mate that a philosopher who as such denies Divine revelation, adheres to Islam for example, i.e., complies in deed and speech with the requirements of that religion and therefore, if an emergency arises, defends that faith which he cannot but call the true faith, not only with the sword, but with arguments, viz., dialectical arguments, as well.[60] The philosopher certainly does not say, or imply, that a genuine philosopher would necessarily openly reject any other religion or law in favor of the rational *nomoi* composed by the philosophers or of "the religion of the philosophers," although he does admit that under certain cir-cumstances he might.

What have we to understand by these rational *nomoi?* They cannot be identical with the *lex naturalis* which binds every man and which is the sum of dictates of right reason concerning ob-jects of action. For how could one say of such dictates that they can be exchanged with any other order of life, the religion of the Khazares, e.g.? Nor can they be identical with the "rational

[58] I 1 (6, 17-22). Cf. II 49 and IV 13 (252, 24-26).

[59] Cf. III 65 (216, 2 f.) with the passages indicated in the preceding note.

[60] This possibility has to be considered for the interpretation of the remark on "the students of philosophy among the adherents of the religions" in IV 3 (242, 23-26). Cf. Bahya ibn Pakuda, *Al-hidāya ilā farā'iḍ al-ḳulūb,* III 4, ed. by Yahuda, p. 146.—Cf. notes 44 and 11 above.

116   *Persecution and the Art of Writing*

laws," with those elementary rules of social conduct which have
to be observed equally by all communities, by the most noble
community as well as by a gang of robbers; for the rational
nomoi which the philosopher has in mind, are not merely the
framework of a code, but a complete code: they are identical
with "the religion of the philosophers."[61] It is evident that the
philosopher does not consider the rational *nomoi*, or the religion of the philosophers, in any way obligatory. This does not
mean that he considers them absolutely arbitrary: the rational
nomoi have not been "invented" to satisfy a passing need of a
particular man or group, but, being emphatically "rational,"
they have been set up by the philosophers with a view to the
unchanging needs of man as man; they are codes fixing the
political or other conditions most favorable to the highest perfection of man: Plato's *Laws* were known in Halevi's period as
Plato's rational *nomoi*.[62] Now, if the highest perfection of man
is indeed philosophy, and a life devoted to philosophy is essentially asocial, the rational *nomoi* would be the *regimen solitarii*:
the philosopher certainly does not mention any social relations
when speaking of the rational *nomoi*, whereas he does mention
such relations when speaking of the religion which the king
might invent.[63] The ambiguity of the term "rational *nomoi*,"
viz., that it might designate an essentially political code, such as
that suggested in Plato's *Laws*, which contains a political theology, and an essentially apolitical rule of conduct destined for
the guidance of the philosopher alone, would at any rate be
easily understandable on the basis of Plato's own teaching: just
as the philosopher's city is not necessarily an earthly city, a political community, the philosopher's law is not necessarily a

61 Cf. I 3 with I 1 (6, 21).
62 Cf. Moritz Steinschneider, *Die arabischen Uebersetzungen aus dem Griechischen*, Leipzig 1897, 19, and *Die hebräischen Uebersetzungen des Mittelalters*,
Berlin 1893, 848 f., as well as Alexander Marx, "Texts by and about Maimonides,"
Jewish Quarterly Review, N. S., XXV, 1934/5, 424.—Consider Fârâbî's account
of Plato's *Laws* in his treatise on Plato's philosophy (the Hebrew translation in
Falkera's *Reshit Hokmah*, ed. by David, 77).
63 Cf. I 1 (6, 22) with III 1 (140, 11-16) and IV 18. Cf. Aristotle, *Eth. Nic.*,
1177a27-34 (and *Politics* 1267a10-12), and the remarks of medieval writers which
are quoted by I. Efros, "Some textual notes on Judah Halevi's Kusari," *Proceedings of the American Academy for Jewish Research*, 1930/1, 5. Cf. note 72
below.

political law.[64] From the philosopher's point of view, the way of
life of the philosopher who is a member of the most excellent
political community, or the way of life of the philosopher who
leads an absolutely private life, is without any question preferable to any other religion; but their being preferable does not
make these ways of life indispensable and hence obligatory:
Socrates led the philosophic life although he was an active member of a political community which he considered very imperfect.[65] Or, to state this fact in the language of a medieval philosopher, one can live in solitude both by retiring from the
world completely and by partaking of the political community,
of the city, be that city excellent or defective.[66] It is for this
reason that the philosopher in the *Kuzari* declares it to be fairly
irrelevant whether the philosopher adopts the rational *nomoi*
composed by the philosophers or any other religion.

The philosopher takes leave of the king, and of the readers,
with his second speech which consists of one short sentence
only. That sentence is to the effect that "the religion of the
philosophers" does not approve of, or command, the killing of
the adherents of other religions as such.[67] No other conclusion
could be drawn from the premise that the religion of the philosophers is not obligatory for the very philosophers, let alone
for other human beings; this being the case, it would be most
unjust to impose it by force on people who do not freely choose
it. The quiet and clear assertion with which the philosopher
leaves the stage, is not without effect on the later happenings
in the *Kuzari*, as appears from the passages in the conversations

[64] Cf. *Republic* IX *in fine* with *Laws* 739b8 and d3.
[65] Cf. the discussion of the two ways of life—the apolitical and the political—
which Socrates successively adopted in Muhammad b. Zakariyya al-Rāzī's
K.al-sīrat al-falsafiyya, ed. by Paul Kraus, *Orientalia*, N. S., IV, 1935, 309 f.
[66] See Narboni's remarks introducing his excerpts from Ibn Baǧǧa's *k. tadbir
al-mutawaḥḥid*, ed. by Herzog, 7 f.
[67] I 3. Ibn Tibbon's translation הריגת אדם for קתל ואחר מן האולאי is inaccceptable.
האולאי refers back to the Christians and Muslims and their religious wars which
had been mentioned by the king in the preceding speech. The philosopher does
not say that the religion of the philosophers objects to the killing of any human
beings. The killing of bestial men, of men on the lowest level of humanity—cf.
I 1 (4, 14 f.)—was considered legitimate by the philosophers; see Fârâbî,
k.al-siyâsât al-madaniyya, Hyderabad 1346, 57 f. The view expressed by Ibn
Tibbon's translation is in accordance with Plato's *Phaedo* 66 c5-d3; cf. also Râzî's
account of the attitude of the young Socrates in the *k.al-sîrat al-falsafiyya*.

between the king and the Jewish scholar where war and killing and enemies are mentioned.

III. THE LAW OF REASON AS A THEOLOGICO-POLITICAL CODE

THE Law of Reason which is not mentioned at all in the conversations of the king with the Christian and the Muslim, occurs more than once in his conversations with the Jewish scholar.[68] At first glance, the scholar's attitude toward the Law of Reason seems to be self-contradictory: in one passage he opposes the rational *nomoi*, while in the other passages where he mentions them, he approves of them.[69] One does not solve this difficulty by saying that the rational *nomoi* of which he approves are not identical with the rational *nomoi* which he rejects; for this does not explain why he uses one and the same term for two so greatly different things. This ambiguity which could easily have been avoided, is due, as all ambiguities occurring in good books are, not to chance or carelessness, but to deliberate choice, to the author's wish to indicate a grave question. It is therefore wise to retain to begin with the ambiguous term and to understand the different attitudes of the scholar to *the* rational *nomoi* in the light of the different conversational situations in which they express themselves. The remark unfavorable to the rational *nomoi* occurs in the first makâla, whereas the remarks which are favorable to them, occur in the subsequent makâlât. Now, the first makâla contains the conversations preceding the king's conversion, whereas the later makâlât contain the conversations

[68] Cf. n. 25 above.

[69] He opposes them in I 81 (cf. the context: 79 f.). He approves of them in II 48, III 7 and V 14 (330, 7). In IV 19 (262, 17) the original merely speaks of *nomoi*, not, as Ibn Tibbon's translation does, of rational *nomoi*. But even if the reading of the translation should have to be preferred, the statements made in the text would not have to be materially altered, as appears from a comparison of the passage with the other passages mentioned: in I 81, he opposes the rational *nomoi*, and in II 48 and III 7, he approves of them, without mentioning the philosophers; IV 19, where *nomoi*, and perhaps even rational *nomoi*, of the philosophers are mentioned with a certain disapproval, is destined to prepare the eventual approval (in V 14) of the rational *nomoi* as observed or established by the philosophers.—Cf. below note 139.—"Rational laws" are alluded to by the king in III 60.

following it. This means: while the scholar adopts a negative attitude toward the rational *nomoi* as long as the king is outside of the Jewish community, as long as he can reasonably be suspected of doubting the truth of Judaism, he adopts a positive attitude toward them after the king's fundamental doubts have been definitely overcome. This is in accordance with another, more visible feature of the *Kuzari*, viz., that the scholar gives his sketch of the philosophic teaching almost at the end of his conversations with the king, i.e., considerable time after the king had begun to consider himself a normal Jew.[70] The scholar shows, not merely by "speech," by his explicit utterances, but by "deed," by his conduct, that only on the basis of faith can allowances be made for reason, or that it is hazardous, if not futile, to make reason the basis of faith.[71]

Immediately after the beginning of his first conversation with the king, the scholar attacks "the religion . . . to which speculation leads" in the name of the right kind of religion or law. That speculative "religion" is certainly, in so far as it regulates both "actions" and "beliefs" the same thing as a "law" or a *"nomos."* He calls that religion "syllogistic" with a view to its basis: it is based on demonstrative, rhetorical and other syllogisms. He calls it "governmental"[72] with a view to its purpose: it is in the service of government, either of political government, or of the government of the reason of the individual over his passions. He implies that that religion is the work of the philosophers. He objects to it because it leads to doubt and anarchy: the philosophers do not agree as to a single action or a single belief. He

[70] Cf. the allusions to this crucial event in IV 26 (282, 19: *"we say"*) on the one hand, and in IV 22 *vers. fin.* ("O Jewish scholar . . . the Jews") on the other: it was the scholar's account of the *Sefer Yeṣirah* that brought about the king's complete and final conviction of the truth of the Jewish faith.—The fact that the scholar gives a sketch of the philosophic teaching in the fifth makâla, requires an explanation, since the king had asked him to give a sketch, not of the philosophic teaching, but of the kalâm; see V 1.

[71] Cf. II 26 end and V 16. Cf. p. 104 ff., and note 47 above.

[72] *Siyâsî,* derived from *siyâsa (government* or *rule). Siyâsa* may mean πολιτεία (the title of Plato's *Republic* was rendered in Arabic by "siyâsa" or "on the siyâsa"; see Fârâbî, *Iḥṣâ al-'ulûm,* ch. 5, and *K.taḥṣîl al-saʿâda,* Hyderabad 1345, 44) as well as the rule of reason over passion (see V 12 [318, 20 f.] and III 5 beg.). Accordingly, *siyâsî* can sometimes be rendered by "political" as in IV 13 (254, 12): צרורה סיאסיה ("political necessity").—The Arabic translation of πολιτεία in the sense of πολίτευμα seems to be *riyâsa.*

traces that deficiency to the fact that the arguments supporting the philosophers' assertions are only partly demonstrative.[73] It is probably with a view to this fact that he refrains from calling that religion, or *nomos*, rational. His statements lead one to suspect that each philosopher, or at least each philosophic sect,[74] elaborated a religion of that kind. He does not say anything as to whether the philosophers themselves were aware of the rhetorical or sophistical character of some of their arguments which accounts for their religion as a whole being untrue or at least unfounded; but it is hard to believe that that character of the syllogisms in question should have escaped the notice of the very men who have taught mankind the difference between syllogisms which are demonstrative and syllogisms which are not. However this may be, the scholar makes it abundantly clear that the philosophers' religion is governmental and that the arguments supporting that religion are partly rhetorical.

When reading the scholar's remarks concerning the speculative religion, one cannot help recalling the remarks, made by the philosopher himself, concerning the rational *nomoi* composed by the philosophers or the religion of the philosophers. The philosopher himself did not consider that religion obligatory, for he considered it legitimate for the philosopher to exchange it with any other religion, and hence to adhere in his speeches as well as in his actions to a religion to which he does not adhere in his thoughts. Now the scholar tells us almost explicitly what the philosopher had hardly intimated—for the adversary of such a view can disclose its implications with greater safety than an adherent of it can—that the religion of the philosophers prescribes, not merely actions, but beliefs as well.[75] Since the religion of the philosophers is, according to the philosopher's own admission, exchangeable with any other religion,

---

[73] I 13. Cf. I 79 (34, 7 f.) and 103 (56,12).

[74] IV 25 end.

[75] The philosopher himself indicates that the philosophers' religious indifference extends itself, not merely to mute actions, but to speeches as well; see I 1 (6, 17-22). He distinguishes however between the invariable "belief" of the philosophers and the variable "religions," one of the latter being the religion of the philosophers. The scholar supplies us with the additional information that "beliefs" are an integral part of the philosophers' religion. Evidently the philosopher and the scholar do not understand by "belief" the same thing. As regards the ambiguity of "belief," cf. Maimonides, *Guide*, I 50.—Cf. also note 25 above.

the beliefs contained in the religion of the philosophers cannot be identical with the philosophic teaching proper which, being true, cannot be exchanged by a philosopher, a lover of the truth, with a teaching which he must consider untrue (e.g., the teaching that God is a lawgiver). It does seem that the religion of the philosophers is identical with, or at least partly consists of, the exoteric teaching of the philosophers.[76] Regarding that exoteric teaching, we learn from the scholar why it is exoteric and for what purpose it is necessary. It is exoteric because of the rhetorical, dialectical or sophistical character of some of the arguments supporting it; it is, at best, a likely tale. And the essential purpose of any exoteric teaching is "government" of the lower by the higher, and hence in particular the guidance of political communities.[77] It is from here that we understand why the scholar speaks of *"the* religion to which speculation leads" although there were apparently as many religions of that kind as there were philosophic sects: differences between philosophers as regards the exoteric teaching do not imply a fundamental difference between them; in fact, the admission of the possibility, and necessity, of an exoteric teaching presupposes agreement concerning the most fundamental point.[78]

Before the scholar actually uses for the first time the term "rational *nomoi,"* he makes us understand in which sense the rational *nomoi* might be called rational. For they are evidently not rational *simpliciter.* When speaking of the rational faculty of man, he states that by the exercise of that faculty "governments" and "governmental *nomoi"* come into being. What he calls in his context "reason," is evidently practical reason only.[79] It is with a view to their provenience from practical reason that

---

[76] Cf. pp. 110-111 above.

[77] Just as "the rational *nomoi"* may designate either political codes or the *regimen solitarii,* the exoteric teaching embodied in such *nomoi* may be in the service either of political government and hence be addressed to citizens as citizens, or of the (highest form of the) rule of reason over the passions, i.e., of the philosophic life, and hence be addressed to potential philosophers. The most outstanding example of the latter type of exoteric teaching is to be found in Plato's *Phaedo.*

[78] Cf. I 13 with 62.

[79] I 35. Cf. V 12 (318, 20 f.). In the former passage in which he speaks in his own name, the scholar "forgets," i.e., tacitly disregards, theoretical reason altogether by tacitly identifying reason with practical reason; in the latter passage, in which he summarizes the philosophers' views, he speaks explicitly of the difference between theoretical and practical reason. (Cf. note 14 above).

the (good) laws of political communities—the (just) positive laws—as well as any other sound rules of conduct can be called rational.[80] Now, the legislator may supplement the purely political laws, the "governmental *nomoi*," with a "governmental religion,"[81] in order to strengthen the people's willingness to obey the purely political laws; that religion would not be rational at all from the point of view of theoretical reason, because its tenets are bound to be based on arguments of doubtful validity; yet it may rightly be called rational from the point of view of practical reason, because its tenets are of evident usefulness.

The scholar's first mention of the Law of Reason occurs considerable time after he had convinced the king of the truth of the most striking presuppositions, or implications, of the Jewish faith, and thus somewhat shaken his initial doubts.[82] In that situation, the scholar contrasts first the right approach to God which is based on "Divine knowledge . . . proceeding from God" with the wrong approach by means of "syllogism" and "thinking" as it is taken by astrologers and makers of talismans; he makes it clear that the wrong approach is the basis of the pre-Mosaic "astrological and physical *nomoi*" whose very variety seems to prove their illegitimacy. It is in this context that he contrasts the *nomos* which is of Divine origin with "the rational *nomoi*" which are of human origin.[83] As far as "*nomos*" and "religion" are used in that context synonymously, one may say that the scholar repeats his initial confrontation of the syllogistic religion with revealed religion. But the repetition is not an identical reproduction: he no longer ascribes the syllogistic religion to philosophers, but to astrologers and other types of superstitious people, and he does not mention its political character. It may be added in passing that in the scholar's initial remark concerning the syllogistic religion, that religion was not called a *nomos* or a law, and its provenience from the philosophers was merely implied. Whatever this may mean, the scholar

[80] Cf. *Eth. Nic.* 1180a21 f.

[81] Cf. I 13 with Maimonides' commentary on Aboda zara IV 7 (ed. Wiener, p. 27) and Falkera, *Sefer ha-mebakkesh*, ed. Amsterdam 1779, 29b.

[82] Cf. I 48, 52 and 58 with the preceding statements of the Kuzari; cf. moreover I 76, 62 and 60.

[83] I 81 and 79 (32, 15-21 and 34, 6-8). Cf. I 80, 97 (46, 24 ff. and 50, 7-10), 98; II 16 (82, 11 f.) and 56 (116, 14-16).

seems to admit two kinds of syllogistic religion or of rational *nomoi:* one being the work of philosophers,[84] and the other being the work of superstitious people. In fact, it is with a view to the latter rather than to the former, that he uses for the first time the term "rational *nomoi.*"[85]

Halevi, or the Jewish scholar, was not the only medieval writer who asserted an affinity between works such as Plato's *Laws* and books regulating, or dealing with, superstitious practices: a book called by some "Plato's *Nomoi*" which deals with witchcraft, alchemy etc., is still extant.[86] From the point of view of Halevi, or of any adherent of any revealed religion, Plato's *Laws* and superstitious *nomoi* would naturally belong to one and the same genus: the genus of *nomoi* of human origin. As far as the rational *nomoi* are the same thing as the syllogistic religion, we have to describe the genus embracing works such as Plato's *Laws* as well as the superstitious *nomoi* more precisely as that of such codes as are of human origin and as consist partly or wholly of rules regulating religious beliefs or actions; and we have to distinguish two species of that genus: one which is chiefly concerned with ceremonial or magical practices (the superstitious *nomoi*), and another which does not place too strong an emphasis on them (the *nomoi* composed by the philosophers).[87] The codes of both kinds are called rational, because they are the work of practical reason. Of the superstitious "books of the astrologers," the scholar mentions one by name, *The Nabataean Agriculture,* to which he seems to ascribe Hindu origin; and of the Hindus he says in that context that they are people who deny Divine revelation (the existence of a "book from God").[88] The affinity of the philosophic *nomoi* and of at

---

[84] At the beginning of I 97 and at the end of I 99, in contexts similar to that of I 81, the philosophers are explicitly referred to.

[85] From II 20 (88, 10-13) which is the most direct parallel to I 81, it appears that the *nomoi* which the scholar contrasts with the true *nomos*, are those of the Persians, Hindus and Greeks. Cf. also V 2 beg.

[86] Cf. M. Steinschneider, "Zur pseudepigraphischen Literatur des Mittelalters," *Wissenschaftliche Blätter,* Berlin 1862, 51 ff., and *Die arabischen Uebersetzungen aus dem Griechischen,* 19.

[87] See O. Apelt's index to his German translation of Plato's *Laws* s. vv. *Delphi, Feste, Gebet, Gott, Grab, Opfer, Priester, Reinigung, Wahrsager,* etc.

[88] I 79 (32, 19 f.) and 61. As regards the influence of Hindu literature on Ibn Waḥshiyya, the author of the *Nabatean Agriculture,* cf. Bettina Strauss, "Das Giftbuch des Ŝânâq," *Quellen und Studien zur Geschichte der Naturwissenschaften und der Medizin,* IV, Berlin 1934, 116 f. Cf. note 34 above.

least some of the superstitious *nomoi* is then not limited to the human origin and the religious intention of both; both species of literature have moreover in common that their authors explicitly deny Divine revelation. And, last but not least, the possibility is by no means excluded that the originators of some of the superstitious practices or beliefs, and hence perhaps the authors of some of the superstitious codes, were themselves philosophers addressing the multitude.[89]

For a more adequate understanding of the relation between rational *nomoi* composed by philosophers and superstitious rational *nomoi*, recourse should be had to Maimonides' *Guide*. According to Maimonides, the *Nabataean Agriculture* is the most important document of the Sabean literature. The Sabeans were people of extreme ignorance and as remote from philosophy as possible. They were given to all sorts of superstitious practices (idolatry, talismans, witchcraft). There existed *"nomoi* of the Sabeans"* which were closely related to their "religion," and their "delirious follies" represented, just as "the *nomoi* of the Greeks," forms of "political guidance."[90] They did not hesitate to assert the reality of the most strange things which are "impossible by nature." Thus one might be tempted to ascribe to them an extreme credulity with regard to miracles.[91] Yet, as Maimonides does not fail to point out, their willingness to assert the reality of the most strange things which are "impossible by nature," is itself very strange; for they believed in the eternity of the world, i.e., they agreed with the philosophers over against the adherents of revelation as regards the crucial question.[92] Those who follow this trend of the argument up to its necessary conclusion, are not surprised to read in Maimonides' *Treatise on Resurrection*, the most authentic commentary on the *Guide*, that the Sabeans inferred from the eternity of the world the impossibility of miracles, and that they were far indeed from any credulity as regards miracles: it was their radical unbelief as regards miracles which induced God to postpone the announce-

---

[89] Cf. I 97 beg. (46, 24-48, 4) and III 53 (204, 9-15). Cf. Avicenna, *De anima* . . . , tr. by Alpagus, Venice 1546, 60b-61a.

[90] *Guide* III 29 (63a and b, 64b, 66b). Cf. II 39 end.

[91] As regards miracles which are "impossible by nature," cf. Maimonides' *Treatise on Resurrection*, ed. by Finkel, pp. 34-36 and 27-30.

[92] III 29 (63a). Cf. III 25 end.

ment of the future miracle of resurrection until a long time after
the Sinaitic revelation, i.e., until the belief in miracles had
firmly taken root in the minds of men.[93] In accordance with
this, Maimonides indicates in the *Guide* that the author of the
Nabatean Agriculture presented his ridiculous nonsense in order
to cast doubt on the Biblical miracles, and, in particular that
some of the stories contained in that work serve the purpose of
suggesting that the Biblical miracles were performed by means
of tricks.[94] It is certainly not difficult to understand why a man
who denies miracles, should collect Sabean information about
natural happenings more marvellous than the most impressive
Biblical miracles. It is perhaps not absurd to wonder whether
books such as the *Nabatean Agriculture* were written, not by
simple-minded adherents of superstitious creeds and practices,
but by adherents of the philosophers.[95] It might therefore be
rash to brush aside without any further discussion, the suspicion
that at least some of the superstitious *nomoi,* and of the apparently superstitious interpretations of such *nomoi,* were rational,
not so much from the point of view of practical reason, as from
that of theoretical reason. The same would hold true *mutatis
mutandis* of the rational *nomoi* composed by the philosophers
in so far as they served the purpose of undermining the belief
in Divine legislation proper.[96] However this may be, Maimonides opens his exposition of Sabeanism with the statement that
the Sabeans identified God with the stars or, more precisely, with
the heavens.[97] That is to say: the basic tenet of the Sabeans is

[93] *Resurrection*, pp. 31-33.

[94] III 29 (65a).

[95] Accordingly, at least a part of the "Sabean" literature would be comparable
as regards both tendency and procedure to Ibn Ar-Râwandî's account of the
Brahmanes (cf. Paul Kraus, "Beiträge zur islamischen Ketzergeschichte," *Rivista
degli Studi Orientali,* XIV, 1934, 341-357). The Sabeans and the Brahmanes are
mentioned together in *Kuzari* II 33; cf. I 61. Maimonides states that the Hindus
are remnants of the Sabeans: *Guide* III 29 (62b, 63a, 65a) and 46 (101b).

[96] Compare Plato's discussion of the Divine origin of the laws of Minos and
Lycurgus in the first book of the *Laws.*

[97] *Guide* III 29 (62a-b). Note in particular on p. 62b bottom the distinction
between *"all* Sabeans" and "the philosophers" of the Sabean period: only the
latter identified God with the spirit of the celestial sphere; the large majority
evidently identified God with the body of the celestial sphere. Cf. *Mishneh
Torah,* H. 'Abodah zarah I 2 (ed. Hyamson 66b 1-7). On the "atheism" of the
Sabeans, cf. also *Guide* III 45 (98b-99a).

identical with what adherents of Avicenna declared to be the basic tenet of Avicenna's esoteric teaching, viz., the identification of God with the heavenly bodies. Avicenna's esoteric teaching was expounded in his *Oriental Philosophy*, and he is said to have called that teaching "oriental," because it is identical with the view of "the people of the Orient."[98]

IV. THE LAW OF REASON AS THE FRAMEWORK OF EVERY CODE

THE scholar's first approving mention of the Law of Reason occurs some time after the king had joined the Jewish community and begun to study the Torah and the books of the prophets. The scholar, answering "Hebraic questions"[99] of the king, had explained to him the superiority of Israel to the other nations. The king is on the whole convinced; but he feels that precisely because of Israel's superiority one should expect to find more monks and ascets among the Jews than among other people. It is in connection with a critique of asceticism and anachoreticism, that the scholar's first and second approving mentions of the Law of Reason occur.[100] That critique is the central part of the critique of philosophy; for it concerns, not this or that set of dogmas of this or that philosophic sect, but the philosophic life itself: the life of contemplation which is essentially asocial and hence anachoretic.[101]

The king had assumed, partly on the basis of such Biblical passages as Deuteronomy 10:12 and Micah 6:8, that the right way of approaching God consists in humility, self-mortification and justice as such, or, to make full use of the Biblical passages which are alluded to rather than quoted by him, that it consists in fearing God, in walking in His ways, in loving Him and in serving Him with all one's heart and all one's soul, in doing

[98] Averroes, *Tahâfut al-tahâfut*, X (ed. by M. Bouyges, Beyrouth 1930, 421). Cf. *Kuzari* IV 25 (282, 1 f.).— Maimonides touches upon the oriental orientation of the Sabeans, as opposed to the occidental orientation of Abraham and his followers, in *Guide* III 45 (98a).
[99] II 1 *vers. fin.* Cf. II 81.
[100] Cf. II 48 with 45 and 50 beginning, and III 7 with 1-17.
[101] Cf. note 63 above.

justly, in loving mercy and in walking humbly with God.[102] The
scholar's answer runs as follows: "These and similar things are
the rational *nomoi;* they are the preamble and the introduction
to the Divine law, they are prior to it in nature and in time, they
are indispensable for the government of any human community
whatsoever; even a community of robbers cannot dispense with
the obligation to justice in their mutual relations: otherwise
their association would not last." He understands then by rational *nomoi* the sum of rules which describe the indispensable
minimum of morality required for the preservation of any
society. He considers their relation to any society comparable
to the relation of such "natural things" as food, drink, movement, rest, sleep and waking to the individual:[103] one is tempted
to say that he considers the rational *nomoi* as *iura quasi naturalia.*[103a] In the second approving mention of the rational *nomoi*
which occurs some time after the conclusion of the discussion
of the "Hebraic questions," he adds the remark that the rational
nomoi are known independently of revelation as regards their
substance, but not as regards their measure: the precise speciali-
zation of these evidently very general rules is beyond the power
of man.[104] By linking together the two remarks, we are led to
think that the rational *nomoi* of which the scholar approves,
are but the framework of any code, and not a code.

In his first statement on the question, the scholar calls the
rational *nomoi* also "the rational and governmental laws," "the
laws which (even) the smallest and lowest community observes,"
"the governmental and rational law," "the rational law," "the
rational (laws)." In that context, he uses the term *"nomoi"*
once only and he substitutes for it consistently "laws" or "law."
By this, he indicates that he is following the kalâm rather than
philosophy. For it is in accordance with the kalâm-tradition
that he contrasts what he almost calls "the rational laws" with

[102] The king merely quotes the following: "What doth the Lord thy God
require of thee, but to fear the Lord thy God and so forth" and "What doth
the Lord require of thee." In Ibn Tibbon's translation the following words of
Micah's are added: "but to do justly and to love mercy."
[103] II 48.
[103a] They are not natural precisely because they are *nomoi.*
[104] III 7. Cf. Saadya, *K. al-amânât,* III, ed. by Landauer, 119.

what he almost calls "the revealed laws." Deviating from that tradition, however, he does not use these terms without qualification.[105] This procedure is not surprising since he is a mutakallim indeed, but not a typical mutakallim,[106] and since he does not ascribe his peculiar use of the terms in question either to the mutakallimûn or the philosophers. Nor is it surprising that he, being a mutakallim, seems to include duties toward God among the "rational laws." What does surprise us is, first, that he seems to include the most sublime religious obligations (to fear God, to love Him with all one's soul, and to walk humbly with Him) among those minimum obligations which even the smallest and lowest society performs as necessarily, or almost as necessarily, as every individual eats, drinks and sleeps; and, second, that by using the terms "rational *nomoi*" and "rational laws" synonymously, he seems to identify the rational *nomoi*, or the syllogistic religion, of which he had so definitely disapproved prior to the conversion of the king, with the rational laws, or the rational commandments which are the framework of the Biblical code as well as of any other code. The first difficulty concerns the content of the Law of Reason as the framework of any code; the second difficulty concerns the apparently close relation between that framework of any code and the complete code elaborated by the philosophers.

Do duties toward God belong to the moral minimum required of any society however low?[107] In the first statement on the subject, the scholar adduces as examples of the rational *nomoi*,

[105] Whereas the usual kalâm-term is "revealed laws," the scholar speaks first of "the Divine and revealed laws," then of "the Divine law," and finally of "the laws." (II 48. He does not speak any more of "revealed laws" in the two later statements, III 7 and 11.) Whereas the kalâm-terminology implies that the Divine law as a whole consists of rational and revealed laws, the scholar considers the rational laws as preparatory to, and hence outside of, the Divine law: he insists on the independence of the rational laws with regard to the Divine law.—Cf. the mention of "revealed laws" in IV 13 end and the allusion to them in III 60.

[106] See p. 99 f. above.

[107] The scholar's answer to this question cannot be established by reference to the seven Noahidic commandments; for, as he intimates in I 83 (36, 17-20), i.e., shortly after his first mention of the rational *nomoi* (in I 81), he considers the Noahidic commandments as "inherited," and hence as not merely rational (cf. I 65). Cf. also III 73 near the beginning with II 48, III 7 and 11. The same applies to the Decalogue, "the mothers and roots of the laws"; cf. I 87 (38, 19 f.), II 28 and IV 11 beginning with II 48, III 7 and 11.

or the rational and governmental laws, the following points in this illuminating order which anticipates explanations given later on: "justice, goodness and recognition of God's grace," "justice and recognition of God's grace," and "to do justly and to love mercy."[108] When speaking explicitly of the community of robbers, he mentions the obligation to justice only, while when speaking of the smallest and lowest community, he mentions justice, goodness and recognition of God's grace. In his second statement, he does not mention any duties toward God among the "governmental actions and rational *nomoi*" or "governmental and rational (*nomoi* or actions)" as distinguished from the "Divine (*nomoi* or actions)." In a third statement, in which he does not as much as allude to rational *nomoi* or rational laws, he distinguishes between Divine laws, governmental laws and psychic laws; he does not mention any duties toward God among the governmental laws, whereas the Divine and the psychic laws are concerned exclusively with such duties.[109] The crucial question which was left open in the first statement is not decided in the two later statements, since nothing is said in them as to whether the "governmental actions and rational *nomoi*" or the "governmental laws" which do not appear to include duties toward God, exhaust the indispensable and unchangeable minimum of morality required of any society.[110]

Under the circumstances one can hardly do more than to discuss the alternatives. But even this is not quite easy, since the scholar's statements are of a strange elusiveness. This applies not merely to the question as to whether religion belongs

[108] Cf. also n. 128 below.

[109] II 48, III 7 and 11 (152, 9-154, 24). These three passages will be referred to on the following pages as the first, second and third (or last) statement respectively.—The distinction between Divine, governmental and psychic laws is akin to that used by Bahya ibn Pakuda between "revealed duties of the limbs," "rational duties of the limbs," and "duties of the heart." The Divine laws are practically identical with the ceremonial laws; the most important examples of the psychic laws are the first three commandments of the Decalogue.

[110] In the middle of the first statement, the scholar seems to distinguish "the rational law" whose object is justice and recognition of God's grace, from "the governmental and the rational law" whose object is justice, goodness and recognition of God's grace; thus the specific object of the governmental law as such would be "goodness." (As regards the close relation between "goodness" and "city," cf. III 2-3.) The second and third statements contain an interpretation of this implication.

to the minimum of morality required of any society, or to the *iura naturalia,* but likewise to the question as to whether the *iura naturalia* can be called rational. For the alternative that religion is not essential to society as such is closely linked in his argument with the thesis that the *iura naturalia* are not rational, and *vice versa.*[111] The connection between the two questions is as close as that between religion as such and morality as such.

The scholar's embarrassment can easily be accounted for. To deny that religion is essential to society, is difficult for a man of Halevi's piety, and, we venture to add, for anyone who puts any trust in the accumulated experience of the human race. To assert it, would amount to ascribing some value even to the most abominable idolatrous religion; for the proverbial gang of robbers, or the lowest and smallest community, cannot be supposed to adhere to the one true religion or to any of its imitations. From his point of view, it is, I believe, impossible to decide the question as to whether the denial, not accompanied by the assertion of the existence of any other deity, of the existence, say, of Moloch is better or worse than a living faith in Moloch.[112] This embarrassment arises from the fact that he raises at all the philosophic question of the basis of any and every society; but this could hardly be avoided in a conversation with a king who had barely ceased to be a pagan. Or, to disregard for one moment the conversational setting, the defence of religion by means of argument is, as Halevi himself does not fail to indicate, not without danger to unadulterated faith.[113]

The very term "governmental laws" indicates that the group of laws which it designates, is more directly connected with government, and in particular with political government, than are the other groups: the governmental laws by themselves seem to be the indispensable moral minimum of any government, or

---

[111] The thesis that religion is not essential to society, means that the *iura naturalia* are identical with the non-revealed governmental laws; now, one cannot establish the precise meaning of the non-revealed governmental laws, if one does not assume that the non-revealed governmental laws are not identical with the rational *nomoi,* and hence that the former are not rational laws.

[112] Cf. also the elusive handling of the question as to whether Islam or philosophy are preferable in IV 12 f.

[113] Cf. p. 109 f. above.

the evidently necessary and sufficient, and the always identical, framework of both the many man-made codes and the one Divine code. In order to grasp more clearly the purport of the governmental laws which, be it said, occupy the central place in the last statement,[114] one has to overcome this difficulty. Precisely the last statement which is the only one to deal unambiguously with governmental laws, does not deal unambiguously with their non-revealed elements, for it deals with the governmental laws as contained in the Divine code without distinguishing between their revealed and their non-revealed elements. On the other hand, the second statement, in which the scholar does distinguish between laws known by revelation only and laws known independently of revelation, deals with "governmental actions and rational *nomoi*" without distinguishing between governmental laws and rational *nomoi;* and the distinction, made in the last statement, between governmental laws and psychic laws, leads one to suspect a corresponding, although by no means identical, distinction between governmental laws and rational *nomoi*.[115] To find out which unambiguously governmental laws are considered by the scholar to be known independently of revelation, one has to compare the second and the third statement: laws occurring in the second statement under the heading "governmental actions and rational *nomoi*" as well as in the third statement under the heading "governmental laws" are without any doubt such governmental laws as are known independently of revelation.

The scholar mentions among the governmental and rational *nomoi* which are known independently of revelation, the duty to train one's soul by means of fasting and humility, whereas he does not mention it among the governmental laws of the

---

[114] The last statement is the only one of the three in which an odd number of groups of laws are mentioned.

[115] The psychic laws are not rational laws; for they direct man toward God as legislator and judge, and God as legislator and judge is not known to unassisted human reason; cf. III 11 (154, 5 ff.) with IV 3 (228, 18 ff.) and 16. To assert the rationality of the psychic laws because of II 47 f., would amount to asserting that even a gang of robbers cannot dispense with belief in, fear of, and love to, the God of Abraham as distinguished from the God of Aristotle.—Ibn Tibbon adds to "psychic laws" "and they are the philosophic laws"; this addition is either based on a complete misunderstanding of the author's intentions, or else it is meant as a hint which I for one have not been able to grasp.

Divine code; by this he seems to indicate that that duty does not belong to the *iura naturalia;* this is not surprising, since it is fairly absurd to imagine a gang of robbers training their souls by means of fasting and humility in order to guarantee the preservation of their gang. On the other hand, he mentions among the governmental laws of the Divine code the prohibition against murder, e.g., while he does not mention it among the governmental and rational *nomoi* which are known independently of revelation; this again is easily understandable considering that the Bible prohibits murder absolutely, whereas a gang of robbers, e.g., would merely have to prohibit the murder of other members of the gang. This explains also why he mentions in both enumerations the prohibition against deceit or lying; for the Bible itself speaks on the occasion of that prohibition merely of the neighbor.[116] He mentions in both enumerations the duty to honor one's parents: "the household is the primary part of the city."[117] Or, if we follow the hint supplied by Ibn Tibbon's translation, we have to say—and this seems to be preferable—that he mentions among the governmental laws of the Bible the commandment to honor father and mother, and among the governmental laws known independently of revelation the duty to honor "the fathers," understanding "fathers" probably also in the metaphoric sense of "adviser" or "teacher";[118] accordingly, he would signify that even a gang of robbers cannot last if they do not respect those of their fellows who are their intellectual superiors. To sum up: the *iura naturalia* are really not more than the indispensable and unchangeable minimum of morality required for the bare existence of any society.[119]

[116] The prohibition against deceit occupies the central place in the enumeration in III 7, and, probably, also in the enumeration of the governmental laws in III 11, i.e., if one counts each item as a law by itself ("honoring the father" and "honoring the mother," e.g., as two distinct laws; cf. n. 118 below).

[117] Maimonides, *Guide,* III 41 (90b) in a discussion of similar Biblical commandments.

[118] "Honoring the parents is a duty" (III 7); "is a duty" is missing in the original; besides, Ibn Tibbon translates אלואלדין by האבות.

[119] A more explicit presentation of this "low" view of the natural law occurs in Joseph Albo's *'Ikkarim,* I 7. Cf. Julius Guttmann's critical remarks on Saadya's and others' failure to distinguish between "juridical norms of a purely technical nature" and "moral norms" (*Die Philosophie des Judentums,* Munich 1933, 80 f.).

The foregoing remarks are based on the distinction between governmental laws and rational *nomoi,* and hence on the assumption, forced upon us by the trend of the argument, that the (non-revealed) governmental laws cannot be called, in the last analysis, rational laws.[120] This assumption can be justified by a number of reasons. The term "rational laws" has a clear meaning, as long as the rational laws are contrasted with Divinely revealed, or supra-rational laws; but it ceases to be clear if it is used for distinguishing such different groups of non-revealed laws as are natural laws and civil laws e.g.; for all laws which deserve that name, are the work of reason[121] and hence rational: a law solving justly a problem which exists in a given country at a given time only, is not less rational, it is in a sense more rational, than a law valid in all countries at all times. Moreover, if universal validity is taken as an unambiguous sign of rationality, the answer is obvious that not a single of those most universal laws which the scholar mentions among the non-revealed governmental laws, is truly universally valid:[122] almost all men admit that one may deceive a potential murderer as to the whereabouts of his potential victim. Finally, it is doubtful whether one may call rational in an emphatic sense such laws as are not, as such, directed toward the perfection of man as man; now, the governmental laws are, as such, directed toward man's physical well-being only and do not pay any attention to the well-being of his soul.[123]

We have now disentangled the following view of the *iura naturalia:* they do not comprise any duties toward God,[124] they do not go beyond delimiting the essential elements of any "Binnenmoral," and they cannot be called rational. We shall call

[120] Maimonides (*Eight Chapters,* VI) mentions among those laws which are erroneously called by the mutakallimûn rational laws and which ought to be called generally accepted laws, such laws only as would be called by Halevi governmental laws; i.e., deviating from his talmudic source (b. Yoma 67b), he does not mention among them any duties toward God. Cf. also note 136 below.

[121] I 35. Cf. *Eth. Nic.* 1180a12f.

[122] Cf. IV 19.

[123] Cf. Maimonides, *Guide,* II 40 (86b) on the governmental codes.

[124] Cf. Thomas Aquinas, *Summa Theologica,* 1 2, quaest. 104., art. 1.: "praeceptorum cujuscumque legis quaedam habent vim obligandi ex ipso dictamine rationis, . . . et hujusmodi praecepta dicuntur moralia . . . . . etiam in his quae ordinant ad Deum, quaedam sunt moralia, quae ipsa ratio *fide informata* dictat, sicut Deum esse amandum et colendum."

this view the philosophic view.[125] It is certainly not the kalâm-view. And it might seem as if would suffice to state it explicitly in order to prove that the scholar, this atypical mutakallim, cannot have accepted it, although it is one alternative interpretation of his statements. What one can say with certainty is that he virtually rejects the first of the reasons which we mentioned in the preceding paragraph. But this merely leads to a new difficulty.

In the central statement, the scholar makes it clear that the outline supplied by the *iura naturalia* which are known independently of revelation, cannot be filled in adequately but by God alone; he thus seems to admit that the distinction between rational and non-rational (revealed) laws is legitimate. The remark referred to implies however that even a merely governmental code, if it is to be good for the community, must be the work of revelation. Since no society however low or small can last if it does not observe the *iura naturalia*, and since these rules must be determined precisely by Divine revelation in order to become good for the community, i.e., in order to become applicable at all, we are driven to the conclusion that no society which is not ruled by a revealed code, can last, or, that not only religion, but revealed religion, is essential for the lasting of any society. This conclusion is not completely surprising: according to the scholar, only the Jewish nation is eternal, all other nations are perishable; all other nations are dead, only the Jewish nation is living.[126]

To find our way back from his ultimate answer to his explanation of how a society can humanly speaking be lasting, we have to recall the connection between the assertions that the *iura naturalia* are rational, and that religion belongs to these *iura naturalia:* by accepting the first of these assertions, he must have accepted, if with some hesitation, the second as well. We shall then say that, according to him, the rational *iura naturalia* are not exhausted by the non-revealed governmental laws as described above, but that they include what may be called the demands of natural piety[127] as well. Unassisted reason is able

---

125 Cf. p. 95 ff. and notes 120 ff. above.
126 II 32-34; III 9-10; IV 3 (230, 12-20) and 23.
127 How little definite as regards the object of worship these demands are, can be seen from IV 15 and IV 1-3.

to perceive that without religious beliefs and actions no society whatsoever can last, but reason is unable to determine the right kind of such actions and beliefs: specific laws concerning religious actions and beliefs are, as all specific laws are, either suprarational and hence good, or else irrational and hence bad. Reason when perceiving the necessity of religion tries to satisfy that need by devising a syllogistic-governmental religion of one kind or another; in this way, the rational *nomoi* disposed of in the first makâla, come into being. In contradistinction to these rational *nomoi* which are complete codes, the rational *nomoi* which are merely the framework of any code, be it man-made or revealed, are legitimate. Although this interpretation comes nearer than anything else I can think of, to the scholar's profession of faith, it remains exposed to the difficulties which have been indicated.[128]

What has been said about the close connection, in the scholar's argument, between the assertions that religion is essential to society and that the moral minimum of social life can be called "the rational laws," must not be understood to mean that these two assertions are altogether inseparable. The philosophers would not have devised governmental religions in addition to the governmental laws, if they had not admitted the social necessity of religion. On the other hand, nothing said, or implied, by the scholar would justify us in distrusting our initial impression that the philosophers denied the rational character of the *iura naturalia.*

V. THE LAW OF REASON AND THE NATURAL LAW

The scholar uses one and the same term "rational *nomoi*" first for designating the man-made pagan codes, of which he thoroughly disapproves, and then for designating rules akin to the

[128] According to the first two statements (I 1 and 81), the rational *nomoi* are religious codes, either the religion of the philosophers or ordinary pagan codes. According to the third statement (II 48), the rational *nomoi* probably contain duties toward God. According to the fourth statement (III 7), the rational *nomoi* almost certainly do not contain duties toward God. According to the fifth statement (III 11), the governmental laws are clearly distinguished from the Divine and the psychic laws, i.e., from the laws regulating religion. According to the sixth statement (IV 19), the philosophers' *nomoi* are clearly distinguished from the philosophers' (esoteric) religion which is "assimilation to God," i.e., to the God of Aristotle. The final statement (V 14) is completely silent on the subject.

"rational laws," the "rational commandments" in the sense of
the kalâm, or for the framework of every code, of which he
naturally approves. Nothing would have been easier for him
than to use two different terms for these two so greatly different
things. Considering the gravity of the subject, his failure to do
so cannot be due to carelessness. His strange and perplexing
usage compels us to raise the question as to how complete codes,
which are utterly irreconcilable with the Divine code, can be
interpreted in such a way as to become identical with the framework of every code, and hence of the Divine code in particular.
As far as the answer to this question cannot possibly be borne
out by an explicit statement of the scholar, or of the author, it
will of necessity be hypothetical. To clarify the issue, we shall
avoid as far as possible the ambiguous term "rational *nomoi*":
we shall call the complete codes in question the Law of Reason,
and the framework of every code the Natural Law.

It is evidently impossible to identify the Law of Reason in
the full sense of the term[129] with the Natural Law. The scholar
must therefore have distinguished between the religiously neu-
tral core of the Law of Reason and its pagan periphery,[130] and
he must have identified its core only with the Natural Law. We
assume that the Law of Reason is primarily the sum of rules of
conduct which the philosopher has to observe in order to become capable, and to be capable, of contemplation. These rules
are addressed to the philosopher as such without any regard to
place and time; hence they cannot but be very general in charac-

129 That is to say: the "rational" (practically wise) presentation of the "rational"
(theoretical-demonstrative) teaching which, according to the philosophers whom
Halevi has in mind, is a refutation of the teaching of the revealed religions.

130 The scholar alludes to the distinction between the Law of Reason proper
and the religion of the philosophers when he first mentions the *nomoi* which are
set up by the philosophers—he does this shortly before giving his summary
explanation of the *Sefer Yeṣirah* (cf. note 70 above)—. In that context he states
that these *nomoi* are "governments" of a certain kind (IV 19), *viz.* they are rules
of conduct of a certain kind—and nothing else. This explanation of "nomoi"
is indispensable because the term might designate, and did in fact designate in
some earlier passages of the *Kuzari*, those rules of conduct plus the man-made
or governmental religion, or even the governmental religion by itself. Cf. p.
123 f. above with I, 1 and 79 (34, 8). Gersonides, *Milhamot hashem*, Introd., ed.
Leipzig 1866, p. 7, says that "the Torah is not a *nomos* compelling us to believe
untrue things." Cf. also Falkera, *Sefer ha-mebakkesh*, ed. Amsterdam 1779, 29b
and 38a-b, and the promiscuous use of "lex," "lex divina" and "secta" in
Marsilius' *Defensor Pacis*, Dictio I., c. 5., §10 f.

ter: their application in given circumstances is left to the discretion of the individual philosopher; they are, as it were, the
framework of all private codes of all individual philosophers.
The way in which these general rules are applied in the individual case, depends considerably on the character of the society
in which the individual philosopher happens to live: that society
may be favorable or unfavorable to philosophy and philosophers.
In case the given society is hostile to philosophy, the Law of
Reason advises the philosopher either to leave that society and
to search for another society, or else to try to lead his fellows
gradually toward a more reasonable attitude,[131] i.e., for the time
being to adapt his conduct, as far as necessary, to the requirements of that society: what at first glance appears to be a repudi-
ation of the Law of Reason in favor of another rule of life,
proves on closer investigation to be one form of observing the
very Law of Reason.[132] The Law of Reason is then not indissolu-
bly bound up with any particular form of society, with that form
e.g. which is sketched in Plato's *Laws*, the rational laws par excellence. As a matter of principle, contemplation requires with-
drawal from society. Therefore, the Law of Reason is primarily
the sum of rules of conduct of the philosophizing hermit, the
regimen solitarii.[133] It is best illustrated by the advice to train
one's soul by means of fasting and humility, and its content, as
distinguished from its purpose which is assimilation to God, or
contemplation, can be reduced to the formula "purity of the
soul": as distinguished from any social or political law, it regulates "the soul," "the intention," the basic attitude of the philosopher rather than any action, anything corporeal.[134] Nat-

[131] Cf. Fârâbî's account of Plato's *Republic* on the one hand, of his *Letters* on
the other in his treatise on Plato's philosophy (the Hebrew translation in
Falkera's *Reshit Ḥokmah*, 76 ff.).

[132] Cf. pp. 115 ff. and 120 f. above.

[133] The philosopher when speaking of the rational *nomoi*, does not mention
any social relations (cf. p. 116 above). Halevi intimates that a life guided by the
rational *nomoi* alone, would be an anachoretic life (cf. p. 126 above). The scholar
states that the rational *nomoi* by themselves are not sufficient for the right
guidance of society, and thus implies that they are sufficient for the right guidance of the individual; cf. III 7 (150, 1-4). Consider also the twofold meaning
of *siyâsa* ("government"); see above note 72.

[134] Cf. III 7 beginning: "governmental actions and rational [intellectual]
nomoi" with the distinction between "practica" and "intellectualia" in III 65
(214, 28). Cf. p. 131 above.

urally, the solitary character of the philosophic life must be understood intelligently, it must be understood *cum grano salis:* Socrates, the model of the philosophic life, loved the company of his pupils,[135] and he had to live together with people who were not, and could not become, his pupils. Hence, the Law of Reason must be supplemented with, or, rather, it comprises, rules of social conduct. It is this social, or governmental, part of the Law of Reason which the scholar calls the Law of Reason and which he identifies with the Natural Law: the rational *nomoi* which he accepts, are purely governmental.[136] He acts as if he were blind to the non-governmental part of the Law of Reason, or to the aim which it is destined to serve: he deliberately disregards that non-governmental part, or its aim, which is assimilation to "the God of Aristotle."[137] For only its governmental part is "visible," i.e., of interest, to men who are not philosophers or even adversaries of the philosophers. But by identifying the governmental part of the Law of Reason, or what we may call briefly the philosophers' social morality, with the

[135] III 1 (140, 13-16).

[136] II 48 beginning. The philosophers would not call the governmental part of the Law of Reason rational (cf. p. 133 above), but the rules of which that part consists, are rational laws according to the mutakallimûn; the scholar, being an atypical mutakallim, identifies the rational laws of the mutakallimûn with what he calls the Law of Reason, *viz.* the governmental part of the Law of Reason. By way of illustration it may be noted that R. Sheshet ha-Nasi in his brief recommendation of Plato's rational *nomoi* (see A. Marx, *op. cit.,* 424) mentions exclusively such Platonic laws as would be called by the scholar governmental laws.—It is doubtful whether the scholar calls the *nomoi* of the philosophers which are rules of conduct and nothing else, rational *nomoi* (IV 19): the term "rational" does not occur in the original, while it occurs in Ibn Tibbon's translation. Both readings are justifiable, if we assume that when mentioning first the philosophers' *nomoi,* the scholar adopted the philosophers' terminology. If he called them rational, he understood by the *nomoi* of the philosophers the complete Law of Reason (i.e. the *regimen solitarii* including the rules of social conduct). If he failed to call them rational, he understood by the *nomoi* of the philosophers the governmental part of the Law of Reason only. The second alternative is borne out by the context in which a distinction is made between the *nomoi* on the one hand and what appears to be the central part of the philosophers' rule of conduct, *viz.* assimilation to God or morality proper, on the other.

[137] One may say that the scholar replaces the non-governmental part of the Law of Reason which regulates man's attitude toward the God of Aristotle, by the psychic laws, i.e. by laws regulating man's attitude toward the God of Abraham. Cf. note 115 above.

Natural Law, i.e., natural morality, or the framework of every code,[188] he is enabled to shed some light on the latter.

For what are the distinctive features of the social part of the Law of Reason? While philosophy presupposes social life (division of labor), the philosopher has no attachment to society: his soul is elsewhere. Accordingly, the philosopher's rules of social conduct do not go beyond the minimum moral requirements of living together. Besides, from the philosopher's point of view, observation of these rules is not an end in itself, but merely a means toward an end, the ultimate end being contemplation. More precisely, these rules are not obligatory; they are valid, not absolutely, but only in the large majority of cases; they can safely be disregarded in extreme cases, in cases of urgent need;[139] they are rules of "prudence" rather than rules of morality proper. The Natural Law is then a rule of social conduct which is only hypothetically valid and whose addressees are "rugged individualists," men with no inner attachment to society, men who are not—citizens: it is in contrast to the essentially solitary philosopher that the truly good or pious man is called "the guardian of his city," φύλαξ πόλεως.[140] It is hardly necessary to add that it is precisely this view of the non-categoric character of the rules of social conduct which permits the philosopher to hold that a man who has become a philosopher, may adhere in his deeds and speeches to a religion to which he does not adhere in his thoughts; it is this view, I say, which is underlying the exotericism of the philosophers.

By calling both the Law of Reason and the Natural Law

---

[188] Compare Abraham b. Hiyya's attempt to interpret the *regimen solitarii* as the framework of the Divine code: the Decalogue which contains *in nuce* all the commandments of the Torah, is by itself the sufficient rule of conduct for the פרושים, the solitary saints (*Hegyon ha-nefesh*, ed. by Freimann, 35b-38a). Cf. note 107 above.

[139] IV 19. Cf. p. 114 f. above.—What we learn from IV 19, the first passage in which the scholar mentions the philosophers' *nomoi*, can be summarized as follows: the philosophers' *nomoi* are distinguished from the philosophers' religion (or from the rational *nomoi* as interpreted by the philosophers); they are only a rule of conduct and nothing else; moreover, these rules regulate social conduct and nothing else; they are not obligatory; and they are not rational. (Cf. above notes 128, 130 and 136.)

[140] Cf. III 2-3 with Avicenna, *Metaphysics*, X 4 beginning and Plato, *Republic*, 414 a-b.

rational *nomoi*, by thus, as matters stand, identifying that part of the Law of Reason which is relevant to men who are not philosophers, with the Natural Law, the scholar tacitly asserts that the Natural Law is not obligatory[141] and does not command, or presuppose, an inner attachment to society. He accepts, at least within these limits, what may be called the philosophers' view of the Natural Law. But precisely by going so far with the philosophers, does he discover the fundamental weakness of the philosophic position and the deepest reason why philosophy is so enormously dangerous. For if the philosophers are right in their appraisal of natural morality, of morality not based on Divine revelation, natural morality is, strictly speaking, no morality at all: it is hardly distinguishable from the morality essential to the preservation of a gang of robbers. Natural morality being what it is, only a law revealed by the omnipotent and omniscient God and sanctioned by the omniscient and omnipotent God can make possible genuine morality, "categoric imperatives"; only revelation can transform natural man into "the guardian of his city," or, to use the language of the Bible, the guardian of his brother.[142] One has not to be naturally pious, he has merely to have a passionate interest in genuine morality in order to long with all his heart for revelation: moral man as such is the potential believer. Halevi could find a sign for the necessity of the connection between morality and revelation in the fact that the same philosophers who denied the Divine lawgiver, denied the obligatory character of what we would call

141 In II 48, the scholar asserts that even a community of robbers cannot dispense with the obligation to justice. Are we then to believe that robbers are more moral than philosophers? The philosophers would not deny that in the large majority of cases the rules of justice are, for all practical purposes, obligatory; the crucial question concerns the crucial cases, the cases of extreme necessity. If even the Torah admits that in the extreme case all governmental laws, with the exception of the prohibitions against murder and inchastity can be transgressed, we are safe in assuming that the community of robbers, and many other communities as well, would drop these two exceptions. (Cf. IV 19 end and III 11 with Maimonides' *Mishneh Torah*, H. Yesode ha-torah V.) Above all, the philosophers would deny that the rules which are called obligatory by the societies, are in fact obligatory strictly speaking: society has to present to its members certain rules as obligatory in order to supply these rules with that degree of dignity and sanctity which will induce the members of the society to obey them as much as possible.

142 Cf. p. 133 f. above.

the moral law. In defending Judaism, which, according to him, is the only true revealed religion, against the philosophers, he was conscious of defending morality itself and therewith the cause, not only of Judaism, but of mankind at large. His basic objection to philosophy was then not particularly Jewish, nor even particularly religious, but moral. He has spoken on this subject with a remarkable restraint: not being a fanatic, he did not wish to supply the unscrupulous and the fanatic with weapons which they certainly would have misused. But this restraint cannot deceive the reader about the singleness of his primary and ultimate purpose.

5

How TO STUDY SPINOZA'S *THEOLOGICO-POLITICAL TREATISE*

I

Before attempting to answer the question of how to proceed in a particular historical investigation, one must clarify the reasons why the investigation is relevant. In fact, the reasons which induce one to study a particular historical subject, immediately determine the general character of the procedure. The reason why a fresh investigation of Spinoza's *Theologico-Political Treatise*[1] is in order, is obvious. The chief aim of the *Treatise* is to refute the claims which had been raised on behalf of revelation throughout the ages; and Spinoza succeeded, at least to the extent that his book has become *the* classic document of the "rationalist" or "secularist" attack on the belief in revelation. The study of the *Treatise* can be of real importance only if the issue discussed in it is still alive. A glance at the present scene is sufficient to show one that the issue which, until a short while ago, was generally believed to have been settled by Spinoza's nineteenth-century successors once and for all, and thus to be obsolete, is again approaching the center of attention. But we cannot help noticing that the most fundamental issue—the issue raised by the conflicting claims of philosophy and revela-

[1] The *Theologico-Political Treatise* will be cited as "the *Treatise*" in the text and as "*Tr.*" in the notes. In the notes Roman figures after "*Tr.*" indicate the chapters of the work, Arabic figures following the comma and preceding the brackets indicate the pages in Gebhardt's edition of the *Opera omnia*, and Arabic figures within the brackets indicate the §§ inserted by Bruder in his edition.

tion—is discussed in our time on a decidedly lower level than was almost customary in former ages. It is with a view to these circumstances that we open the *Treatise* again. We shall therefore listen to Spinoza as attentively as we can. We shall make every effort to understand what he says exactly as he means it. For if we fail to do so, we are likely to substitute our folly for his wisdom.

To understand the words of another man, living or dead, may mean two different things which for the moment we shall call interpretation and explanation. By interpretation we mean the attempt to ascertain what the speaker said and how he actually understood what he said, regardless of whether he expressed that understanding explicitly or not. By explanation we mean the attempt to ascertain those implications of his statements of which he was unaware. Accordingly, the realization that a given statement is ironical or a lie, belongs to the interpretation of the statement, whereas the realization that a given statement is based on a mistake, or is the unconscious expression of a wish, an interest, a bias, or a historical situation, belongs to its explanation. It is obvious that the interpretation has to precede the explanation. If the explanation is not based on an adequate interpretation, it will be the explanation, not of the statement to be explained, but of a figment of the imagination of the historian. It is equally obvious that, within the interpretation, the understanding of the explicit meaning of a statement has to precede the understanding of what the author knew but did not say explicitly: one cannot realize, or at any rate one cannot prove, that a statement is a lie before one has understood the statement in itself.

The demonstrably true understanding of the words or the thoughts of another man is necessarily based on an exact interpretation of his explicit statements. But exactness means different things in different cases. In some cases exact interpretation requires the careful weighing of every word used by the speaker; such careful consideration would be a most inexact procedure in the case of a casual remark of a loose thinker or talker.[2] In

[2] Consider the following statement of Spinoza (ep. 15): ". . . ubi pag. 4. lectorem mones, quâ occasione primam partem composuerim, vellem ut simul ibi, aut ubi placuerit, etiam moneres me eam intra duas hebdomadas composuisse. hoc enim praemonito nemo putabit, haec adeo clare proponi, ut quae clarius explicari non possent, adeoque verbulo uno, aut alteri, quod forte hic illic ofendent [sic], non haerebunt."

order to know what degree or kind of exactness is required for the understanding of a given writing, one must therefore first know the author's habits of writing. But since these habits become truly known only through the understanding of the writer's work, it would seem that at the beginning one cannot help being guided by one's preconceived notions of the author's character. The procedure would be more simple if there were a way of ascertaining an author's manner of writing prior to interpreting his works. It is a general observation that people write as they read. As a rule, careful writers are careful readers and *vice versa*. A careful writer wants to be read carefully. He cannot know what it means to be read carefully but by having done careful reading himself. Reading precedes writing. We read before we write. We learn to write by reading. A man learns to write well by reading well good books, by reading most carefully books which are most carefully written. We may therefore acquire some previous knowledge of an author's habits of writing by studying his habits of reading. The task is simplified if the author in question explicitly discusses the right manner of reading books in general, or of reading a particular book which he has studied with a great deal of attention. Spinoza has devoted a whole chapter of his *Treatise* to the question of how to read the Bible, which he had read and reread with very great care.[3] To ascertain how to read Spinoza, we shall do well to cast a glance at his rules for reading the Bible.

Spinoza holds the view that the method of interpreting the Bible is identical with the method of interpreting nature. The reading of the book of nature consists in inferring the definitions of natural things from the data supplied by "natural history." In the same way, the interpretation of the Bible consists in inferring the thought of the Biblical authors, or the definitions of the Biblical subjects *qua* Biblical subjects, from the data supplied by "the history of the Bible." The knowledge of nature must be derived solely from data supplied by nature herself, and not at all from considerations of what is fitting, beautiful, perfect, or reasonable. In the same way the knowledge of the Bible must be derived solely from data supplied by the Bible itself, and not at all from considerations of what is reasonable.

[3] *Tr.* IX, p. 135 (§31).

For we have no right to assume that the views of the Biblical authors agree with the dictates of human reason. In other words, the understanding of the Biblical teaching and the judgment on whether that teaching is reasonable or not, have to be kept strictly separate. Nor can we identify the thought of the Biblical authors with its traditional interpretation, unless we prove first that that interpretation goes back to oral utterances of the Biblical authors. Besides, seeing that there is a variety of Biblical authors, we have to understand each of them by himself; prior to investigation we have no right to assume that they all agree with each other. The Bible has to be understood exclusively by itself, or nothing can be accepted as a Biblical teaching if it is not borne out clearly by the Bible itself, or the whole knowledge of the Bible must be derived exclusively from the Bible itself.[4]

"The history of the Bible" as Spinoza conceives of it, consists of three parts: a) thorough knowledge of the language of the Bible; b) collection and lucid arrangement of the statements of each Biblical book regarding every significant subject; c) knowledge of the lives of all Biblical authors, as well as of their characters, mental casts, and interests; knowledge of the occasion and time of the composition of each Biblical book, of its addressees, of its fate, etc. These data or, more specifically, the collected and properly arranged Biblical statements understood in the light of grammar, palaeography, history, etc., are the basis of the interpretation proper, which consists in inferring, by legitimate reasoning, from the data mentioned, the thought of the Biblical authors. Here again one has to follow the model of natural science. One has to ascertain first the most universal or most fundamental element of Biblical thought, i.e., what all Biblical authors explicitly and clearly present as a teaching meant for all times and addressed to all men; thereafter one has to descend to derivative or less universal themes, such as the Biblical teaching about less general subjects, and the teachings peculiar to the individual Biblical authors.[5]

Spinoza's formulation of his hermeneutic principle ("the

[4] *Tr.* VII, pp. 98-101, 104-105, 108-109, 114-115 (§§6, 7, 9-14, 16-19, 22, 35, 37-39, 52, 55, 56, 77 ff., 84); XV, pp. 181-182 (§8); XVI, pp. 190-191 (§§10-11); praef., pp. 9-10 (§§20, 25).

[5] *Tr.* VII, pp. 98-104, 106-107, 112 (§§7, 13, 15-17, 23-24, 26-29, 36, 44-47, 70); V, p. 77 (§39).

whole knowledge of the Bible must be derived exclusively from the Bible itself") does not express precisely what he actually demands. In the first place, the knowledge of the language of the Bible has to be derived primarily, as he maintains, not from the Bible, but from a certain tradition.[6] Besides, as for the knowledge of the lives, etc. of the authors, and of the fate of their books, it may not be impossible to derive it partly from the Bible, but there is certainly no reason why it should be an indispensable duty to derive it exclusively from the Bible; Spinoza himself welcomed every reliable extraneous information shedding light on matters of this kind.[7] Furthermore, he does not say a word to the effect that the Biblical statements regarding the various significant subjects must be arranged according to principles supplied by the Bible itself; there are reasons for believing that his own arrangement of Biblical subjects would have had no Biblical basis whatever, but would have corresponded to what he considered the natural order of the subjects in question.[8] Above all, the interpretation proper, as he conceives of it, consists in ascertaining the definitions of the subjects dealt with by the Bible; but these definitions are admittedly not supplied by the Bible itself; in fact, *qua* definitions they transcend the horizon of the Bible; thus the interpretation of the Bible consists, not in understanding the Biblical authors exactly as they understood themselves but in understanding them better than they understood themselves. We may say that Spinoza's formulation of his hermeneutic principle is not more than an exaggerated and therefore inexact expression of the following view: the only meaning of any Biblical passage is its literal meaning, except if reasons taken from the indubitable usage of the Biblical language demand the metaphorical understanding of the passage; certainly the disagreement of the statement of a Biblical author with the teaching of reason, of piety, of tradition, or even of another Biblical author, does not justify one in abandoning the literal meaning. Spinoza's exaggeration is sufficiently justified by the power of the position which he challenges: he

[6] *Tr.* VII, p. 105 (§40).
[7] Compare, e.g., *Tr.* IX, p. 140 (§58).
[8] Compare, e.g., the distinction between histories, revelations, and moral teachings in *Tr.* VII, pp. 98-99 (§§9-11).

had to make himself heard amidst the clamor raised by the myriads of his opponents.

There is a certain agreement between Spinoza's hermeneutic principle ("the Bible must be understood exclusively by itself") and the principle to which we adhere ("the Bible must be understood exactly as it was understood by its authors, or by its compilers"). His demand that the interpretation of the Biblical teaching and the judgment on the truth or value of that teaching be kept strictly separate, partly agrees with what we meant by distinguishing between interpretation and explanation. Yet, as we have indicated, the difference between the two principles is fundamental. According to our principle, the first questions to be addressed to a book would be of this kind: what is its subject matter, i.e. how is its subject matter designated, or understood, by the author? what is his intention in dealing with his subject? what questions does he raise in regard to it, or with what aspect of the subject is he exclusively, or chiefly, concerned? Only after these and similar questions have found their answer, would we even think of collecting and arranging the statements of the author regarding various topics discussed or mentioned in his book; for only the answers to questions like those we have indicated, would enable us to tell what particular topics referred to in his book are significant or even central. If we followed Spinoza's rule, we would start to collect and to arrange the Biblical statements regarding all kinds of subjects without any guidance supplied by the Bible itself, as to what subjects are central or significant, and as to what arrangement agrees with the thought of the Bible. Furthermore, if we followed Spinoza, we would next look out for the most universal or most fundamental teaching of the Bible as a teaching clearly presented everywhere in the Bible. But is there any necessity, or even likelihood, that the most fundamental teaching of a book should be constantly repeated? In other words, is there any necessity that the most universal or most fundamental teaching of a book should be its clearest teaching?[9] Be this as it may, we need not dwell on what we consider the deficiencies of Spinoza's Biblical hermeneutics. For any objections which we could raise against that hermeneutics would be based on the premise that

[9] *Tr.* VII, pp. 100, 102-104, 112 (§§16, 27-29, 36, 70).

the Bible is substantially intelligible, and Spinoza denies that very premise. According to him, the Bible is essentially unintelligible, since its largest part is devoted to unintelligible matters, and it is accidentally unintelligible since only a part of the data which could throw light on its meaning is actually available. It is the essential unintelligibility of the Bible—the fact that it is a "hieroglyphic" book—which is the reason why a special procedure has to be devised for its interpretation: the purpose of that procedure is to open up an indirect access to a book which is not accessible directly, i.e. by way of its subject matter. This implies that not all books, but only hieroglyphic books require a method of interpretation that is fundamentally the same as that required for deciphering the book of nature. Spinoza is primarily concerned with what the Bible teaches clearly everywhere, because only such a ubiquitous teaching could supply a clue to every hieroglyphic passage that might occur in the Bible. It is because of its essential unintelligibility that the Bible must be understood exclusively by itself: the largest part of the Bible is devoted to matters to which we have no access whatever except through the Bible.[10] For the same reason it is impossible merely to try to understand the Biblical authors as they understood themselves; every attempt to understand the Bible is of necessity an attempt to understand its authors better than they understood themselves.

There is probably no need for proving that Spinoza considered his own books, and in particular the *Treatise,* intelligible and not hieroglyphic. Hieroglyphic subjects, he indicates, are a matter of curiosity rather than useful, whereas the subjects of the *Treatise* are eminently useful.[11] In order to find out how he wants his own books to be read, we must therefore turn from his Biblical hermeneutics to his rules for reading intelligible books.

[10] Compare especially *Tr.* VII, adnot. 8 (§66 n.) with VII, pp. 98-99, 105 (§§9-10, 37), and VII, pp. 109-111 (§§58-68) with *ib.*, p. 101 (§23). See also *ep.* 21 (34§3): "plane et sine ambagibus profiteor me sacram scripturam non intelligere." Cf. *Tr.* VII, pp. 98-99, 114 (§§6-10, 78).—The distinction between what we have called the essential unintelligibility of the Bible, which is due to its subject matter (or its origin), and its accidental unintelligibility, which is due to the condition of the text, etc., is underlying also Isaac de la Peyrère's Biblical criticism. See his *Systema theologicum, ex Praeadamitarum hypothesi. Pars Prima.* (1655), IV 1.

[11] *Tr.* praef., p. 12 (§33); VII, pp. 111-112 (§69).

He does not think that there can be any difficulty that might seriously obstruct the understanding of books devoted to intelligible subjects, and hence he does not see any need for elaborate procedures conducive to their understanding. To understand a book of this kind, one does not need perfect knowledge, but at most "a very common and, as it were, boyish knowledge" of the language of the original; in fact, reading of a translation would suffice perfectly. Nor does one have to know the life of the author, his interests and character, the addressee of his book, its fate, nor the variant readings, etc. Intelligible books are self-explanatory. Contrary to what Spinoza seems to say, not hieroglyphic books, to whose subjects we have no access through our experience or insight, but intelligible books, to whose understanding the reader naturally contributes by drawing on his experience or insight "while he goes," can and must be understood by themselves. For while the meaning of hieroglyphic books must be inferred indirectly from data which are not necessarily supplied by the book itself (the life of the author, the fate of the book, etc.), the meaning of intelligible books can and must be ascertained directly by consideration of its subject matter and of the intention of the author, i.e. of things which become truly known only through the book itself.[12] If we apply this information, as we must, to Spinoza's own books, we realize that according to his view the whole "history" of his works, the whole historical procedure as employed by the modern students of his works, is superfluous; and therefore, we may add, rather a hindrance than a help to the understanding of his books.

We add a few words of explanation. Spinoza says that for the understanding of intelligible books knowledge of the variant readings is superfluous. But he also says that there never was a book without faulty readings. He must have thought that errors which have crept into books or passages dealing with intelligible matters will easily be detected and corrected by the intelligent reader "while he goes."[13] Spinoza says that for the understanding of intelligible books knowledge of the character

---

[12] *Tr.* VII, pp. 98-99, 109-111 (§§9-10, 59-60, 67-68).
[13] *Tr.* IX, p. 135 (§32); X, p. 149 (§42); XII, pp. 165-166 (§§34-35, 37).—Carl Gebhardt (Spinoza, *Opera*, vol. II, p. 317) says: "Dieses Fehlen der Controlle (des Drucks durch den Autor) macht sich namentlich bei der *Ethica* bemerkbar. Zum Teil gehen die dadurch verschuldeten textkritischen Zweifel so tief, dass selbst die Interpretation spinozanischer Lehren von ihrer Entscheidung abhängt."

or mental cast of an author is superfluous. But when discussing
the intention of Machiavelli's *Prince*, which he could not have
considered a hieroglyphic book, he comes to a decision only by
taking into account the author's "wisdom" or "prudence," as
well as his love of political liberty.[14] Spinoza would probably
answer that he based his decision not on any previous or at any
rate extraneous knowledge of Machiavelli's life and character,
but on what every intelligent reader of the *Prince* and the
Discourses on Livy would notice. Spinoza says that even obscure
presentations of intelligible matters are intelligible. But he
doubtless knew that no negligible number of authors dealing
with intelligible matters contradict themselves. He probably
would reply that, if an author contradicts himself, the reader
does well to suspend his judgment on what the author thought
about the subject in question, and to use his powers rather for
finding out by himself which of the two contradictory assertions
is true. Consideration of whether the usage of the author's language permits the metaphorical interpretation of one of the two
contradictory assertions is clearly out of place in the case of
intelligible books, since for their understanding it is not even
necessary to know in what language they were originally composed.[15]

Our study of Spinoza's rules of reading seems to have led to
an impasse. We cannot read his books as he read the Bible
because his books are certainly not hieroglyphic. Nor can we
read them as he read Euclid and other intelligible books, because his books are not as easily intelligible to us as the non-
hieroglyphic books which he knew were to him. If an author of
Spinoza's intelligence, who speaks with so much assurance about

---

[14] *Tr. pol.* V 7. Cf. *Tr.* VII, pp. 102, 111 (§§24, 67, 68); *ep.* 43 (49§2).

[15] *Tr.* VII, pp. 101, 111 (§§21, 66-68).—Spinoza implies that in the case of
intelligible books one need not know in what manner and on what occasion
they were written—*Tr.* VII, pp. 102, 111 (§§23, 67)—; but compare what he says
about his own *Renati Des Cartes Principia Philosophiae* (see note 2 above).—When
Spinoza indicates in *Tr.* XVII adnot. 38 (§55 n.) that one has to consider the
different "states" in which the Hebrews were at different times in order not to
ascribe to Moses, e.g., such institutions as originated at a much later time, he
does not formally contradict what he implies in *Tr.* VII adnot. 8 (§65 n.), *viz.*
that the understanding of institutions does not require "history." For in the
former passage he is speaking only of institutions recorded in the Bible, i.e., in
a book which is altogether unintelligible without "history."

the most important Biblical subjects, simply confesses that he
does not understand the Bible, we on our part have to confess
that it cannot be easy to understand him. His rules of reading
are of little or no use for the understanding of books that are
neither hieroglyphic nor as easy of access as a modern manual of
Euclidean geometry. One could say of course that by laying
down rules for the two extreme cases Spinoza has given us to
understand how books of moderate difficulty have to be read:
books of this kind are neither absolutely intelligible nor absolutely unintelligible without "history"; "history" is required for
the understanding of a book to the extent to which the book is
not self-explanatory. But, if one does not want to suppress
completely the spirit of Spinoza's statements, one would have to
add in the most emphatic manner that according to him the
contribution of "history" to the understanding of truly useful
books cannot but be trivial.

The modern interpreter of Spinoza on the other hand considers it most useful, and even necessary, to understand Spinoza's
books, and is at the same time convinced that "history" makes
a most important contribution to their understanding. The interpreter thus contradicts Spinoza in a point which, apparently,
is of no small importance: he holds that Spinoza's books cannot
be understood on the basis of Spinoza's own hermeneutic principles. Thus the question becomes inevitable, whether it is
possible to understand Spinoza on the basis of the rejection of
these principles. One's answer will depend on what importance
one attaches to the controversial issue. If it is true that the
problem of "history," fully understood, is identical with the
problem of the nature of philosophy itself, the modern interpreter is separated from Spinoza by a fundamental difference of
orientation. The modern interpreter takes it for granted that in
order to be adequate to its task, philosophy must be "historical,"
and that therefore the history of philosophy is a philosophic
discipline. He presupposes then from the outset—by the very
fact that he is a philosophic historian of philosophy and not a
mere antiquarian—that Spinoza's whole position as Spinoza
himself presented and understood it, is untenable because it is
manifestly not "historical." He lacks then the strongest incentive

for attempting to understand Spinoza's teaching as Spinoza himself understood it, that incentive being the suspicion that Spinoza's teaching is *the* true teaching. Without that incentive no reasonable man would devote all his energy to the understanding of Spinoza, and without such devotion Spinoza's books will never disclose their full meaning.

It would seem then that one cannot understand Spinoza if one accepts his hermeneutic principles, nor if one rejects them. To find a way out of this difficulty, we must first understand why Spinoza could rest satisfied with his unsatisfactory remarks about the manner in which serious books must be read. It does not suffice to say that he was exclusively concerned with *the* truth, the truth about the whole, and not with what other people taught about it. For he knew too well how much he was indebted for his grasp of what he considered *the* truth to some books written by other men. The true reason is his contempt for that thought of the past which can become accessible only through the reading of very difficult books. Other things being equal, one needs more of "history" for understanding books of the past than for understanding contemporary books. If a man believes that the most useful or important books are contemporary ones, he will hardly ever experience the need for historical interpretation. This was the case of Spinoza. The only book which he published under his name is devoted to the philosophy of Descartes. The only books (apart from the Bible) on which he ever wrote extensively, were books by Descartes and Boyle, i.e. by contemporaries. The authority of Socrates, Plato and Aristotle, to say nothing of their followers, did not carry much weight with him. He admired Epicurus, Democritus, Lucretius and their followers much more.[16] Yet there are hardly any unambiguous traces of his having studied their works, or the remnants of their works, with any assiduity; he had easy access to their teaching through the writings of Gassendi, a contemporary. As regards political philosophy in particular, he flatly declares that all political philosophy prior to his own is useless.[17] He confesses to owe much to certain "outstanding men who have

---

[16] *Ep.* 56 (60 §13). Cf. *Tr.* praef., p. 9 (§§18-19); I, p. 19 (§19).
[17] *Tr. pol.* I 1.

written many excellent things about the right way of life, and who have given counsels full of wisdom to mortals";[18] he probably has in mind authors like Seneca and Cicero; but the doctrines to which he refers are by their nature easy for everyone to understand. Regarding a much more difficult and basic teaching, *viz.* the thesis that God is the immanent cause of all things, he surmises that he says the same thing as "all ancient philosophers, although in a different manner," and as "all ancient Hebrews, as far as one can conjecture from some traditions, which however have been adulterated in many ways." This is not the way in which one would speak of definite literary sources. Besides, he was probably more sincere when he indicated that his doctrine of God deviated radically from all other teachings which he knew.[19] Naturally, he had read a considerable number of old books, especially in his youth; but the question is what importance the mature Spinoza attached to them and to their study. His attitude is not surprising: the conviction that they were achieving a progress beyond all earlier philosophy or science, a progress condemning to deserved oblivion all earlier efforts, was rather common among the men who were responsible for the emergence of modern philosophy or science.

But Spinoza, who wrote for posterity rather than for his contemporaries, must have realized that the day would come when his own books would be old books. Yet, if they contain *the* true, i.e. *the* clear and distinct account of the whole, there seems to be no reason why they should not be directly intelligible at all times, provided they survive at all. This very reply however seems to prove conclusively that Spinoza did not consider a crucial possibility which to us is so obvious: the possibility that the whole orientation of a period may give way to a radically different orientation, and that after such a change has taken

---

[18] *Ethics* III praef. Cf. *Tr.* VII, p. 111 (§68).

[19] *Ep.* 73 (21 §2). Cf. *Ethics* II 7 schol. Cf. *ep.* 6 *vers. fin.*: "dico quod multa attributa quae ab iis (*sc.* concinnatoribus) et *ab omnibus mihi saltem notis* deo tribuuntur; ego tanquam creaturas considero, et contra alia, propter praejudicia ab iis tanquam creaturas considerata, ego attributa dei esse . . . contendo. et etiam quod Deum a natura non ita separem ut *omnes, quorum apud me est notitia,* fecerunt." Cf. also Spinoza's polemics against what "all" teach regarding the infinite in *ep.* 12 (29§2). As for the reference to "all ancient Hebrews," cf. *Tr.* III, p. 48 (§18) and XI, p. 158 (§24).

place one cannot bridge the gulf between the thought of the later age and that of the earlier age but by means of historical interpretation. From Spinoza's point of view one would have to retort that he denied, not the possibility of such a change occurring after the emergence of his doctrine, but its legitimacy. The abandonment of his approach in favor of a radically different one would have been in his eyes a manifest blunder, and not more than a new example of the frequently experienced relapse of human thought into the servitude of superstition.

Spinoza's rules of reading derive from his belief in the final character of his philosophy as *the* clear and distinct and, therefore, *the* true account of the whole. If we reject Spinoza's belief *a limine*, we will never be able to understand him because we will lack the necessary incentive for attempting to understand him properly. On the other hand, if we open our minds, if we take seriously the possibility that he was right, we can understand him. Apart from the fact that we would have the indispensable incentive, we would be in a position to correct his insufficient rules of reading without having to fear that in doing so we would deviate radically from his fundamental principles. For if these principles are sound, questions of hermeneutics cannot be central questions. More precisely, the need for a correction of Spinoza's hermeneutics follows directly from the assumption that his teaching is *the* true teaching. On the basis of this assumption, *the* true teaching is accessible to us only through certain old books. Reading of old books becomes extremely important to us for the very reason for which it was utterly unimportant to Spinoza. We shall most urgently need an elaborate hermeneutics for the same reason for which Spinoza did not need any hermeneutics. We remain in perfect accord with Spinoza's way of thinking as long as we look at the devising of a more refined historical method as a desperate remedy for a desperate situation, rather than as a symptom of a healthy and thriving "culture."

Our argument implies the suggestion that today *the* truth may be accessible only through certain old books. We still have to show that this suggestion is compatible with Spinoza's principles. Spinoza knew that the power of the natural obstacles to philosophy, which are the same at all times, can be increased by specific mistakes.[20] The natural and sporadic outbursts against philosophy may be replaced by its deliberate and relentless suppression. Superstition, the natural enemy of philosophy, may arm itself with the weapons of philosophy and thus transform itself into pseudo-philosophy. Of pseudo-philosophies there is an indefinitely large variety, since every later pseudo-philosopher can try to improve on the achievements, or to avoid certain blunders of his predecessors. It is therefore impossible even for the most far-sighted man to foresee which pseudo-philosophies will emerge, and gain control of the minds of men in the future. Now, not indeed philosophy, but the way in which the introduction to philosophy must proceed, necessarily changes with the change of the artificial or accidental obstacles to philosophy. The artificial obstacles may be so strong at a given time that a most elaborate "artificial" introduction has to be completed before the "natural" introduction can begin. It is conceivable that a particular pseudo-philosophy may emerge whose power cannot be broken but by the most intensive reading of old books. As long as that pseudo-philosophy rules, elaborate historical studies may be needed which would have been superfluous and therefore harmful in more fortunate times.

Before we consider whether the dominant thought of the present age would have to be described from Spinoza's point of view as a pseudo-philosophy of this kind, we shall venture to express our suggestion in terms of the classic description of the natural obstacles to philosophy. People may become so frightened of the ascent to the light of the sun, and so desirous of making that ascent utterly impossible to any of their descendants, that they dig a deep pit beneath the cave in which they were born, and withdraw into that pit. If one of the descendants desired to ascend to the light of the sun, he would first have to try to reach the level of the natural cave, and he would have to invent new and most artificial tools unknown and unnecessary to those who dwelt in the natural cave. He would be a fool, he would never see the light of the sun, he would lose the last

[20] *Tr.* XI end, and praef., p. 7 (§9). Compare Maimonides, *Guide of the Perplexed* I 31 (34 b Munk).

vestige of the memory of the sun, if he perversely thought that
by inventing his new tools he had progressed beyond the ancestral cave-dwellers.

According to Spinoza, the natural obstacle to philosophy is
man's imaginative and passionate life, which tries to secure itself
against its breakdown by producing what Spinoza calls superstition. The alternative that confronts man by nature, is then that
of a superstitious account of the whole on the one hand, and of
the philosophic account on the other. In spite of their radical
antagonism, superstition and philosophy have this in common,
that both attempt to give a final account of the whole, and both
consider such an account indispensable for the guidance of
human life. Philosophy finds itself in its natural situation as long
as its account of the whole is challenged only by superstitious
accounts and not yet by pseudo-philosophies. Now, it is obvious
that that situation does not exist in our time. The simplicity and
directness of the two original antagonists who fought their secular struggle for the guidance of mankind on the one plane of
truth, has given way to a more "sophisticated" or a more "prag-
matic" attitude. The very idea of a final account of the whole—
of an account which necessarily culminates in, or starts from,
knowledge of the first cause or first causes of all things—has been
abandoned by an ever-increasing number of people, not only as
incapable of realization but as meaningless or absurd. The authorities to which these people defer are the twin-sisters called
Science and History. Science, as they understand it, is no longer
the quest for the true and final account of the whole. Accordingly, they are used to distinguish between science and philosophy, or between the scientist and the philosopher.[21] Thus they
tacitly, and sometimes even openly, admit the possibility of an
unphilosophic science and of an unscientific philosophy. Of
these two endeavors, science naturally enjoys a much higher
prestige: it is customary to contrast the steady progress of science
with the failure of philosophy. The philosophy which is still
legitimate on this basis, would not be more than the handmaid
of science called methodology, but for the following considera-

---

[21] As for Spinoza's synonymous use of "philosophy" and "science," cf., e.g.,
Tr. II, pp. 35-36 (§§26-27); IV, p. 60 (§11); XIII, pp. 167-168, 172 (§§4, 7, 27);
XIV, p. 174 (§§5, 7); XV, p. 187 (§38); XIX, pp. 237-238 (§§54, 62).

tion. Science, rejecting the idea of a final account of the whole, essentially conceives of itself as progressive, as being the outcome of a progress of human thought beyond the thought of all earlier periods, and as being capable of still further progress in the future. But there is an appalling discrepancy between the exactness of science itself, and the quality of its knowledge of its progressive character as long as science is not accompanied by the effort, at least aspiring to exactness, truly to prove the fact of progress, to understand the conditions of progress, and therewith to secure the possibility of future progress. Science in the present-day meaning of the term is therefore necessarily accompanied by history of human thought either, as originally, in a most rudimentary form or, as today, in a much more elaborate form. It is the history of human thought which now takes the place formerly occupied by philosophy or, in other words, philosophy transforms itself into history of human thought. The fundamental distinction between philosophy and history which was implied in the original meaning of philosophy, gives way to a fusion of philosophy and history. If the history of human thought is studied in the spirit of modern science, one reaches the conclusion that all human thought is "historically conditioned," or that the attempt to liberate one's thought from one's "historical situation" is quixotic. Once this has become a settled conviction constantly reinforced by an ever-increasing number of new observations, the idea of a final account of the whole, of an account which as such would not be "historically conditioned," appears to be untenable for reasons which can be made manifest to every child. Thereafter, there no longer exists a direct access to the original meaning of philosophy, as quest for the true and final account of the whole. Once this state has been reached, the original meaning of philosophy is accessible only through recollection of what philosophy meant in the past, i.e., for all practical purposes, only through the reading of old books.

As long as the belief in the possibility and necessity of a final account of the whole prevailed, history in general and especially history of human thought did not form an integral part of the philosophic effort, however much philosophers might have appreciated reports on earlier thought in their absolutely ancillary function. But after that belief has lost its power, or after a complete break with the basic premise of all earlier philosophic thought has been effected, concern with the various phases of earlier thought becomes an integral part of philosophy. The study of earlier thought, if conducted with intelligence and assiduity, leads to a revitalization of earlier ways of thinking. The historian who started out with the conviction that true understanding of human thought is understanding of every teaching in terms of its particular time or as an expression of its particular time, necessarily familiarizes himself with the view, constantly urged upon him by his subject matter, that his initial conviction is unsound. More than that: he is brought to realize that one cannot understand the thought of the past as long as one is guided by that initial conviction. This self-destruction of historicism is not altogether an unforeseen result. The concern with the thought of the past gained momentum, and increased in seriousness, by virtue of the late eighteenth- and early nineteenth-century critique of the modern approach, of modern natural science and of the moral and political doctrines which went with that science. Historical understanding, the revitalization of earlier ways of thinking, was originally meant as a corrective for the specific shortcomings of the modern mind. This impulse was however vitiated from the outset by the belief which accompanied it, that modern thought (as distinguished from modern life and modern feeling) was superior to the thought of the past. Thus, what was primarily intended as a corrective for the modern mind, was easily perverted into a confirmation of the dogma of the superiority of modern thought to all earlier thought. Historical understanding lost its liberating force by becoming historicism, which is nothing other than the petrified and self-complacent form of the self-criticism of the modern mind.

We have seen how one has to judge of the predominant thought of the present age in the light of Spinoza's principles, or how one can enlarge, in strict adherence to his principles, his view regarding the obstacles to philosophy and therewith to the understanding of his own books. One thus acquires the right in reading his books to deviate from his own rules of reading. One realizes at the same time that one cannot simply replace his rules of reading by those actually followed by numerous modern historians. It is true that what today is frequently meant by historical understanding of Spinoza's thought, *viz.* the understanding of his thought in terms of his time, could be described as a more elaborate form of what he himself would have called the "history" of his books. But it is also true that he limited the need for "history" to the understanding of hieroglyphic books. We have no right simply to disregard his view according to which books like his own can and must be understood by themselves. We merely have to add the qualification that this must be done within the limits of the possible. We have to remain faithful to the spirit of his injunction. Contrary to what he implies, we need for the understanding of his books such information as is not supplied by him and as is not easily available to every reasonable reader regardless of time and place. But we must never lose sight of the fact that information of this kind cannot have more than a strictly subordinate function, or that such information has to be integrated into a framework authentically or explicitly supplied by Spinoza himself. This holds of all knowledge which he did not supply directly and which he did not therefore consider relevant for the understanding of his books: information regarding his life, character and interests, the occasion and time of the composition of his books, their addressees, the fate of his teaching and, last but not least, his sources. Such extraneous knowledge can never be permitted to supply the clue to his teaching except after it has been proved beyond any reasonable doubt that it is impossible to make head and tail of his teaching as he presented it. This principle creates from the outset a healthy suspicion against the attempts, so vastly different among themselves, to understand Spinoza's teaching as a modification of the Kabbala or of Platonism, or as an expression of the spirit of the barocco, or as the culmination of mediaeval scholasticism. Every deviation from that principle exposes one to the danger that one tries to understand Spinoza better than he understood himself before one has understood him as he understood himself; it exposes one to the danger that one understands, not Spinoza, but a figment of one's imagination.

Historical understanding, as it is frequently practiced, seduces one into seeing the author whom one studies, primarily as a contemporary among his contemporaries, or to read his books as if they were primarily addressed to his contemporaries. But the books of men like the mature Spinoza, which are meant as possessions for all times, are primarily addressed to posterity. Hence he wrote them in such a manner as not to require for their understanding the previous knowledge of facts which, to the best of his knowledge, could be really relevant and easily accessible only to his contemporaries. The flight to immortality requires an extreme discretion in the selection of one's luggage. A book that requires for its adequate understanding the use, nay, the preservation of all libraries and archives containing information which was useful to its author, hardly deserves being written and being read at all, and it certainly does not deserve surviving its author. In particular, there must have been facts and teachings which were very important to Spinoza during his formative years when he was naturally less capable than later of distinguishing between the merely contemporary—which from Spinoza's point of view probably included much of what he knew of mediaeval philosophy—and what he considered deserving preservation. Information about his "development" can justly be regarded as irrelevant until it has been shown that Spinoza's final teaching remains mysterious without such information. Since his teaching is primarily addressed to posterity, the interpreter has always to be mindful of the difference in specific weight of the books of the mature Spinoza and his letters. The letters are primarily addressed, not to posterity, but to particular contemporaries. Whereas the works of his maturity may be presumed to be addressed primarily to the best type of readers, the large majority of his letters are obviously addressed to rather mediocre men.

The need for extraneous information derives from the fact that a man's foresight as to what could be intelligible to posterity is necessarily limited. To mention only the most striking and at the same time most important example: Spinoza could not have foreseen, or at any rate he could not have taken effective precaution against the fact that the traditional terminology of philosophy, which he employed while modifying it, would become obsolete. Thus the present-day reader of Spinoza has to learn the rudiments of a language which was familiar to Spinoza's contemporaries. To generalize from this, the interpreter of Spinoza has to reconstruct that "background" which from Spinoza's point of view was indispensable for the understanding of his books, but could not reasonably be supplied through his books, because no one can say everything without being tedious to everyone. This means that in his work of reconstruction the interpreter must follow the signposts erected by Spinoza himself and, secondarily, the indications which Spinoza left accidentally in his writings. He must start from a clear vision, based on Spinoza's explicit statements, of Spinoza's predecessors as seen by Spinoza. He must pay the greatest attention to that branch of "the philosophic tradition" that Spinoza himself considered most important or admired most highly. For instance, he cannot disregard with impunity what Spinoza says about Plato and Aristotle on the one hand, and about Democritus and Epicurus on the other. He must guard against the foolish presumption, nourished by unenlightened learning, that he can know better than Spinoza what was important to Spinoza, or that Spinoza did not know what he was talking about. He must be willing to attach greater weight to mediocre textbooks quoted by Spinoza than to classics which we cannot be sure that Spinoza has even known of. In attempting to interpret Spinoza, he must try his utmost not to go beyond the boundaries drawn by the terminology of Spinoza and of his contemporaries; if he uses modern terminology in rendering Spinoza's thought, or even in describing its character, he is likely to introduce a world alien to Spinoza into what claims to be an exact interpretation of Spinoza's thought. Only after one has completed the interpretation of Spinoza's teaching, when one is confronted with the necessity of passing judgment on it, is one at liberty, and even under the obligation, to disregard Spinoza's own indications. Spinoza claims to have refuted the central philosophic and theologic teaching of the past. To judge of that claim, or of the strength of the arguments in support of it, one must naturally consider the classics of the tradition regardless of whether or not Spinoza has known or studied them. But the understanding of Spinoza's silence about a fact or a teaching with which he must have been familiar, and whose mention or discussion would have been essential to his argument, belongs to the interpretation proper. For the suppression of something is a deliberate action.

II

ACCORDING to Spinoza, his rules for reading the Bible are not applicable to the study of his own writings for the additional reason that the Bible is addressed to the vulgar, whereas his own writings are addressed to philosophers. In the preface to the *Treatise* he explicitly urges the vulgar to leave that book alone, and he explicitly recommends the book to "the philosophic reader" or "the philosophers."[22] Books addressed to the vulgar must be adequately intelligible if read in the way in which the vulgar is used to read, i.e., their substance must disclose itself to very inattentive and careless reading. In other words, in vulgar books written for instruction the most fundamental teaching must be written large on every page, or it must be the clearest teaching, whereas the same does not hold of philosophic books.

Spinoza held that intelligible books can be fully understood without the reader's knowing to whom they are addressed. By stressing the fact that the *Treatise* is addressed to a specific group of men, he supplies us with the first clue to the specific difficulty of the work. He says that the work is meant especially for those "who would philosophize more freely if this one thing did not stand in the way, that they think that reason ought to serve as handmaid to theology." Those who think that reason or philosophy or science ought to be subservient to theology, are characterized by Spinoza as skeptics, or as men who deny the certainty of reason, and the true philosopher cannot be a skeptic.[23] Thus, the *Treatise* is addressed, not to actual philosophers,

[22] *Tr.* praef., p. 12 (§§33-34); V, pp. 77-79 (§§37-46); XIV, pp. 173-174 (§§1-2, 10); XV, p. 180 (§§2-3).

[23] *Tr.* praef., p. 12 (§34); XV, p. 180 (§§1-3); XX, p. 243 (§26). *Tr. de intellectus emendatione* pp. 18, 29-30 (§§47-48, 78-80).—Spinoza frequently uses "philosophy" and "reason" synonymously, implying of course that philosophy is the perfection of man's natural capacity of understanding; cf. *Tr.* VII, p. 117 (§94) with XV, pp. 180, 182-184, 187 (§§1-3, 12, 17, 21, 38); XIV, p. 179 (§38); praef., p. 10 (§27). Cf. IV, p. 59 (§10).—That Spinoza understands by "philosopher" a man who is not limited in his investigations by any regard whatsoever for theology, is indicated in passages such as these: *Tr.* VI, pp. 88, 95 (§§34, 37, 67-68); XII, p. 166 (§40); XIII, p. 167 (§5); XV, p. 188 (§42); *ep.* 23 (36§2).

but to potential philosophers. It is addressed to "the more prudent sort" or to those who cannot easily be duped,[24] i.e., to a class of men which is clearly more comprehensive than, and therefore not identical with, the class of the actual philosophers. The potential philosophers to whom the *Treatise* is addressed, believe in the authority of theology, i.e., of the Bible. By the Bible Spinoza understands the Old Testament and the New Testament.[25] The *Treatise* is then addressed to the potential philosophers among Christians. According to Spinoza's explicit declaration, it was the contrast between Christian belief and Christian practice that induced him to write that work.[26] If we could trust numerous explicit statements of Spinoza, his addressing Christian potential philosophers would have to be explained as follows. Christianity, and not Judaism, is based on the most perfect divine revelation. Both its universalist and its spiritual character, as contrasted with the particularist and carnal character of Judaism in particular, explain why the ascent to philosophy is easier or more natural for the Christian than for the Jew, who as such "despises" philosophy. Moreover, Spinoza's aim is to liberate philosophy from the theological domination which culminates in the persecution of philosophers by theologians and their disciples. If Christianity is the religion of love par excellence, whereas the Old Testament commands "thou shalt love thy neighbor, and hate thine enemy," Spinoza's plea for toleration is more naturally addressed to Christians than to Jews.[27]

In spite of this, the subject matter of the *Treatise* is obviously much more Jewish than Christian. Not only does Spinoza speak more fully of the Old than of the New Testament; he also refers in numerous cases, either polemically or approvingly, to Jewish commentators in the widest sense of the term, and hardly, if ever, to Christian ones. Moreover, he is much more indebted for

[24] *Ep.* 30. Cf. *Tr.* XVII, pp. 205, 219 (§§24, 103); XVIII, p. 223 (§11); X, adnott. 21, 25 (§§1 n., 43 n.).

[25] *Tr.* XII, p. 163 (§24); XIV, p. 174 (§6); XV, pp. 180, 184-185 (§§1-3, 24).

[26] *Tr.* praef., pp. 7-8 (§§13-14). Cf. XIX, pp. 234-235 (§§38-39).

[27] *Tr.* I, p. 21 (§§23, 25); cf. II, p. 43 (§§56-57) and XI, p. 158 (§23) with II, pp. 42-43 (§§52-55); III, p. 48 and adnot. 5 (§§21, 21 n., 22); IV, pp. 64-65 (§§30-34); V, pp. 70, 77 (§§8, 38); XI, pp. 152, 158 (§§4, 24); XII, pp. 158-159, 163 (§§3, 24); XVII, pp. 214-215, 221 (§§77-82, 115); XVIII, p. 221 (§2); XIX, pp. 233-234 (§§29-30, 38). Cf. *epp.* 73 (21§§4, 7) and 19 (32§10).

his interpretations to Jewish than to Christian sources. He indicates that he is so well versed in Jewish lore that he can safely rely on his memory when speaking of Jewish subjects, or of what he had ascertained about them "a long time ago." Probably the most striking example of this Jewish background of the *Treatise* is the fact that, in illustrating the two opposed views of the relation between Bible and philosophy, Spinoza refers only to the two men whom he considered the leaders of the two camps within Judaism. He explains his refraining from philologic examination of the New Testament by his insufficient knowledge of the Greek language.[28] Generalizing from this remark, we may explain the preponderance of Jewish subject matter in the *Treatise* by the fact that Spinoza was much more versed in the Jewish than in the Christian tradition. One may go a step further in the same direction and surmise that he incorporated into that work a considerable amount of materials which he had originally used for justifying his defection from Judaism. Certain incongruities which strike the reader of the *Treatise* do not seem to admit of any other explanation. For our purpose it suffices to mention the two most outstanding examples. Spinoza says that the subject of the third chapter (the election of the Jews) is not required by the guiding purpose of the work; and one could consider applying this statement to the fourth and fifth chapters as well, which culminate in the critique of the Jewish ceremonial law. Chapters III-V would thus appear to be relics of a work primarily addressed to Jews. Besides, the *Treatise* stands or falls by the principle that the true meaning of any Biblical passage has to be established exclusively out of the Bible, and not at all with regard to the philosophic or scientific truth. But in discussing the question of miracles, Spinoza asserts, in striking contradiction to that principle, that the Biblical teaching fully agrees with the philosophic teaching, and that any Biblical passage which contradicts the philosophic teaching has to be rejected as a sacrilegious addition to Holy Writ. This method of solving the conflict between philosophy and Bible had been used with particular energy by Spinoza's older Jewish contemporary Uriel da Costa. It would seem that Spinoza's occa-

[28] *Tr.* I, p. 18 (§13); IX, pp. 135-136 (§§30-31, 36); X, p. 150 (§48); XV, pp. 180-181 (§§1-5).

sional use of that method is another relic of his youthful, as it were intra-Jewish, reflections.

The assertion that Spinoza incorporated into his *Treatise* parts of his youthful apology for his defection from Judaism is at best a plausible hypothesis. Besides, no author who deserves the name will incorporate into a book parts of an earlier writing which do not make sense in the new book. Every concern with the question of what parts of the *Treatise* might have been taken from Spinoza's early apology, seduces the interpreter into escaping from his plain duty to understand the book as composed and published by Spinoza, to the questionable pleasures of higher criticism. While it can only be surmised what parts, if any, of the *Treatise* were taken from an earlier writing of Spinoza, it can be known what function these parts fulfill in the *Treatise* itself. Let us discuss from this point of view the two difficulties to which we have referred.

Spinoza says that his principal aim in the *Treatise* is the separation of philosophy from theology, and that this aim requires the discussion of "prophets and prophecy" but does not require the discussion of the questions as to whether the prophetic gift was peculiar to the Jews and as to what the election of the Jews means.[29] This is perfectly correct as far as the surface argument of the *Treatise* is concerned. Yet the deeper argument requires the proof, as distinguished from the assertion, that prophecy is a natural phenomenon. The proof offered in the first two chapters of the *Treatise* remains unsatisfactory as long as it has not been shown that prophecy is a universal phenomenon, i.e., that it is not peculiar to the Jews. This in its turn cannot be demonstrated without previous discussion of what kind of phenomena can possibly be peculiar to a nation, or a discussion of the privileges to which a nation as nation can be chosen. Not only the third chapter, however, but the fourth and fifth chapters as well are indispensable for the fully understood argument of the *Treatise*. The largest part of the work is in fact devoted more directly to an investigation of the Old rather than of the New Testament. In his discussion of the Old Testament, or of Judaism in general, Spinoza quite naturally follows a tra-

[29] Cf. *Tr.* II, p. 44 (§58) with the heading as well as the plan of III. Cf. XIV, p. 180 (§40).

ditional Jewish arrangement of the subject matter. According to the tradition in question (which ultimately goes back to the Islamic kalâm), what we may call "theology" is divided into two parts, the doctrine of God's unity and the doctrine of God's justice. The doctrine of divine justice deals especially with prophecy, law and providence. This order is necessary because providence, or divine reward and punishment, presupposes the existence of a divine law, and the divine law in its turn presupposes divine revelation or prophecy. It is this order which underlies the plan of the first six chapters of the *Treatise* as one sees at once if one considers the connection, clearly indicated by Spinoza, between "miracles" and "providence."[30]

It is equally possible to understand from the context of the *Treatise* why Spinoza disregards in his discussion of miracles the principle of his Biblical hermeneutics. For reasons which we shall state later, Spinoza tries to present his views about theological subjects with a great deal of restraint. There is, however, one fundamental point regarding which he consistently refuses to make any unambiguous concessions, and this is precisely the possibility of miracles as supra-natural phenomena. Whereas he speaks without hesitation of supra-rational teachings, he consistently rejects the possibility of miracles proper. If he had always rejected the possibility of supra-rational teachings, he would have had no choice but either simply to identify the Biblical teaching with the rational teaching—and this would have been fatal to the separation of philosophy from theology—or else simply to deny all truth to all Biblical teachings as revealed teachings. The utmost he could dare was not always to deny the fact of supra-rational revelation but always to deny

[30] *Tr.* I-III: prophecy; IV-V: law; VI: miracles. As for the connection between miracles and providence, cf. *Tr.* VI, pp. 82, 88-89 (§§6, 34, 37, 39). Spinoza could be familiar with the order which he adopted, of the three cardinal subjects, partly from the plans of Maimonides' discussion and partly from explicit utterances of that authority; cf. *Guide* III 17 (34b-35a Munk) and 45 (98b-99a). In the light of the tradition in question, the theological part par excellence of the *Treatise* proves to be devoted to the subject of Divine justice as distinguished from the subject of Divine unity. That this inference is justified, appears from a comparison of *Tr.* I-VI with *Ethics* I appendix. It would be an exaggeration, but it would not be misleading if one were to say that the subject of the *Treatise* as a whole is Divine justice and human justice; consider *Tr.* XIX, pp. 229-232 (§§5-20).

its supra-natural or miraculous character, and he could not do this consistently or conveniently without denying the possibility of miracles proper altogether. To avoid the break with the Bible in the crucial point, he had to assert that the possibility of miracles proper is denied by the Bible itself. To maintain this assertion in the presence especially of the New Testament accounts of the resurrection of Jesus—of accounts which, as Spinoza admitted, are incompatible with his spiritualistic interpretation of Christianity—, he had no choice but to suggest that any Biblical accounts of miracles proper cannot be really Biblical but must be sacrilegious additions to Holy Writ.[31]

There are no valid reasons for doubting that the *Treatise* and all its parts are addressed to Christians. As a consequence, one does not sufficiently explain the preponderance of Jewish subject matter in the *Treatise* by referring to the fact that Spinoza had greater knowledge of the Jewish than of the Christian tradition. For this very fact would disqualify him from speaking with authority to Christians on the central subject of Christianity. The peculiarly "Jewish" character of the work must be understood in the light of Spinoza's guiding intention. If one assumes that he believed in the superiority of Christianity to Judaism, one cannot help suggesting that he wanted to give to Christians the following counsel: that they should abandon the Jewish carnal relics which have defaced Christianity almost from its beginning, or that they should return to the purely spiritual teaching of original Christianity. If the chief aim of the *Treatise* is the liberation of Christianity from its Jewish heritage, Jewish subjects will quite naturally be in the fore-

---

[31] Cf. *Tr.* VI, p. 91 (§51) with *epp.* 75 and 78 (23 §§5-7 and 25 §6). Cf. *Tr.* XV, p. 185 (§27). The explicit denial of the resurrection of Jesus in the cited letters is confirmed by the implication of *Tr.* XII, pp. 163, 166 (§§24, 39).—What we have said in the text throws light on another difficulty presented by Spinoza's discussion of miracles. In his thematic discussion of the Biblical teaching, he says that the Bible teaches only indirectly that there are no miracles proper, and yet he adds that any contradictory Biblical passage must be rejected as a sacrilegious addition. But in the concluding section of the chapter on miracles he says that the Bible teaches directly that there are no miracles proper, and yet he adds that this explicit Biblical teaching is not in any way obligatory. That is to say, the Biblical teaching is either merely implicit and at the same time sacred, or it is explicit and at the same time indifferent from a religious point of view: it is certainly not explicit and at the same time obligatory. Cf. *Tr.* VI, pp. 89-91 (§§39-51) with *ib.*, 95-96 (§§66-71).

ground of the discussion, and the author's qualification as a teacher of things Christian to Christians will be enhanced rather than diminished by the fact that he is more deeply versed in the Jewish than in the Christian tradition.

The modern historian is inclined to interpret the purpose of the *Treatise,* and therewith to answer the question regarding its addressees, in terms of the particular circumstances of Spinoza's life or of his time. There are even some statements of Spinoza which apparently support such an approach. But the statements in question are necessarily misunderstood if they are not grouped around the central fact that the *Treatise* is not addressed to Spinoza's contemporaries in particular. It is addressed to potential philosophers who are Christians. Men of this kind, and hence Spinoza's problem as well as its solution, are coeval with Christianity, and not peculiar to Spinoza's age. This does not do away with the fact that, according to Spinoza's explicit statement, not only philosophy and the subject matter itself, but "the time" as well required of him the investigations presented in the *Treatise.*[32] We have to see how this agrees with what one might call the timeless character of the purpose, and of the thesis, of the work.

Spinoza starts from the contrast between the Christian preaching of universal love and the Christian practice of persecution, especially the persecution of philosophers. This contrast existed at all times except at the very beginning of Christianity. For the decline of Christianity began very early, and its primary cause was not any guilty action. Since the Gospel was unknown to their contemporaries, the apostles were compelled to introduce it by appealing to views that were well-known and accepted at that time. Thus they laid the foundation for that fusion of faith and philosophy that contradicts the original intention of the Gospel and justifies the persecution of philosophy in the name of religion. Since the power of errors increases with the length of the time during which they remain uncontested, things became worse and worse as time went on and, but for certain facts to be mentioned immediately, the situation is worse in Spinoza's time than it had ever been before. Still, there are reasons for hoping that just in "our age" Christian society will

[32] *Tr.* II, p. 29 (§2).

return for the first time to the pure teaching of the Gospel. This hope is grounded on facts such as these: there are now in existence Christian republics or democracies, i.e., societies which by their nature require freedom of public discussion; there are no longer any prophets whose authoritative demeanor is incompatible with urbanity; the unitary ecclesiastical system of Christianity has been dissolved.[33] All this does not mean more, however, than that the chances of a general acceptance by Christian society of the true Christian teaching in its purity, or the possibilities of its publication, are greater in Spinoza's time than ever before. It does not mean at all that that teaching was not equally accessible to the free minds of all ages since the beginnings of Christianity.

III

THE THEOLOGICAL part of the *Treatise* opens and concludes with the implicit assertion that revelation or prophecy as certain knowledge of truths which surpass the capacity of human reason is possible. This assertion is repeated, explicitly or implicitly, in a considerable number of other passages of the work.[34] Yet there are also passages in which the possibility of any supra-rational knowledge is simply denied.[35] Spinoza contradicts himself then regarding what one may call the central subject of his book. To suspend one's judgment on what he thought about that subject would be tantamount to throwing away the *Treatise* as a completely unintelligible book. Now, there is no reason why a sincere believer in revealed and supra-rational teachings should declare that man has no access whatever to truth except through

[33] *Tr. praef.*, pp. 7-9 (§§12, 14-20); I, p. 16 (§7); VII, pp. 97-98, 105, 112 (§§1-5, 38-39, 70); VIII, p. 118 (§§2-3); XI, pp. 153, 157-158 (§§8, 21-24); XII, p. 159 (§4); XIV, pp. 173, 180 (§§2, 4, 40); XVIII, pp. 225-226 (§§24-25); XIX, pp. 235-237 (§§43, 50, 52-53); XX, pp. 245-246 (§§39-40).

[34] *Tr.* I, pp. 15-16, 20-21, 28 (§§1-4, 6-7, 22-23, 45); XV, pp. 184-185, 188 (§§22, 26-27, 44). Cf., e.g., VI, p. 95 (§65); VII, pp. 98-99, 114 (§§8-10, 78); XI, pp. 155-156 (§§14-15); XII, pp. 162-163 (§§21-22); XIII, pp. 168, 170 (§§6-8, 20); XVI, pp. 198-200 (§§53-56, 61, 64). Cf. *ep.* 21 (34 §§3, 23).

[35] *Tr.* V, p. 80 (§49); XIII, p. 170 (§17); XIV, p. 179 (§38); XV, pp. 184, 188 (§§21, 23, 42). Cf. IV, p. 62 (§20); VII, p. 112 (§72); also L. Meyer's preface to *Renati Des Cartes Principiorum etc., vers. fin.*

sense-perception and reasoning, or that reason or philosophy alone, as distinguished from revelation or theology, possesses and justly claims for itself the realm of truth, or that belief in invisible things which cannot be demonstrated by reason is simply absurd, or that what are said to be teachings "above reason" are in truth dreams or mere fictions and "by far below reason." This observation by itself solves the difficulty: Spinoza did not admit the possibility of any supra-rational teachings. Yet we cannot dispense with a more detailed discussion of Spinoza's self-contradictions. For there occur in the *Treatise* a considerable number of them, some of which cannot be disposed of as easily as the one just mentioned. We are in need of an exact and universal rule that would enable us to decide with certainty in all cases which of two given contradictory statements of Spinoza expresses his serious view.

We shall first enumerate a few additional examples of important contradictions. Spinoza asserts that once philosophy and theology (or reason and faith) are radically separated from each other or restricted to their peculiar realms, there will be no conflict between them. Philosophy, and not theology, aims at truth; theology, and not philosophy, aims at obedience. Now, theology rests on the fundamental dogma that mere obedience, without the knowledge of the truth, suffices for salvation, and this dogma must be either true or untrue. Spinoza asserts that it is a supra-rational truth. But he also asserts that supra-rational truths are impossible. If the second assertion is accepted, it follows that the very foundation of theology is an untruth.[36] Hence, philosophy and theology, far from being in perfect accord with each other, actually contradict each other. Another form of the same contradiction is presented by the assertions that theology (or the Bible or prophecy) is not authoritative regard-

---

[36] This conclusion is confirmed by the facts that obedience (*viz.*, to God) presupposes that God is a lawgiver or ruler, and that reason refutes this presupposition; cf. *Tr.* IV, pp. 62-65 (§22-37) and XVI adnot. 34 (§53 n.). In accordance with the conclusion that we have drawn in the text, Spinoza says that faith requires, not so much true dogmas, as pious ones, "although there may be among them very many which have not even a shadow of truth"; cf. XIV, p. 176 (§20) and XIII, p. 172 (§29).—Cf. XV, pp. 182, 187, 188 (§§11-12, 38, 43); XII, p. 159 (§6); *ep.* 21 (34 §§3, 23) on the one hand with XV, p. 185 (§§26-27) and the passages cited in the preceding note on the other.

ing any merely speculative matters, and that theology is authoritative regarding some merely speculative matters.[37]—Spinoza asserts that the Biblical teaching regarding providence is identical with the philosophic teaching. On the other hand, he asserts that only philosophy (and hence not the Bible) teaches the truth about providence; for only philosophy can teach that God cares equally for all men, i.e., that one fate meets the just and the unjust;[38] in other words, that there is no providence at all. This agrees with the implicit thesis that there is a fundamental antagonism between reason and faith.—Spinoza uses "prophecy" and "Bible" as virtually synonymous terms, and he asserts that the only source for our knowledge of the phenomenon of prophecy is the Bible. But he also asserts that the augurs of the pagans were true prophets,[39] and thus implies that the first book of Cicero's *De divinatione*, for example, would be as good a source for the study of prophecy as the Bible.

The contradictions regarding Christianity, or the New Testament, require a somewhat more extensive treatment. Spinoza asserts first that no one except Jesus (whom he regularly calls Christ) has reached the superhuman excellence sufficient for receiving, without the aid of the imagination, revelations of supra-rational content; or that he alone—in contradistinction to the Old Testament prophets in particular—truly and adequately understood what was revealed to him. He is therefore prepared to say that the wisdom of God has taken on human nature in Christ, and that Christ is the way of salvation.[40] These statements must be understood, i.e., corrected, in the light of Spinoza's denial of supra-natural phenomena. Since the laws of nature in general, and of human nature in particular, are always and everywhere the same, or since there is never anything radically "new," the mind of Jesus, who had a human body, cannot

[37] Cf. *Tr.* XV, p. 188 (§42) and II, p. 35 (§24) with V, p. 77 (§38), XIII, p. 168 (§6), and XX, p. 243 (§22).

[38] Cf. *Tr.* VI, pp. 82, 95-96 (§§6, 66-71) with VI, pp. 87-88 (§§37, 32-34, 36); XIX, pp. 229, 231-232 (§§8, 20); XIV, pp. 177-178 (§27); *Ethics* I app.

[39] Cf. *Tr.* III, p. 53 (§39) with I, pp. 15, 16 (§§1, 7); VI, p. 95 (§63); VII, p. 98 (§6); XII, p. 163 (§27); XIV, p. 179 (§38); XV, p. 188 (§44).—Cf. also the contradiction between XVII, p. 219 (§§105-106) and XI, p. 152 (§§5-6).

[40] *Tr.* I, pp. 20-21 (§§22-25); IV, pp. 64-65 (§§30-32). Cf. *epp.* 73 (21 §4) and 75 (23 §9).

have been superhuman.[41] In other words, since man has no higher faculty than reason, or since there cannot be suprarational truths, Jesus cannot possibly have been more than the greatest philosopher who ever lived. The second of the two thematic treatments of Jesus which occur in the *Treatise* fully confirms this conclusion. If Spinoza affirms "with Paul" that all things are and move in God, he can be presumed to have believed that his own doctrine of God as the immanent cause of all things goes back to Jesus himself. He even proves that Jesus' knowledge was of necessity purely rational, because Jesus was sent to teach the whole human race and therefore he had to conform to the opinions common to the whole human race, i.e., to the fundamental principles of reason; whereas the Old Testament prophets had to conform merely to the opinions of the Jews, i.e., to a particular set of prejudices.[42] Or, more precisely, whereas the Old Testament prophets were themselves under the spell of the popular prejudices, Jesus and the apostles only adapted freely the expression of their rational thoughts to the popular prejudices.[43] Not indeed the exoteric teaching of the New Testament but its esoteric teaching is genuinely philosophic. This conclusion is, however, strikingly at variance with the chief purpose of the *Treatise*. The radical separation of philosophy and Bible would be a preposterous demand if the esoteric teaching of the New Testament were the peak of philosophic wisdom. Besides, when Spinoza affirms "with Paul" that all things are and move in God, he adds that the same view was perhaps held by all ancient philosophers and by all ancient Hebrews. He speaks with high regard of Solomon's teaching about God and he calls Solomon simply "the philosopher." Yet philosophy, as Spinoza conceives of it, presupposes the knowledge of mathematics, and Solomon had hardly any mathematical knowledge; moreover, the people accepted Solomon's sayings as religiously as those of the prophets, whereas the people would

[41] *Tr.* I, p. 16 (§3). Consider the use of the *modus irrealis* in I, pp. 20-21 (§22) and I adnot. 3 (§40 n.). Cf. III, p. 47 (§12); VI, p. 95 (§§66-67); XII, pp. 159-160 (§7); *Ethics* III praef.

[42] *Tr.* IV, pp. 64-65 (§§30-36). Cf. XI, p. 154 (§11). Cf. also the preface to the *Ethics* in the *Opera posthuma*.

[43] *Tr.* II, pp. 42-43 (§§52-57); V, pp. 77-78 (§§37-40); XI, p. 158 (§23). Cf. the argument of XI as a whole.

deride rather than respect philosophers who lay claim to authority in religious matters. Thus it would be more accurate to ascribe to Solomon, not philosophy, but popular wisdom, and accordingly to apply the same description to the teaching of Jesus.[44] This agrees with the facts that, according to Spinoza, the doctrine of "the Scripture," i.e., of both Testaments, contains "no philosophic things but only the most simple things," and that he probably regarded his teaching, i.e., the true philosophic teaching, about God as opposed to all earlier teachings.[45] The rational teaching that Spinoza would seem to have seriously ascribed to Jesus, was hardly more than rational morality. Yet he does not consistently maintain that the true moral teaching was discovered, or preached for the first time, by Jesus. To say nothing of the fact that it is by nature accessible to all human beings at all times, it was certainly known to, and preached by, the prophets and wise men of the Old Testament.[46] The teaching that is characteristic of Jesus or of the New Testament in general is not rational morality itself but its combination with such a "history" as permitted its being preached to the common people of all nations. In other words, the substance of the teaching of the two Testaments is identical. They differ only in this: the Old Testament prophets preached that identical teaching by virtue of the Mosaic Covenant, and therefore addressed it only to the Jews, whereas the apostles preached it by virtue of the passion of Jesus, and therefore addressed it to all men.[47] Now the combination of rational morality with a "historical" basis of either kind implies that the rational morality is presented in the form of a divine command, and hence that God is presented as a lawgiver. Thus the New Testament demands obedience to God as does the Old, and therefore both Testaments are equally in conflict with the philosophic teaching according to which God cannot be conceived as a lawgiver. "To know Christ according to the spirit" means to believe that God is merciful; but philosophy teaches that it does not make sense

[44] *Tr.* II, pp. 36, 41 (§§29, 48); IV, p. 66 (§40); VI, p. 95 (§67); VII, p. 114 (§79); XI, p. 156 (§15). *Ep.* 73 (21 §2).

[45] *Tr.* XIII, p. 167 (§4); XIV, p. 174 (§8); XV, p. 180 (§2). Cf. page 153 above.

[46] *Tr.* IV, pp. 66-68 (§§40-46, 48); V, pp. 71-72 (§§10-13); VII, p. 99 (§11); XII, p. 162 (§19); XIX, p. 231 (§16).

[47] *Tr.* XII, pp. 163, 165-166 (§§24, 37); XIX, p. 231 (§16).

to ascribe mercy to God.[48] In short, the New Testament is not more rational than the Old. There is then no reason why the apostles, for example, should have been more emancipated from the prejudices of their age than the Old Testament prophets had been. In defending his *Treatise* in one of his letters, if not in the *Treatise* itself, Spinoza admits that all apostles believed in the bodily resurrection of Jesus and hence were under the spell of popular prejudices.[49] There may be more of reasoning in the New Testament than in the Old, and the greatest Old Testament prophet may never have produced a single legitimate argument; but this does not mean of course that there are no illegitimate arguments in the New Testament.[50] Philosophic statements occur especially in Paul's Epistles, but no more than in the writings ascribed to Solomon. Paul's philosophic utterances could be traced to his desire to be a Greek with the Greeks, or to make the Gospel acceptable to a multitude tainted by philosophy; the most philosophic utterances of the New Testament would thus appear to be simply borrowings from Greek philosophy. Furthermore, since these utterances were made in deliberate accommodation to the prejudices of their addressees, they do not necessarily agree with Paul's own views. Above all, Paul's pedagogic use of philosophy seems to have laid the foundation for the fatal fusion of philosophy and theology against which the whole *Treatise* is directed. Certainly Paul's teaching of justification "by faith alone" contradicts what Spinoza considers the central and most useful teaching of the Bible.[51] One could think for a moment that by insisting on the universalistic character of the New Testament, as distinguished from the particularistic character of the Old, Spinoza denies the identity, which he elsewhere asserts, of the moral teaching of the two Testaments. Yet he quotes the statement "love thy neighbour and hate thine enemy" in order to prove, not the difference, but the basic identity of the teaching of the Sermon on the Mount with that of Moses. The difference between the commands "hate thine

[48] *Tr.* IV, p. 64 (§30); XIII, pp. 171-172 (§26); XIV, pp. 174, 178 (§§6-8, 28).
[49] *Epp.* 75 (23 §5) and 78 (25 §6).
[50] *Tr.* XI, pp. 152-153 (§§5-7); XIV, pp. 175-176 (§§17-18). Cf. *ep.* 75 (23 §7).
[51] *Tr.* XI, pp. 156-158 (§§15, 21, 23-24); XII, p. 166 (§40); XIII, p. 167 (§3); XIV, pp. 175-176 (§§14-19); III, p. 54 (§46). Cf. the implicit criticism of Paul in I, pp. 21, 28-29 (§§25, 46).

enemy" (i.e., the foreigner) and "love thine enemy" is exclusively due to the changed political circumstances of the Jewish people: Moses could think of the establishment of a good polity, whereas Jesus (just as Jeremiah before him) addressed a people which had lost its political independence.[52] Spinoza does not consistently grant that what the New Testament teaches in regard to private morality is superior to the Old Testament teaching. But even if he did, this would be outweighed in his opinion by the fact that Christianity, owing to the circumstances of its origin, offers much stronger support for the dualism of spiritual and temporal power, and therewith for perpetual civil discord, than the Old Testament teaching, which was originated by Moses, who was king in fact if not in name. For the safety of the community is the highest law.[53] To sum up: Spinoza's identification of the teaching, or the esoteric teaching, of the New Testament with the true teaching is contradicted in numerous passages of the *Treatise*.

Our last example shall be a contradiction which we have been forced to imitate in our own presentation and which has the advantage that we can resolve it by having recourse to Spinoza's own explanation of a similar difficulty. In one set of passages of the *Treatise* Spinoza suggests that the Bible is hieroglyphic, i.e., unintelligible on account of its subject matter. In accordance with this view, he explicitly says in one of his letters that he simply does not understand the Bible. This view exposes him to the danger of being forced to admit that the Bible is rich in mysteries and requires for its understanding supra-rational illumination;[54] it is at any rate incompatible with the whole meaning and purpose of the *Treatise*. There is another set of passages in which Spinoza says with equal definiteness that the Bible is easily intelligible on account of its subject matter, that all difficulties obstructing its understanding are due to our insufficient knowledge of the language, the poor condition of the text and similar causes,[55] and that almost all these difficulties can be

[52] *Tr.* XIX, p. 233 (§§29-30); XII, pp. 165-166 (§37); VII, pp. 103-104 (§§30-33).
[53] *Tr.* XVIII, pp. 225-226 (§25); XIX, pp. 232, 236-238 (§§22-24, 50-59). Cf. V, pp. 70-72 (§§8-9, 13-14).
[54] *Tr.* VII, pp. 98, 112 (§§9, 23); XII, p. 159 (§4); II, pp. 35, 36 (§§25, 29).
[55] *Tr.* V, pp. 76-77 (§§35-39); VII, p. 112 (§§70, 73); XIII, p. 167 (§§3-4). Cf. XIV, p. 174 (§§6-8) and II, p. 34 (§21).

overcome by the use of the right method: there is no need whatsoever for supra-rational illumination nor for an authoritative
tradition. What then does he mean by saying that he does not
understand the Bible? When mentioning in the *Treatise* the
Christology of "certain Churches," he says that he does not speak
at all about these things nor deny them, "for I willingly confess
that I do not understand them." In what is the authentic commentary on this passage, he first repeats his statement that he
does not understand the Christology of "certain Churches," but
then adds that, "to confess the truth," he considers the doctrines
in question absurd, or evidently self-contradictory.[56] Accordingly, he says that he does not understand the Bible because he
does not want "to confess the truth" that he regards the Biblical
teaching as self-contradictory. His view concerning the intelligi-
bility of the Bible must then be stated as follows: since one
cannot realize that the teaching of a book is absurd if one does
not understand that teaching, the Bible is certainly intelligible.
But it is easier to understand a book whose teaching is lucid
than a book whose teaching is self-contradictory. It is very
difficult to ascertain the meaning of a book that consists to a
considerable extent of self-contradictory assertions, of remnants
of primeval prejudices or superstitions, and of the outpourings
of an uncontrolled imagination.[57] It is still more difficult to
understand a book of this kind if it is, in addition, poorly compiled and poorly preserved. Yet many of these difficulties can
be overcome by the use of the right method.

Spinoza, who regarded the Bible as a book rich in contradictions, has indicated this view in a book that itself abounds in
contradictions. We have to see whether his treatment of Biblical
contradictions does not supply us with some help for the understanding of his own work. We must limit ourselves to what he
has to say about contradictions between non-metaphoric statements of one and the same speaker. His rule is that in such
cases one has to suspend one's judgment as to what the speaker
thought about the subject in question, unless one can show that

---

[56] *Tr.* I, p. 21 (§24); *ep.* 73 (21 §5).

[57] *Tr.* XV, pp. 180, 184 (§§3, 20); VI, pp. 81-82, 88 (§§1-5, 36). See especially the
explicit addition to the teaching of the *Treatise* in *ep.* 73 (21 §3), an addition
clarifying the meaning of "superstition."

the contradiction is due to the difference of the occasion or of the addressees of the two statements.[58] He applies this rule to the (real or alleged) contradiction between certain views of Jesus and Paul: while one of the views is addressed to the common people, the other is addressed to the wise. But Spinoza goes beyond this. The mere fact that Paul says on some occasions that he speaks "after the manner of man," induces Spinoza to dismiss all statements of Paul which agree with what Spinoza considers the vulgar view, as mere accommodations on the part of Paul and to say of them that they are spoken "after the manner of man."[59] If we reduce this procedure to its principle, we arrive at the following rule: if an author who admits, however occasionally, that he speaks "after the manner of man," makes contradictory statements on a subject, the statement contradicting the vulgar view has to be considered as his serious view; nay, every statement of such an author which agrees with views vulgarly considered sacred or authoritative must be dismissed as irrelevant, or at least it must be suspected even though it is never contradicted by him.[60]

Spinoza himself is an author of this kind. The first of the three "rules of living" which he sets forth in his *Treatise on the improvement of the understanding* reads as follows: "To speak with a view to the capacity of the vulgar and to practice all those things which cannot hinder us from reaching our goal (*sc.* the highest good). For we are able to obtain no small advantage from the vulgar provided we make as many concessions as possible to their capacity. Add to this that in this way they will lend friendly ears to the truth,"[61] i.e., the vulgar will thus be induced to accept such truths as the philosopher may wish to communicate to them, or they will not resent occasional heresies of the philosopher. At any rate, Spinoza means not merely that the choice of the form of his external worship, or of his religious affiliation, is a matter of mere expediency for the philosopher, but, above all, that he will adapt the expression of his thought to

---

[58] *Tr.* VII, pp. 101, 103-104 (§§21, 29-33).

[59] *Tr.* IV, p. 65 (§§33-36); II, p. 42 (§51); XVI, adnot. 34 (§53 n.).

[60] For a somewhat different formulation of the same principle, see E. E. Powell, *Spinoza and Religion*, Boston 1941, 65.

[61] *Tr. de int. em.*, p. 9 (§17). Cf. *Tr. pol.* III 10.

the generally accepted opinions by professing, as far as it is possible or necessary, these very opinions, even though he considers them untrue or absurd. That this is the correct interpretation of the phrase "ad captum vulgi loqui," appears from what Spinoza says on the subject in the *Treatise*. For in the *Treatise* he teaches that God, and Jesus and Paul as well, in speaking to men who held vulgar opinions, accommodated themselves to the capacity of their addressees by professing or at any rate not questioning those opinions. Even in the case of Moses Spinoza suggests that he may have taught things which he did not believe ("Moses believed, or at least he wished to teach . . .").[62] And he calls this kind of communication to speak "ad captum vulgi" or, more frequently, "ad captum alicuius." For to speak with a view to the capacity of the vulgar necessarily means to argue *ad hominem*, or to accommodate oneself to the particular prejudices of the particular vulgar group or individual whom one happens to address.[63] The author or authors of the Bible speak "ad captum vulgi" by communicating a salutary or pious teaching, while not only not questioning but even professing, and thus confirming, the untrue or absurd principles or premises of the addressees.[64]

It is no accident that practically the only authentic information about the precise character of Spinoza's method of communication is supplied by the *Treatise*. A full and direct explanation of this subject was, for obvious reasons, out of the question. But it was possible to assert that in the Bible, a superior mind or superior minds condescend to speak in the language of ordinary people, and that there occur in the Bible a number of statements which contradict those Biblical statements that are adapted to vulgar prejudices. Spinoza was thus led to assert

[62] *Tr.* VII, p. 101 (§22). This statement is prepared by an allusion in II, pp. 38-39 (§§36, 38). Cf. IV, pp. 45, 53 (§§6, 41).

[63] "Ad captum vulgi": VI, p. 84 (§14); XV, p. 180 (§2). "Secundum captum vulgi": XIII, p. 172 (§26); XV, pp. 178-179 (§33). "Ad captum plebis": V, p. 77 (§§37-38). "Ad captum alicuius": II, pp. 37, 43 (§§31-33, 53, 55, 57); III, pp. 44-45, 54 (§§3, 6, 46). "Ad hominem sive ad captum alicuius": II, p. 43 (§57). In III, p. 45 (§6) Spinoza applies the expression "ad captum (Hebraeorum) loqui" to a remark of his own.—Cf. XIV, p. 173 (§§1-2); VII, pp. 104, 115 (§§35, 81-82); praef., p. 6 (§§7-8).

[64] *Tr.* VI, p. 88 (§36); XV, p. 180 (§§2-3). Cf. II, pp. 32-33, 35-43 (§§15, 24, 29, 31-35, 41-45, 47, 50, 52-57); IV, p. 65 (§§33-37); V, pp. 76-78 (§§35-40); VII, pp. 98-99 (§10); XI, pp. 156, 158 (§§15, 23-24); XIV, p. 173 (§§1-3).

that at least some of the Biblical contradictions are conscious or deliberate, and therewith to suggest that there is an esoteric teaching of the Bible, or that the literal meaning of the Bible hides a deeper, mysterious meaning. By contradicting this ultimate consequence,[65] he leaves no doubt in the reader's mind as to the ironical or exoteric character of his assertion that the statements of the Bible are consciously adapted by its authors to the capacity of the vulgar. But the temporary device has fulfilled its most important function which is to supply the reader with an urgently needed piece of information. We may say that Spinoza uses the sketch of his exoteric interpretation of the Bible for indicating the character of his own exoteric procedure.

There must be scholars who believe that "to speak with a view to the capacity of the vulgar" merely means to express oneself in not too technical a language, and who argue that the alternative interpretation would be a reflection on Spinoza's .character. Those scholars are requested to consider that, if their reason were valid, Spinoza would impute to the author or authors of the Bible a morally questionable practice. Whatever may be the sound moral rule, Spinoza had certainly no compunctions to refrain from "confessing the truth," or to reveal his views while hiding them behind more or less transparent accommodations to the generally accepted opinions. When he says that the wise man will never, not even in the greatest danger, act *dolo malo*, he does not mean that the wise man will never employ any ruses; for he explicitly admits that there are good or legitimate ruses.[66] If the statesman is under an obligation to employ all kinds of ruses in the interest of the material welfare of the ruled,[67] the same duty must be incumbent on those to whom nature has entrusted the spiritual guidance of mankind, i.e., on the philosophers, who are much more exposed to the

[65] *Tr.* praef., p. 9 (§18); II, pp. 36-37 (§30); VII, p. 105 (§37); X, p. 149 (§41); XII, p. 163 (§27); XIII, pp. 167-168 (§§4-5).—When saying that God spoke with a view to the capacity of the prophets, or of the vulgar, Spinoza himself is speaking "ad captum vulgi" by accommodating himself to the belief, which he rejects, in Divine revelation. The fact that he refers with particular emphasis to Paul's speaking "after the manner of man" does not prove that, in his opinion, Paul was emancipated from the vulgar opinions as such, as will have appeared from what we said on page 174 above.

[66] *Tr.* XVI, p. 192 and adnot. 32 (§§16 n., 18). *Tr. pol.* III 17. Cf. *Ethics* IV 72.

[67] Cf. *Tr.* XVI, p. 197 (§46). *Tr. pol.* I 2, III 14, 17.

suspicions of the multitude[68] than statesmen, and therefore in greater need of caution than anyone else. "Caute" was the inscription of Spinoza's signet. By this he did not primarly mean the caution required in philosophic investigations but the caution that the philosopher needs in his intercourse with nonphilosophers. The only reason which he can find for showing that the reading of histories is most useful is that we may learn through their study "to live more cautiously among men and more successfully to accommodate our actions and our life, within the limits of reason, to their way of thinking."[69] For he considered caution, and especially caution in speech, extremely difficult: "not even the most learned or experienced, to say nothing of the common people, know how to be silent. This is a common vice of men, to confide their intentions to others, even though silence is needed." If it is of the essence of the wise man that he is able to live under every form of government, i.e., even in societies in which freedom of speech is strictly denied, it is of his essence that he is able to live without ever expressing those of his thoughts whose expression happens to be forbidden.[70] The philosopher who knows the truth, must be prepared to refrain from expressing it, not so much for reasons of convenience as for reasons of duty. Whereas truth requires that one should not accommodate the words of the Bible to one's own opinions, piety requires that everyone should accommodate the words of the Bible to his own opinions,[71] i.e., that one should give one's own opinions a Biblical appearance. If true religion or faith, which according to him requires not so much true dogmas as pious ones, were endangered by his Biblical criticism, Spinoza would have decided to be absolutely silent about this subject; nay, he would have gladly admitted—in order to escape from all difficulties—that the deepest mysteries are hidden in the Bible.[72] That is to say, he would have suppressed the truths

[68] *Tr.* praef., p. 12 (§§7-8); II, pp. 29-30 (§2); VII, p. 114 (§79); XX, pp. 244-245 (§§32-35); *ep.* 30.
[69] *Tr.* IV, pp. 61-62 (§19). Cf. *Ethics* IV 69, 70 and schol.—Regarding Spinoza's caution, see also *epp.* 7 (7 §§4-5), 13 (9 §§1-4), 82 (71 §2). Compare the discussion of this subject by Powell, *op. cit.*, 51-65.
[70] *Tr.* XX, p. 240 (§§8-9); XVI, adnot. 33 (§34 n.).
[71] Cf. *Tr.* XIV, pp. 173, 178-179 (§§3, 32-33) with VII, pp. 115, 101 (§§85, 22).
[72] *Tr.* XII, p. 159 (§4).

in question and asserted their contraries, if he had felt that these truths could do harm to the mass of readers.

If we disregard, as we must, Spinoza's references to his alleged Biblical models, the only man to whom he almost explicitly refers in the *Treatise* as a predecessor regarding his technique of presentation is Abraham ibn Ezra, of whom he speaks with unconcealed respect. Ibn Ezra "did not dare to explain openly" what he thought about the authorship of the Pentateuch, but indicated his view "in rather obscure words." One cryptic statement of ibn Ezra that is quoted by Spinoza, ends with the words "He who understands, should be silent." A certain allusion made by Spinoza himself ends with the words that he wished to remain silent on the subject in question for reasons which the ruling superstition or the difficult times do not permit to explain, but that "it suffices to indicate the matter to the wise."[73] Spinoza did not indicate what he owed to Maimonides, to whom he refers more frequently than to ibn Ezra, although in a much less friendly tone. But when saying that Moses "believed or at least wished to teach" that God is zealous or angry, he merely makes explicit what Maimonides had implied when intimating that the belief in God's anger is required, not for man's ultimate perfection, but for the good ordering of civil society.[74] For Moses, whom Maimonides considered the wisest of all men, was necessarily aware of the particular character of the belief in question, to which he gave so forceful an expression. In his *Guide of the Perplexed*, Maimonides presents his teaching by using deliberate contradictions, hidden from the vulgar, between non-metaphoric statements; it is in this way that he reveals the truth to those who are able to understand by themselves, while hiding the truth from the vulgar. He raises the question as to whether the same kind of contradiction is also used in the Bible, but he does not answer it.[75] If he has answered it in the affirmative—as, in a sense, he necessarily did—the *Guide* would be the model for Spinoza's sketch of an exoteric interpretation of the Bible, an interpretation according to which

---

[73] *Tr.* VIII, pp. 118-119 (§§4-5, 9); X, adnot. 21 (§1 n.). As regards the use of "openly" (*aperte*), compare the parallels in II, p. 36 (§27); IV, p. 65 (§35); V, p. 80 (§49); XV, p. 180 (§4); *ep.* 13 (9 §1).

[74] *Tr.* VII, p. 101 (§§21-22). *Guide* III 28 (61a Munk).

[75] *Guide* I Introduction (11 b, 3 b, 8 b Munk). Cf. *Tr.* VII, p. 113 (§75).

the Bible consists partly of vulgar statements and partly of philosophic statements which deliberately and secretly contradict the vulgar ones. At any rate, there can be no doubt that, generally speaking, Maimonides' method of presentation is meant to be an imitation of what he declared to be the method of the Bible. Maimonides in his turn was indebted for his method to "the philosophers" of his period. The typical philosopher, as presented in Yehuda Halevi's *Kuzari*, considered it perfectly legitimate for the philosopher to adhere in his speeches as well as in his actions to a religion to which he does not adhere in his thought, and he took it for granted that the philosophic teaching proper is necessarily accompanied by an exoteric teaching. Fârâbî, whom Maimonides regarded as the greatest philosophic authority of his period, virtually denied all cognitive value to religion, and yet considered conformity with the laws and the beliefs of the religious community in which one is brought up as a necessary qualification for the future philosopher.

But it would be a mistake to think that one has to look for Spinoza's models exclusively in Islamic philosophy. Fârâbî himself traces the procedure to which we have referred to Plato. Practically the same expression that Spinoza applies to Moses ("he believed, or at least he wished to teach . . .") is applied to Socrates by Lessing, who had studied Spinoza very closely, and who stated that there is no other philosophy than that of Spinoza. According to Lessing, Socrates "believed in eternal punishment in all seriousness, or at least believed in it to the extent that he considered it expedient to teach it in words that are least susceptible of arousing suspicion and most explicit." Lessing held that "all ancient philosophers" had made a distinction between their exoteric and their esoteric teaching and he ascribed the same distinction to Leibniz.[76] Spinoza's rules of living which open with "ad captum vulgi loqui" are modeled on the rules of Descartes' "morale par provision" which open with the demand for intransigent conformism in everything except in the strictly private examination of one's own opinions.[77] We can barely allude to the question of Descartes' technique of writing, to a

[76] "Leibniz von den ewigen Strafen," *Werke*, edd. Petersen and von Olshausen, XXI, 147 and 160.
[77] *Discours de la méthode*, III and VI *in princ.*

question which seems to baffle all his students because of the extreme caution with which that philosopher constantly acted. The traditional distinction between exoteric (or "disclosed") and esoteric (or "enigmatical") presentation was accessible to Spinoza also through Bacon, who insisted especially on the "secret and retired" character of the science of government. The student of Spinoza must pay particular attention to Bacon's principles regarding the use of terms: "it seemeth best to keep way with antiquity *usque ad aras;* and therefore to retain the ancient terms, though I sometimes alter the uses and definitions, according to the moderate proceeding in civil government; where although there be some alteration, yet that holdeth which Tacitus wisely noteth, *Eadem Magistratuum vocabula.*"[78] It is well-known how much Spinoza silently complied with this politic rule. He seems to allude to it when saying that if a man wishes to alter the meaning of a term to which he is accustomed, he will not be able "without difficulty" to do it consistently in speech and in writing.[79] We merely have to remember the fact that "all excellent things are as difficult as they are rare."

Spinoza's caution or thrift in communicating his views is far from being excessive if we judge his procedure by the standards admitted by a number of earlier thinkers. In fact, judged by these standards, he proves to be extraordinarily bold. That very bold man Hobbes admitted after having read the *Treatise* that he himself had not dared to write as boldly. Spinoza was very bold in so far as he went to the extreme to which he could go as a man who was convinced that religion, i.e., positive religion, is indispensable to society, and who took his social duties seriously. He was cautious in so far as he did not state the whole truth clearly and unequivocally but kept his utterances, to the best of his knowledge, within the limits imposed by what he considered the legitimate claims of society. He speaks then in all his writings, and especially in the *Treatise,* "ad captum vulgi." This

---

[78] *Advancement of Learning,* Everyman's Library ed., 92, 141-142, 205-206. Cf. *De augmentis* III 4 and VI 2.

[79] *Tr.* VII, p. 106 (§42).—v. Dunin-Borkowski, *Spinoza,* II, 217-218: "Nur im Notfall brachte (Spinoza) eine selbstersonnene Terminologie auf . . . Die altgewohnte Form sollte gleichsam die gefährliche Beunruhigung beschwichtigen. Die Leser konnten zuerst meinen, dass sie sich in einer ihnen wohl bekannten philosophischen Welt bewegten."

is not at variance with the fact that the *Treatise* is explicitly addressed, not to the vulgar, but to philosophers. For Spinoza was not in a position effectively to prevent the Latin-reading part of the vulgar from reading the *Treatise* and from thus becoming obnoxious to him. Accordingly, that book serves the purpose, not merely of enlightening the potential philosophers, but also of counteracting the opinion which the vulgar had of Spinoza, i.e., of appeasing the *plebs* itself.[80] Furthermore, the *Treatise* is addressed, not so much to philosophers simply, as to potential philosophers, i.e., to men who, at least in the early stages of their training, are deeply imbued with the vulgar prejudices: what Spinoza considers the basic prejudice of those potential philosophers whom he addresses in the *Treatise,* is merely a special form of the basic prejudice of the vulgar mind in general.[81]

In the *Treatise* Spinoza addresses potential philosophers of a certain kind while the vulgar are listening. He speaks therefore in such a way that the vulgar will not understand what he means. It is for this reason that he expresses himself contradictorily: those shocked by his heterodox statements will be appeased by more or less orthodox formulae. Spinoza boldly denies the possibility of miracles proper—in a single chapter. But he speaks of miracles throughout the work without making it clear in the other chapters that he understands by miracles merely such natural phenomena as seemed to be strange to the particular vulgar thinkers who observed or recorded them. To exaggerate for purposes of clarification, we may say that each chapter of the *Treatise* serves the function of refuting one particular orthodox dogma while leaving untouched all other orthodox dogmas.[82] Only a minority of readers will take the trouble of keeping firmly in mind the results of all chapters and of adding them up. Only a minority of readers will admit that if an author makes contradictory statements on a subject, his view may well be expressed by the statements that occur least frequently or only

---

[80] *Epp.* 30 and 43 (49 §2).

[81] Cf. *Tr.* praef., p. 12 (§34) with I, p. 15 (§2). Cf. V, p. 69 (§3). Cf. the analyses of superstition in *Tr.* praef., p. 5 (§4) and in *Ethics* I app.

[82] Fundamentally the same procedure is followed by Hobbes in the Third Part of his *Leviathan.*

once, while his view is concealed by the contradictory statements
that occur most frequently or even in all cases but one; for many
readers do not fully grasp what it means that the truth, or the
seriousness, of a proposition is not increased by the frequency
with which the proposition is repeated. One must also consider
"the customary mildness of the common people,"[83] a good-
naturedness which fairly soon shrinks from, or is shocked by, the
inquisitorial brutality and recklessness that is required for ex-
torting his serious views from an able writer who tries to conceal
them from all but a few. It is then not misleading to say that the
orthodox statements are more obvious in the *Treatise* than the
heterodox ones. It is no accident, for example, that the first
sentence of the first chapter is to the effect that prophecy or
revelation is such certain knowledge of any subject as is revealed
by God to human beings. We may call the more or less orthodox
statements the first statements, and the contradictory statements
the second statements. Of the two thematic statements about
Jesus, the first is definitely nearer to the orthodox Christian view
than is the second one.[84] This rule must be taken with a grain
of salt: the conclusion of the theological part of the *Treatise* is
hardly less orthodox than its opening. The "second statements"
are more likely to occur—according to a rule of forensic rhetoric[85]—somewhere in the middle, i.e., in places least exposed to
the curiosity of superficial readers. Thus even by presenting
his serious view in one set of explicit statements, while contradicting it in another set, Spinoza could reveal it to the more
attentive readers while hiding it from the vulgar. But not all of
Spinoza's contradictions are explicit. In some cases, not the
explicit statements, but the necessary consequences from explicit
statements contradict other explicit statements. In other cases,
we are confronted with a contradiction between two explicit
statements, neither of which is necessarily heterodox or expresses
directly Spinoza's view on the subject; but the incongruity
presented by the contradiction points to an unexpressed and

---

[83] Aristotle, *Resp. Ath.* 22. 4.

[84] Compare also *Tr.* VII, pp. 98-99 (§§6-10) with *ib.*, pp. 109-111 (§§58-66)—
note the "consulto omisi" on p. 109 (§59)—; and XIV, p. 173 (§3: licet) with *ib.*,
pp. 178-179 (§§32-33: tenetur).

[85] Cicero, *Orator* 15. 50. Cf. *De oratore* II 77. 313.

unambiguously heterodox view, by which the surface contradiction is resolved, and which thus proves to be obliquely presented by the surface contradiction.[86]

The sound rule for reading the *Treatise* is, that in case of a contradiction, the statement most opposed to what Spinoza considered the vulgar view has to be regarded as expressing his serious view; nay, that even a necessary implication of a heterodox character has to take precedence over a contradictory statement that is never explicitly contradicted by Spinoza.[87] In other words, if the final theses of the individual chapters of the *Treatise* (as distinguished from the almost constantly repeated accommodations) are not consistent with each other, we are led by the observation of this fact and our ensuing reflection to a consistent view that is no longer explicitly stated, but clearly presupposed, by Spinoza; and we have to recognize this view as his serious view, or as the secret par excellence of the *Treatise*. Only by following this rule of reading can we understand Spinoza's thought exactly as he himself understood it and avoid the danger of becoming or remaining the dupes of his accommodations.

Since Spinoza states the rule "ad captum vulgi loqui" without any qualification, there is a reasonable presumption that he acted on it also when writing his *Ethics*. This presumption cannot be disposed of by reference to the "geometric" character of that work, for "ad captum vulgi loqui" does not mean to present one's thoughts in a popular garb, but to argue *ad hominem* or *ex concessis*, i.e., from a covered position. Spinoza presented the teaching of Descartes' *Principia* also in "geometric" form, although he did not even pretend that that teaching was the true teaching.[88] Nor is the strictly esoteric or scientific character of the *Ethics* guaranteed by the fact that Spinoza did not explicitly address that work to a human type other than actual or mature philosophers, for there are many other ways in which an author can indicate that he is speaking "ad captum

[86] An example would be the statements "I understand the Bible" and "I do not understand the Bible." Regarding implicit contradictions, cf. *Tr.* XV, p. 184 (§20).

[87] Cf. page 177 above.

[88] *Ep.* 13 (9 §§1-2). Cf. L. Meyer's preface to the *Renati Des Cartes Principiorum* etc.

alicuius." To mention one of them, there has scarcely ever been a serious reader of the *Ethics* who has not also read the *Treatise;* those for whom indications suffice understood from the *Treatise* what Spinoza seriously thought of all positive religions and of the Bible, and they recognized at once from the pious references to Biblical teachings which occur in the *Ethics*[89] that this book is by no means free from accommodations to the accepted views. In other words, one cannot leave it at the impression that while the *Treatise* is, of course, exoteric, the *Ethics* is Spinoza's esoteric work simply, and that therefore the solution to all the riddles of the *Treatise* is presented explicitly and clearly in the *Ethics.* For Spinoza cannot have been ignorant of the obvious truth which, in addition, had been pointed out to him if not by Plato, at any rate by Maimonides,[90] that every book is accessible to all who can read the language in which it is written; and that therefore, if there is any need at all for hiding the truth from the vulgar, no written exposition can be strictly speaking esoteric.

In the absence of statements of Spinoza which refer specifically to the manner of communication employed in the *Ethics,* most students will feel that the question regarding the esoteric or exoteric character of that work can be settled only on the basis of internal evidence. One of the most learned contemporary students of Spinoza speaks of "the baffling allusiveness and ellipticalness of (the) style" of the *Ethics,* and he notes that in that work "statements are not significant for what they actually affirm but for the denials which they imply." He explains Spinoza's procedure by the circumstance that Spinoza, a Jew, lived in a non-Jewish environment in which he "never felt himself quite free to speak his mind; and he who among his own people never hesitated to speak out with boldness became cautious, hesitant and reserved." In the spirit of this "historical" reason (i.e., of a reason primarily based, not on Spinoza's explicit statements, but on the history of the author's life), he finally asserts "Little did he understand the real cause of his own behavior," i.e., he admits that he is trying to understand Spinoza

---

[89] *Ethics* IV 68 schol.; V 36 schol. Cf. *Tr. pol.* II 6, 22, III 10, VII 25.
[90] Maimonides, *Guide* I Introduction (4 a Munk). Cf. Plato, *Seventh Letter* 341 d4-e3 and 344c3-d5; *Phaedrus* 275c5 ff.

better than he understood himself. Apart from this, one can
hardly say that Spinoza "never" hesitated to state his views
when speaking to Jews; for only while he was very young did he
have normal opportunities of conversing with Jews, and caution
is not a quality characteristic of youth. On the principle expressed by Spinoza himself, he would have had to be extremely
"cautious, hesitant and reserved" "among his own people" if he
had lived in an age when the separation from the Jewish community was impossible for a self-respecting man of Jewish
origin, who was not honestly convinced of the truth of another
religion. Professor Wolfson also explains the particular style of
the *Ethics* by Spinoza's Talmudic and Rabbinic training, and he
accordingly demands that one must approach the study of the
Ethics in the spirit "in which the old Rabbinic scholars approach
the study of their standard texts." He admits however by
implication the very limited value of this approach by saying
that "we must constantly ask ourselves, with regard to every
statement he makes, what is the reason? What does he intend to
let us hear? What is his authority? Does he reproduce his
authority correctly or not?"[91] For, clearly, Spinoza did not know
of any authorities in philosophic investigation. There is all the
difference in the world between an author who considers himself
merely a link in the chain of a venerable tradition, and for this
very reason uses allusive and elliptical language, i.e., language
that is intelligible only on the basis of the tradition in question,
and an author who denies all value to tradition and therefore
uses various stylistic means, especially allusive and elliptical language, in order to eradicate the traditional views from the minds
of his best readers. Wolfson indicates a much more adequate
reason for the particular style of the *Ethics* by stating that
Spinoza's " 'God' is merely an appeasive term for the most
comprehensive principle of the universe," or that it was merely
a "literary pretension that his entire philosophy was evolved
from his conception of God." For it is easily understandable
that Spinoza could not neutralize accommodations of this magni-
tude but by allusions, ellipses, or similar devices. In other
words, if, as Wolfson consistently suggests, Spinoza's doctrine of

[91] H. A. Wolfson, *The philosophy of Spinoza*, Harvard University Press, 1934, I, 22-24.

God is fundamentally nothing but an "internal criticism" of traditional theology,[92] one has to admit, on the basis of Spinoza's explicit demand for, and authentic interpretation of, "ad captum
vulgi loqui," that Spinoza's doctrine of God—apparently the basis
or starting-point of his whole doctrine—belongs as such to a
mere argument *ad hominem* or *ex concessis*, that rather hides
than reveals his real starting-point. To express this in technical
language, what Spinoza presents in his *Ethics* is the "synthesis,"
whereas he suppresses the "analysis" which necessarily precedes
it.[93] That is, he suppresses the whole reasoning, both philosophic
and "politic," leading up to the definitions by which the reader
is startled and at the same time appeased when he opens that
book. If it is true that Spinoza's " 'God' is merely an appeasive
term," one would have to rewrite the whole *Ethics* without
using that term, i.e., by starting from Spinoza's concealed
atheistic principles. If it is true that Spinoza's " 'God' is merely
an appeasive term," one certainly has no longer any right to
assume that, according to Spinoza, the idea of God, to say
nothing of God's existence, is "immediately known as an intu-
ition,"[94] and therefore the legitimate starting-point for philosophy. However this may be, Spinoza's general principle of accommodation to the generally accepted views imposes on the
interpreter the duty to raise the question as to what are the
absolute limits to Spinoza's accommodation; or, in more specific
terms, as to what are the entirely non-theological considerations
that brought Spinoza into conflict with materialism, and to what
extent these considerations vouch for the explicit teaching of the
Ethics. In other words, one has to see whether there are not
anywhere in Spinoza's writings indications, however subtle, of a
strictly atheistic beginning or approach. This is, incidentally,
one reason why the *Treatise* should be read, not merely against
the background of the *Ethics*, but also by itself. Precisely the
more exoteric work may disclose features of Spinoza's thought
which could not with propriety be disclosed in the *Ethics*. While
former generations publicly denounced Spinoza as an atheist,

---

[92] Wolfson, *op. cit.*, I, 20-22, 159, 177; II, 4. Cf. *Tr.* II, p. 43 (§§56-57); VI, p.
88 (§36).
[93] Cf. the end of Descartes' "Secundae Responsiones" to objections to his
Meditationes. Cf. also *Regulae* IV.
[94] Wolfson, *op. cit.*, I, 375.

today it is almost a heresy to hint that, for all we know prior to a fresh investigation of the whole issue, he may have been an atheist. This change is due not merely, as contemporary self-complacency would have it, to the substitution of historical detachment for fanatical partisanship, but above all to the fact that the phenomenon and the causes of exotericism have almost completely been forgotten.

To return to the *Treatise*, we are now in a position to state the true reasons for certain features of that work which have not yet been sufficiently clarified. The *Treatise* is addressed to Christians, not because Spinoza believed in the truth of Christianity or even in the superiority of Christianity to Judaism, but because "ad captum vulgi loqui" means "ad captum hodierni vulgi loqui" or to accommodate oneself to the ruling opinions of one's time, and Christianity, not Judaism, was literally ruling. Or, in other words, Spinoza desired to convert to philosophy "as many as possible,"[95] and there were many more Christians in the world than there were Jews. To this one may add two "historical" reasons: after his open and irrevocable break with the Jewish community, Spinoza could no longer with propriety address Jews in the way in which, and for the purpose for which, he addresses Christians in the *Treatise;* in addition, there existed in his time a considerable group of Christians, but not of Jews, who were "liberal" in the sense that they reduced religious dogma to a minimum, and at the same time regarded all ceremonies or sacraments as indifferent, if not harmful. At any rate, Spinoza was "a Christian with the Christians" in exactly the same way in which, according to him, Paul was "a Greek with the Greeks and a Jew with the Jews."[96] It is the political and social power of Christianity which also explains why the subject matter of the *Treatise* is Jewish rather than Christian. It was infinitely less dangerous to attack Judaism than to attack Christianity, and it was distinctly less dangerous to attack the Old Testament than the New. One has only to read the summary of the argument of the first part of the *Treatise* at the beginning of the thirteenth chapter in order to see that while the explicit argument of that part is chiefly based upon, or directed against, the Old Testa-

---

[95] *Tr. de int. em.*, pp. 8-9 (§14); cf. *Ethics* V 20.—Cf. page 177 f. above. As to the oppressed condition of the Jews, cf. *Tr.* III, pp. 55, 57 (§§47, 55); VII, p. 106 (§45).
[96] Cf. *Tr.* III, p. 54 (§46); VI, p. 88 (§36).

ment, the conclusions are meant to apply to "the Scripture," i.e., to both Testaments alike.[97] When Spinoza criticizes at relatively great length the theological principle accepted by "the greatest part" of the Jews, he clearly has in mind "the greatest part" of the Christians as well, as appears from his reference, in the passage in question, to the doctrine of original sin, and from parallels elsewhere in the *Treatise*.[98] After having indicated the doubtful character of the genealogies of Jeconiah and Zerubbabel in 1 Chronicles 3, Spinoza adds the remark that he would rather have wished to remain silent on this subject, for reasons which the ruling superstition does not permit to explain. Since he had not felt any hesitation to point out the doubtful character of other Old Testament records of a similar nature, his cryptic remark can only refer to the connection between the genealogy in question and the genealogy of Jesus in the first chapter of the Gospel according to Matthew.[99] The preponderance of Jewish subject matter in the *Treatise* is then due to Spinoza's caution rather than to his insufficient knowledge of Christianity or of the Greek language.[100] His relative reticence about specifically Christian subjects could be expected to protect him against persecution by the vulgar, while it was not likely to disqualify him in the eyes of the "more prudent" readers, who could be relied upon to understand the implication of his attack on Judaism, and especially on the Old Testament.

From Spinoza's authentic interpretation of "ad captum vulgi loqui" it follows that he cannot have meant the exoteric teaching

[97] To this may be added that the accusation of tampering with the Biblical text, or of pious fraud, is directed by Spinoza not only against the Jews in regard to the Old Testament, but also against the Christians in regard to the New Testament; cf. *Tr.* VI, p. 91 (§51) with *epp.* 75 (23 §5) and 78 (25 §6).

[98] *Tr.* XV, pp. 181-182 (§§4, 10). Cf. the brief reference to fundamentally the same theological principle in V, p. 80 (§49), a reference characteristically concluding with the words: "Sed de his non est opus apertius loqui." Cf. praef., p. 8 (§§14-17).

[99] *Tr.* X, adnot. 21 (§1 n.). For the use of "superstition" in this passage, cf. *ep.* 76 (74 §§4, 14).

[100] At the end of the tenth chapter of the *Treatise,* Spinoza explains his refraining from literary criticism of the New Testament by his insufficient knowledge of the Greek language. But this does not explain why he limits his remarks on the New Testament in the eleventh chapter to the Epistles of the apostles. The reason of this striking fact is his desire to remain silent about the Gospels. Cf. also V, p. 76 (§34).—Hermann Cohen (*Jüdische Schriften*, Berlin 1924, III, 367): "Die Furcht hat (Spinoza) zu zweierlei Mass am Alten und Neuen Testament getrieben."

of the *Treatise* as a "timeless" teaching. But for the same reason the *Treatise* is linked to its time, not because Spinoza's serious or private thought was determined by his "historical situation" without his being aware of it, but because he consciously and deliberately adapted, not his thought, but the public expression of his thought, to what his time demanded or permitted. His plea for "the freedom of philosophizing," and therefore for "the separation of philosophy from theology," is linked to its time in the first place because the time lacked that freedom and simultaneously offered reasonable prospects for its establishment. In another age, or even in another country, Spinoza would have been compelled by his principle of caution to make entirely different proposals for the protection of philosophy, without changing in the least his philosophic thought. The weakening of ecclesiastical authority in Christian Europe, the great variety of Christian sects in certain Protestant countries, the increasing unpopularity of religious persecution, the practice of toleration in Amsterdam in particular, permitted Spinoza to suggest publicly "the separation of philosophy from theology" in the interest, not merely of philosophy or of the philosophers, but of society in general; and to suggest it, not merely on philosophic grounds, but on Biblical grounds as well.[101] Spinoza's argument is linked to his time especially because his plea for "the freedom of philosophizing" is based on arguments taken from the character of the Biblical teaching. For, as is shown by his references to classical authors, he believed that the legitimation of that freedom on social grounds alone was also possible in classical antiquity, and hence would be possible in future societies modeled on the classical pattern. More exactly, Spinoza considered this particular kind of legitimation of the freedom of inquiry a classical rather than a Biblical heritage.[102] Apart from this, it follows from our previous argument

---

[101] *Tr.* XIV, pp. 173, 179 (§§2, 34); XX, pp. 245-246 (§40). *Ep.* 30.

[102] Cf. the heading of *Tr.* XX with Tacitus, *Histories* I 1, and *Tr.* XVII, p. 201 (§9) with Curtius Rufus VIII 5. 17. Cf. also XVII, p. 206 (§32); XVIII, pp. 225-226 (§25); XIX, pp. 236-237 (§§50-53); XI, pp. 157-158 (§§22-24); II, p. 43 (§§55-57).—Cf. Machiavelli, *Discorsi* I 11: in the age of the good Roman emperors everyone could hold and defend every opinion he pleased; also Hobbes, *Leviathan* ch. 46 (Everyman's Library ed. p. 374), and the argument of Milton's *Areopagitica* as a whole.

that the exoteric teaching of the *Treatise* is not meant to be "contemporaneous" with Christianity. The *Treatise* is "contemporaneous" not with the specific assumptions which it attacks, but with those to which it appeals. The assumptions to which Spinoza appeals in the most visible part of the argument of the *Treatise,* are these: the good life simply is the practice of justice and charity, which is impossible without belief in Divine justice; and the Bible insists on the practice of justice and charity combined with the belief in Divine justice as the necessary and sufficient condition of salvation. At the moment these assumptions cease to be publicly defensible,[103] the exoteric teaching of the *Treatise* would lose its *raison d'être.*

Almost everything we have said in the present essay was necessary in order to make intelligible the particular complexity of the argument of the *Treatise.* A considerable part of that argument is actually an appeal from traditional theology to the Bible, whose authority is questioned by the other part of the argument. The hermeneutic principle that legitimates the whole argument and thus blurs the fundamental difference between its heterogeneous parts, is expressed by the assertion that, as a matter of principle, the literal meaning of the Bible is its only meaning. The return to the literal sense of the Bible fulfills an entirely different function within the context of the criticism, based on the Bible, of traditional theology on the one hand and within the contrary context of the attack on the authority of the Bible on the other. Arguing from the conceded premise that the Bible is the only document of revelation, Spinoza demands that the pure word of God be not corrupted by any human additions, inventions, or innovations, and that nothing be considered a revealed doctrine that is not borne out by explicit and clear statements of the Bible.[104] The hidden reason for this procedure is twofold. Spinoza considers the teaching of the Bible partly more rational and partly less rational than that of traditional theology. In so far as it is more rational, he tries to remind traditional theology of a valuable heritage which it has forgot-

---

[103] By a publicly defensible view we understand here, not so much a view whose propagation is permitted by law, as a view backed by the sympathy of a powerful section of society.

[104] *Tr.* I, p. 16 (§7); VI, p. 95 (§65).

ten; in so far as it is less rational, he indicates to the more prudent readers the precarious character of the very basis of all actual theology. He thus leads the reader insensibly toward the criticism of the authority of the Bible itself. This criticism requires the return to the literal meaning of the Bible for the additional reason that the Bible is a popular book: a popular book meant for instruction must present its teaching in the most simple and easily accessible manner.[105] The opposition of the two approaches finds what is probably its most telling expression in the opposite ways in which Spinoza applies the term "ancient" to the Bible: viewed as the standard and corrective for all later religion and theology, the Bible is the document of "the ancient religion"; viewed as the object of philosophic criticism, the Bible is a document transmitting "the prejudices of an ancient nation."[106] In the first case, "ancient" means venerable; in the second case, "ancient" means rude and obsolete. The confusion becomes still greater since Spinoza gives in the *Treatise* the outlines of a purely historical interpretation of the Bible. In fact, his most detailed exposition of hermeneutic rules might seem exclusively to serve the purpose of paving the way for a detached, historical study of the Bible. One is therefore constantly tempted to judge Spinoza's use of the Bible as an authoritative text, as well as his use of the Bible as the target of philosophic criticism, by what he himself declares to be the requirements of a "scientific" study of the Bible; and one is thus frequently tempted to note the utter inadequacy of Spinoza's arguments. Yet one must never lose sight of the fact that the detached or historical study of the Bible was for Spinoza a *cura posterior*. Detached study presupposes detachment, and it is precisely the creation of detachment from the Bible that is Spinoza's primary aim in the *Treatise*. The philosophic criticism of the Biblical teaching, and still more the appeal from traditional theology to the authority of the Bible, cannot be judged in terms of the requirements of the historical study of the Bible, because both uses of the Bible essentially precede that historical study. Whereas the historical study of the Bible, as Spinoza

[105] *Tr.* VII, p. 116 (§87); XIII, p. 172 (§§27-28).
[106] Compare *Tr.* praef., p. 8 (§16); XVIII, p. 222 (§§7-9); XIV, p. 180 (§40) on the one hand, with XV, p. 180 (§2); VI, p. 81 (§4) on the other.

conceives of it, demands that the Bible be not taken as a unity, his two primary purposes require just the opposite; for the claims to which he either defers or which he attacks, are raised on behalf of the Bible as a unitary whole. The first six chapters of the *Treatise,* which lay the foundation for everything that follows, and especially for Spinoza's higher criticism of the Bible, do not in any way presuppose the results of that criticism; in fact, they contradict these results: in these basic chapters, Moses' authorship of the Pentateuch is taken for granted. *Mutatis mutandis* the same applies to Spinoza's attempt to utilize the Bible for political instruction (chapters XVII-XIX).[107] The possible value of Spinoza's philosophic criticism of the Biblical teaching is not impaired by this apparent incongruity; for regardless of who were the authors of the various theological theses asserted in the Bible, or the originators of the institutions recorded or recommended in the Bible, the proof of the absurdity or unsoundness of the theses and institutions in question is the necessary and sufficient condition for the rejection of Biblical authority.

The validity of Spinoza's philosophic criticism of the Bible certainly requires that he has grasped the intention of the Bible as a whole. It is at this point that the distinction between his use of the Bible as authority and his use of the Bible as the target of philosophic criticism becomes decisive for the understanding of the *Treatise.* For it is possible that what Spinoza says about the intention of the Bible as a whole belongs to the context of his appeal from traditional theology to the authority of the Bible. It would certainly not be incompatible with Spinoza's principle "ad captum vulgi loqui" if he had used the Bible in that exoteric context in the way in which counsel for defense sometimes uses the laws: if one wants to bring about an acquittal —the liberation of philosophy from theological bondage—one is not necessarily concerned with ascertaining the true intention of the law. We cannot take it for granted then that Spinoza really identified the fundamental teaching of the Bible with what the Bible teaches everywhere clearly, or that he really believed that

[107] Consider also the difference between the correct sequence of questions to be raised by the interpretation of the Bible—*Tr.* VII, pp. 102-104 (§§26-36)—and the sequence of topics discussed in the *Treatise.*

the moral teaching of the Bible is everywhere clearly expressed
and in no way affected by defective readings and so on.[108]
The fact that he teaches these and similar things regarding the
general character of the Bible does not yet prove that he believed them; for, not to repeat our whole argument, he also
asserts that there cannot be any contradictions between the
insight of the understanding and the teaching of the Bible because "the truth does not contradict the truth,"[109] and we know
that he did not believe in the truth of the Biblical teaching. In
addition, there is some specific evidence that supports the particular doubt we are raising. In his list of those Biblical teachings which allegedly are presented clearly everywhere in the
Bible, Spinoza mentions the dogma that in consequence of God's
decree the pious are rewarded and the wicked are punished; but
elsewhere he says that, according to Solomon, the same fate
meets the just and the unjust, the pure and the impure.[110] He
enumerates among the same kind of teachings the dogma that
God takes care of all things; it is hard to see how this can be
taught in the Bible everywhere clearly if, as Spinoza maintains,
the Bible teaches in a number of important passages that God is
not omniscient, that he is ignorant of future human actions, and
that he takes care only of his chosen people. He also lists among
the teachings in question the dogma that God is omnipotent;
again, it is hard to see how this can be taught in the Bible
everywhere clearly if, as Spinoza suggests, Moses himself believed
that the angels or "the other gods," as well as matter, are not
created by God.[111] Furthermore, Spinoza says that charity is
recommended most highly everywhere in both Testaments, and
yet he also says that the Old Testament recommends, or even
commands, hatred of the other nations.[112] Above all, Spinoza
makes the following assertions: the only intention of the Bible is
to teach obedience to God, or the Bible enjoins nothing but

[108] *Tr.* VII, pp. 102-103, 111 (§§27-29, 68-69); IX, p. 135 (§32); XII, pp. 165-166
(§§34-38).
[109] *Ep.* 21 (34 §3). Cf. *Cogitata metaphysica* II 8 §5.
[110] Cf. *Tr.* XII, p. 165 (§36) with VI, p. 87 (§33); XIX, pp. 229, 231-232 (§§8, 20).
[111] Cf. *Tr.* V, p. 77 (§38); VII, p. 102 (§27); XII, p. 165 (§36) with II, pp. 37-39
(§§32-35, 37-40); III, pp. 44-45 (§3); VI, pp. 81-82 (§§2, 4); XVII, pp. 206, 214-215
(§§30, 77-79).
[112] Cf.*Tr.* XII, p. 166 (§37) with XVII, p. 214 (§77); XIX, p. 233 (§29).

obedience; obedience to God is fundamentally different from love of God; the Bible also enjoins love of God.[113] Precisely because Spinoza openly abandoned in the *Treatise* the belief in the cognitive value of the Bible, his maxim to speak "ad captum vulgi" forced him to assign the highest possible value to the practical or moral demands of the Bible. It is for this reason that he asserts that the practical teaching of the Bible agrees with the true practical teaching, i.e., the practical consequences of philosophy. For obvious reasons, he had to supplement this assertion by maintaining that the practical teaching of the Bible is its central teaching, that it is everywhere clearly presented in the Bible and that it could not possibly be corrupted or mutilated by the compilers and transmitters of the Bible.

The *Treatise* is primarily directed against the view that philosophy ought to be subservient to the Bible, or against "skepticism." But it is also directed against the view that the Bible ought to be subservient, or to be accommodated, to philosophy, i.e., against "dogmatism."[114] Furthermore, while the work is primarily directed against Christianity, it is also directed against Judaism. The *Treatise* is then directed against these four widely different positions: Christian skepticism, Christian dogmatism, Jewish skepticism, and Jewish dogmatism. Now, arguments which might be decisive against one or some of these positions, might be irrelevant if used against the others. For example, arguments taken from the authority of the New Testament might be conclusive against one or the other form of Christian theology, or even against all forms of Christian theology, but they are clearly irrelevant if used against any Jewish position. Hence, one should expect that Spinoza would criticize each of the four positions by itself. But with very few exceptions he directs one and the same criticism against what might appear to be a fantastic hybrid constructed *ad hoc* out of Judaism and Christianity, and of dogmatism and skepticism. His failure to distinguish throughout between the various positions which he attacks, and to pay careful attention to the specific character of

---

[113] Cf. *Tr.* XIII, p. 168 (§§7-8); XIV, p. 174 (§§5-9) with XVI, adnot. 34 (§53 n.). Cf. IV, pp. 59, 60-61, 65 (§§7-8, 14-15, 34); XII, p. 162 (§19); XIV, p. 177 (§§24-25).
[114] *Tr.* XV, p. 180 (§1).

each, might seem to deprive his criticism of every claim to serious attention. For example, he prefaces his denial of the possibility of miracles by such an account of the vulgar view on the subject as probably surpasses in crudity everything ever said or suggested by the most stupid or the most obscurant smatterer in Jewish or Christian theology. Here, Spinoza seems to select as the target of his criticism a possibly non-existent position that was particularly easy to refute. Or, to take an example of a different character, he prefaces his denial of the cognitive value of revelation by the assertion that "with amazing rashness" "all" writers have maintained that the prophets have known everything within the reach of the human understanding, i.e., he imputes to all theologians a view which is said to have been rejected "by all important Christian theologians of the age."[115] The view in question was held by Maimonides, and Spinoza seems, "with amazing rashness," to take Maimonides as the representative of all theologians. Here, he seems to select as the target of his criticism an actual theological position for the irrelevant reason that he had happened to study it closely during his youth.

The *Treatise* remains largely unintelligible as long as the typical difficulties represented by these two examples are not removed. We intend to show that these difficulties cannot be traced to Spinoza's caution, and thus to express our agreement with the view, which we never contradicted, that Spinoza's exotericism is not the only fact responsible for the difficulties of the *Treatise*. We start from the observation that a certain simplification of the theological issue was inevitable if Spinoza wanted to settle it at all. He effects the necessary simplification in two different ways which are illustrated by our two examples. In the first example, he starts from the implicit premise that all possibly relevant Jewish and Christian theologies necessarily recognize the authority, i.e., the truth, of the thematic teaching of the Old Testament; he assumes moreover that the true meaning of any Old Testament passage is, as a rule, identical with its literal meaning; he assumes finally that the most fundamental

<hr/>

[115] v. Dunin-Borkowski, *Spinoza*, IV, 315.—Cf. Maimonides, *Guide*, II 32 and 36. See also Abrabanel's criticism in his commentary on these chapters as well as in his commentary on Amos 1.1 and on 1 Kings 3.14; cf. *Tr.* II, p. 29 (§1).

teaching of the Old Testament is the account of creation. Now, Moses does not explicitly teach creation *ex nihilo;* Genesis 1.2 seems rather to show that he believed that God has made the visible universe out of pre-existing "chaos"; his complete silence about the creation of the angels or "the other gods" strongly suggests that he believed that the power of God is, indeed, superior to, but absolutely different from, the power of other beings. To express Moses' thought in the language of philosophy, the power of nature (which is what he meant by "chaos," and by which he understood a blind "force or impulse") is coeval with the power of God (an intelligent and ordering power), and the power of nature is therefore not dependent on, but merely inferior or subject to, the power of God. Moses taught that uncreated "chaos" precedes in time the ordered universe which is the work of God, and he conceived of God as king. It is therefore reasonable to suppose that he understood the subordination of the power of nature to the power of God as the subjugation of the smaller by the greater power. Accordingly, the power of God will reveal itself clearly and distinctly only in actions in which the power of nature does not cooperate at all. If that only is true which can be clearly and distinctly understood, only the clear and distinct manifestation of God's power will be its true manifestation: natural phenomena do not reveal God's power; when nature acts, God does not act, and *vice versa.* It does not suffice therefore, for the manifestation of God's power, that God has subjugated and reduced to order the primeval chaos; he has to subjugate "the visible gods," the most impressive parts of the visible universe, in order to make his power known to man: God's power and hence God's being can be demonstrated only by miracles. This is the core of the crude and vulgar view which Spinoza sketches before attacking the theological doctrine of miracles. The seemingly non-existent theologian whom Spinoza has in mind when expounding that view is none other than Moses himself, and the view in question is meant to be implied in Genesis 1, in a text of the highest authority for all Jews and all Christians.[116] Spinoza does then not go beyond reminding his opponents of what he considers

[116] Cf. *Tr.* VI, pp. 81-82 (§§1-4) with II, pp. 38-39 (§§37-40); IV, p. 64 (§30). Cf. II, p. 37 (§31); VI, pp. 87-89 (§§34, 39); VII, p. 115 (§§83).

"the original" of their position. As is shown by the sequel in the *Treatise*, he does not claim at all that that reminder suffices for refuting the traditional doctrine of miracles. To conclude, our example teaches us that Spinoza tries to simplify the discussion by going back from the variety of theologies to the basis common to all: the basic doctrine of the Old Testament.

To turn now to the second example, in which Spinoza identifies the view of all theologians with the view of Maimonides, Spinoza here starts from the implicit premise that not all theological positions are of equal importance. He certainly preferred "dogmatism," which admits the certainty of reason, to "skepticism," which denies it: the former ruins the Bible (i.e., it commits only a historical error), whereas the latter ruins reason (i.e., it makes brutes out of human beings).[117] Furthermore, I take it that Spinoza rejected *a limine* the view according to which the teaching of reason is simply identical with the teaching of revelation; for this view leads to the consequence that, in the first place the philosophers, and indirectly all other men, would not need revelation, revelation would be superfluous, and an all-wise being does not do superfluous things.[118] His critical attention was thus limited to the view that the teaching of revelation is partly or wholly above reason but never against reason, or that natural reason is necessary but not sufficient for man's salvation or perfection. At this point he was confronted with the alternative that the process of revelation is, or is not, above human comprehension. Certain Biblical accounts satisfied him that the phenomenon of revelation or prophecy is, in principle, intelligible, i.e., that revelation is effected, not directly by the Divine will, but by the intermediacy of secondary causes. Accordingly, he had to seek for a natural explanation of the fact that certain human beings, the prophets, proclaimed a teaching that was partly or wholly above reason but never against reason. The only possible natural explanation was that the prophets were perfect philosophers and more than perfect philosophers. This view of prophecy was explicitly stated in part, and partly

[117] Cf. *Tr.* XV, p. 180 (§§1-3) with praef., p. 8 (§§16-17) and XIII, p. 170 (§17).
[118] Cf. *Tr.* XV, p. 180 (§§1-3) with praef., p. 8 (§§16-17); XIII, p. 170 (§17).— XV, p. 188 (§44).

suggested by Maimonides.[119] When Spinoza says that "all" theologians have asserted that the prophets have known everything within the reach of the human understanding, he then simplifies the controversial issue by limiting himself, not to the theological position which was easiest to refute, or which he just happened to know best, but to the one which he regarded as the most reasonable and therefore the strongest.

All the difficulties discussed in the preceding pages concern the reasons with which Spinoza justifies the practical proposals made in the *Treatise*. These proposals themselves are very simple. If they were not, they could not reach many readers, and hence they would not be practical. The practical proposals are supported by both the obvious and the hidden reasoning. The practical proposals together with the obvious reasoning are that part of the teaching of the *Treatise* that is meant for all its readers. That part of the teaching of the *Treatise* must be understood completely by itself before its hidden teaching can be brought to light.

[119] Cf. *Tr.* V, pp. 79-80 (§§47-49) with VII, p. 115 (§83); II, p. 29 (§2). Cf. XVI, p. 191 (§11); IV, p. 58 (§4).

INDEX

Abravanel, Isaac, 8, 47, 81, 198
Albo, Joseph, 132
d'Alembert, 29
Alexander Aphrodisiensis, 14, 47
Altmann, A., 42, 52, 69
Anawati, M.-M., 9, 10, 18
Anaxagoras, 33
Apelt, O., 123
Aquinas, Thomas, 8, 14, 19, 20, 48, 95-97, 133
Aristotle, 9, 12-15, 21, 28, 33, 40, 42, 47, 57, 60, 75, 81, 95-97, 105, 106, 111, 112, 116, 131, 133, 135, 138, 152, 161.
Augustine, 35
Averroes, 8-11, 14, 20, 27, 33, 75, 91, 97, 110, 111, 126
Averroism, 14
Avicenna, 9, 10, 33, 48, 50, 99, 111, 124, 126, 139

Bacon, Francis, 57, 183
Bahya ibn Pakuda, 115
Bar Hiyya, Abraham, 85-86, 139
Baron, S. W., 50, 58, 65, 104, 109, 112
Bayle, 33
Bergsträsser, G., 43
Bertolini, 29
Blackstone, Sir William, 22
Blau, L., 82, 85
Bodin, 27
Boyle, 152
Burke, 27

Carlyle, A. J., 27
Catlin, G. E. G., 28
Cicero, 9, 11, 34, 153, 171, 185
Cohen, H., 191
Condorcet, 27
da Costa, Uriel, 164

Curtius, Rufus, 192

Democritus, 152, 161
Descartes, 17, 22, 33, 152, 182, 185, 189
Diesendruck, Z., 49
v. Dunin-Borkowski, 183, 198

Edelstein, L., 28
Efros, I., 81, 116
Elia del Medigo, 109
Ephodi, 57
Epicurus, 152, 161
Eusebius, 28

Falakera, 40, 47, 77, 91, 97, 116, 122, 136
Fārābī, 9-21, 40, 47, 64, 77, 99, 111, 114, 116, 117, 119, 137, 182
Fuerstenthal, 49

Gardet, L., 9, 10, 18
Gassendi, 152
Gauthier, L., 27, 111
Gebhardt, C., 149
Gersonides, 136
Ghazâlî, 111
Gibbon, 28
Ginzberg, L., 81
Goethe, 107
Goldziher, I., 57
Grant, Sir Alexander, 28
Grotius, Hugo, 33, 35, 96
Guttmann, J., 46, 114, 132

Halevi, Yehuda, 11, 19, 98-141, 182
Halkin, A. S., 11
Hegel, 112
Heinemann, I., 42, 112
Helvétius, 29
Hobbes, 27, 33, 34, 96, 183, 184, 192
Hoenigswald, R., 28
Husik, I., 96

Ibn Aknīn, 11
Ibn Ar-Rāwandi, 125, 129
Ibn Baǧǧa, 91, 117
Ibn Daūd, Abraham, 97
Ibn Ezra, Abraham, 181
Ibn Kaspi, Joseph, 56, 70
Ibn Sina. See Avicenna
Ibn Tibbon, 47, 82, 97, 100, 117, 118, 127, 131, 132, 138
Ibn Tufail, 14, 111
Ibn Waḥshiyya, 123

Jaeger, W., 28

Kant, 33
Kraus, P., 99, 111, 125

Laboulaye, 29
Leibniz, 76, 182
Leon, Messer Yehuda, 40
Lessing, 28, 33, 182
Locke, 33
Lubienski, Z., 28
Lucretius, 152

Machiavelli, 15, 22, 150
MacLeish, A., 34
Maimonides, 8-11, 19-21, 33, 38-94, 96, 99, 100, 111-114, 120, 122, 124-126, 132-133, 140, 155, 166, 181, 182, 187, 198, 200
Marsilius of Padua, 15, 95-97, 136
Marx, A., 116, 138
Meinecke, F., 29
Mendelssohn, Moses, 20
Meyer, Ludovicus, 169, 186
Milton, 23, 192
Montesquieu, 28
More, Sir Thomas, 35
Moscato, 101
Munk, S., 49, 66, 70, 76, 78, 97

Nabataean Agriculture, 123, 124, 125
Narboni, Moses, 91, 117
Neo-Kantianism, 28
Neo-Platonism, 18

Parmenides, 23
Pascal, 35
Peritz, 91
Peyrère, Isaac de la, 148
Pines, S., 99
Plato, 9-21, 22, 28, 33-37, 40, 47, 58, 64,

90, 100-101, 103-105, 116-117, 119, 121, 123, 125, 137-139, 152, 161, 182, 187
Powell, E. E., 177, 180
Protagoras, 33

Rāzī, Muhammad b. Zakariyya, 117
Reimarus, H. S., 33
Renan, 27
Rousseau, 33

Saadya, 127, 132
Sabeanism, 81, 124-126
Sabine, G. H., 29
Schechter, S., 104
Schleiermacher, F., 28
Scholasticism, 8
Scholem, G., 51, 79
Schwab, M., 97
Seneca, 153
Shem Tob (author of a Commentary on Maimonides' Guide), 49, 57, 84, 93
Sheshet ha-Nasi, 138
Shotwell, J. T., 28
Sociology of Knowledge, 7-8, 21
Socrates, 16, 33, 37, 64, 104-107, 117, 138, 152
Spinoza, 20, 33, 35, 112, 115, 142-201
Steinschneider, M., 14, 40, 97, 106, 116, 123
Stoicism, 11
Strauss, B., 123
Strauss, L., 28
Suarez, 96

Tacitus, 183, 192
Taylor, Jeremy, 35
Theology of Aristotle, 18
Thrasymachus, 16
Tönnies, F., 28, 34

Vajda, G., 20
Vaughan, C. E., 33
Ventura, M., 99, 110
Voltaire, 33

Wolff, Christian, 33, 96
Wolfson, H. A., 44, 48, 71, 98, 101, 108, 114, 188-189

Xenophon, 29, 33

Zeitlin, S., 85
Zeller, E., 28

Printed in Great Britain
by Amazon